THE BIG IDEAS

OF NANOSCALE

SCIENCE & ENGINEERING

A GUIDEBOOK FOR SECONDARY TEACHERS

THE BIG IDEAS
OF NANOSCALE
SCIENCE & ENGINEERING
A GUIDEBOOK FOR SECONDARY TEACHERS

Shawn Y. Stevens

LeeAnn M. Sutherland

Joseph S. Krajcik

NSTApress

National Science Teachers Association

Arlington, Virginia

National Science Teachers Association

Claire Reinburg, Director
Jennifer Horak, Managing Editor
Andrew Cocke, Senior Editor
Judy Cusick, Senior Editor
Wendy Rubin, Associate Editor

ART AND DESIGN
Will Thomas Jr., Director
Joseph Butera, Senior Graphic Designer, cover and interior design
Cover illustration courtesy of iStock, penfold
All figures are by Shawn Y. Stevens except those identified as adapted from another source
or reprinted with permission.

PRINTING AND PRODUCTION
Catherine Lorrain, Director

NATIONAL SCIENCE TEACHERS ASSOCIATION
Francis Q. Eberle, PhD, Executive Director
David Beacom, Publisher

LIBRARY OF CONGRESS CATALOGING-IN-PUBLICATION DATA

Stevens, Shawn Y.
  The big ideas of nanoscale science & engineering: a guidebook for secondary teachers / by Shawn Y. Stevens,
LeeAnn M. Sutherland, and Joseph S. Krajcik.
     p. cm.
  Includes bibliographical references and index.
  ISBN 978-1-935155-07-2
  1. Science--Study and teaching (Secondary) 2. Nanoscience--Study and teaching (Secondary) 3.
Nanotechnology--Study and teaching (Secondary) I. Sutherland, LeeAnn M. II. Krajcik, Joseph S. III. Title.
  LB1585.S765 2009
  620'.50712--dc22

                        2009026397

eISBN 978-1-936137-94-7

Up-to-the minute online content, classroom ideas, and other materials are just a click away. For
more information go to *www.scilinks.org/Faq.aspx*.

Acknowledgments

This book—a "consensus document"—could not have been completed without the efforts of many people. First and foremost, we thank Patricia Schank of SRI International for co-authoring the grant to support the initial workshop (the Nanoscale Learning Goals Workshop, June 2006, Menlo Park, California), for organizing and hosting a productive and engaging workshop to identify the principle learning goals for nanoscience and nanotechnology, and for helpful comments on drafts of the manuscript. In addition, we appreciate her help facilitating the vetting process.

Nora Sabelli, also from SRI International, made significant contributions throughout the process, from organizing the workshop to designing the framework of this book; she also provided extensive editorial comments.

Molly Yunker, Chris Quintana, César Delgado, and Ramez Elgammal from the University of Michigan and Tina Sanford and Anders Rosenquist from SRI International also supported the workshop, organizing the initial results on the workshop wiki and the subsequent vetting process.

We also thank Carole Stearns and Robert Gibbs, our former and current NSF program officers, respectively, for supporting this work throughout the process.

We appreciate the passionate discussions and intensive work of the participants at the June 2006 workshop. Their efforts provided the foundation for this book. We also thank the participants at subsequent workshops, who carefully considered our questions and goals and made thoughtful suggestions that have shaped the final product.

An extensive amount of work toward defining the content contained in the big ideas was done by many members of the National Center for Learning and Teaching in Nanoscale Science and Engineering (NCLT). We would particularly like to thank Thomas Mason of Northwestern University for his work in identifying the grade 13–16 big ideas. His passion for defining the content helped us focus our definitions of the big ideas. Nicholas Giordano of Purdue University provided extensive editorial comments and many helpful discussions in our effort to define the content of the big ideas. George Bodner, Purdue University; Richard Braatz, University of Illinois at Urbana-Champaign; Carmen Lilley, University of Illinois at Chicago; Greg Light, Northwestern University; Morten Lundsgaard, University of Michigan; and Nate Unterman, Glenbrook North High School, Northbrook, Illinois, all generously provided expertise and advice throughout the process of writing this book.

Several people generously gave their time to provide comments on the document. In particular, we thank Clark Miller, from the Center for Nanotechology in Society at Arizona State University, for helping us clarify the discussion on the relationships between science, technology, and society. Kelly Hutchinson, Purdue University; Shanna Daly, University of Michigan; César Delgado, University of Michigan; and Harold Short, University of Michigan (National Center for Learning and Teaching); Gina Ney, University of Michigan; and Alexa Mattheyses Rockefeller University, also provided valuable comments and helpful discussion on the manuscript.

Many reviewers provided feedback throughout the evolution of this document. However, the conclusions represented herein are ultimately those of the authors and may not be endorsed by all contributors. This work was funded by the National Science Foundation: SGER grant number ESI 0608936, and the National Center for Learning and Teaching in Nanoscale Science and Engineering, grant number 0426328.

CONTENTS

Section 2
Integrating NSE Into the 7–12 Science Curriculum

Section 3
Next Steps

Preface

Nanoscale science and engineering (NSE) is an emerging field. Although defining the nanoscale world is not without debate, *nanoscale* is generally defined as including any material of which at least one dimension is 1 to 100 nanometers. New and refined tools now enable scientists to explore and understand this nanoscale world in ways unforeseeable only a few short years ago. At this scale, materials exhibit novel, often unexpected properties that are not observed at other scales. Based on the discovery of materials' properties and behaviors at this scale, NSE research is rapidly leading to strategies for creating new products and technologies as well as new information likely to have broad societal implications in areas as diverse as healthcare; the environment; and the sustainability of agriculture, food, water, and energy.

The ability to understand the discoveries, technologies, and information resulting from NSE research requires a high degree of science literacy. It is not just today's students but also the adults they will become who will be required to function in a highly technological society. In that society, they will need to make sense of and make decisions about rapid scientific advances. National, state, and local leaders in education must prepare a broad cross section of the U.S. population with the science and engineering knowledge required to meet these demands and to secure an edge in discovery and innovation that will sustain economic prosperity.

While this book sets NSE in the context of larger societal needs for a scientifically informed citizenry, it focuses on the much smaller arena of U.S. schools as a system with a pervasive reliance on traditional means of presenting science education. New, emerging, "big ideas" in the field of NSE require a new approach to science education, an approach outlined in this book for ongoing discussion and debate. It is a text primarily for teachers and others interested in 7–12 science education. But because teachers play the most important role in introducing NSE to students in classrooms, it is they who must understand NSE content and be able to integrate it into the disciplines they teach. NSE is not to be thought of as a separate discipline but as the science of all disciplines at the nanoscale. Its interdisciplinary nature thus requires that teachers learn how the critical ideas of NSE connect across disciplines. In addition, NSE content may require new instructional strategies. The task is more complex than simply adding NSE examples into current lessons or inserting an NSE module into the current curriculum.

Yet this book does not prescribe how nanoscale science and engineering should be taught, nor does it provide lesson plans, activities, or specific strategies or prescribe a curriculum sequence for NSE. Instead, we discuss connections among nanoscience ideas and the current curriculum, as well as new ways of considering traditional science content relevant to NSE. The book is designed to support teachers' development of foundational nanoscience content knowledge and skills and to enable teachers to integrate NSE effectively into their classrooms. It provides a reference for secondary teachers who want to help their students understand the exciting new discoveries and applications from NSE research and development—that is, to truly engage their students in 21st-century science education.

Introduction

The Importance of Nanoscale Science and Engineering (NSE) in 7–12 Education

The emerging fields of nanoscience and nanotechnology promise to have extensive implications for all of society as they apply the unique properties of matter at the nanoscale (i.e., 10^{-9}–10^{-7} meters or 1–100 nanometers) to create new products and technologies. Because nanoscale science and engineering (NSE) research involves the study, control, and fabrication of matter across science and engineering disciplines, NSE researchers explore an extremely diverse range of phenomena. Many industries, including electronics, pharmaceuticals, cosmetics, and textiles, employ nanotechnology to improve products. Examples of products currently on the market include transparent zinc-oxide-based sunscreen, scratch-resistant automobile paint, and stain-resistant clothing. The technical advisory group for the President's Council of Advisors on Science and Technology (PCAST) predicts that by 2020 nanotechnology will also contribute to areas such as water purification, medical diagnostics, targeted drug therapies, and better solar cells (PCAST 2005). Clearly, we live in an exciting time with respect to advances in science and technology at the nanoscale.

Society's Individual and Collective Needs

Although little argument exists about the value of nanomedicines to treat, for example, cancer patients, scientists and conservationists caution that some nanoscale materials may have serious, negative effects on the environment and health of individuals. Nanoscale objects are small enough to cross some biological barriers; thus, familiar materials such as zinc oxide (used in sunscreens) and gold (long used in dental applications) may affect living organisms differently in nanoscale form than in their bulk form. In other words, despite the benefits that result from NSE, legitimate health and environmental concerns also exist.

Understanding these trade-offs is imperative. The need to characterize and to evaluate benefits and risks argues for a scientifically literate citizenry able to consider technological advances in an informed manner. To make wise decisions about the *uses* of science, citizens must be able to consider the consequences and implications of all scientific advances. Most students will not become scientists or engineers, but they will participate in decision making about the work that scientists and engineers do. From privacy concerns related to computerized data storage to stem cell research, citizens are confronting issues related to science and technology in their everyday lives. At the very least, all citizens must be able to read and understand science-based articles in the popular press or on the internet and to make sense of politically charged rhetoric around science-based issues.

Understanding ideas related to NSE is necessary not only for scientific literacy and decision making but also for individual and national

Introduction

prosperity. At the time of this writing (2009), the demand for U.S. workers with science and engineering skills is growing five times faster than the rest of the work force (Foley and Hersam 2006). U.S. economic prosperity is increasingly linked with the growth of technology; a large percentage of future jobs will require technology-based skills. By 2020, scientists, engineers, and policy groups predict that technologies and products derived from nanotechnology will contribute more than $1 trillion each year to the worldwide economy (Roco and Bainbridge 2001). Nearly one million workers knowledgeable in nanoscale science and engineering will be required to support the nanotechnology sector in this country (Roco 2003).

Clearly, future economic prosperity and the ability to make ethical decisions depend on a population with the knowledge required to function in a highly technological society and to produce the knowledge of the future. These conditions are not likely to be met unless preparation begins in schools. The "preparation" aspects are the crux of this book.

As jobs related to science and technology proliferate, education related to these fields is essential. Only if students are educated in growth areas will they have access to predicted career opportunities. This means that NSE education must begin in middle and high school, well before students have chosen a career path in college. This pressing need argues for reviewing the pipeline through which students, particularly those historically underrepresented in science, technology, engineering, and mathematics (STEM) education, come to specialize in STEM-related disciplines. Science education must prepare *all* students to participate not only in the consumption of technological advances but also in the production of these advances. This is especially true in a global economy. The minimal attention paid to STEM education in the United States has long been recognized as an education problem of great consequence (Foley and Hersam 2006; Schmidt, Wang, and McKnight 2005), a problem that will be exacerbated if traditional methods continue to be the *modus operandi* of U.S. schools and if traditional content continues to be the fare offered in U.S. classrooms.

There is no question that the world in which our students live requires a change in what they learn. As such, this book introduces science educators to the "big ideas" of nanoscale science and engineering.

What Are Big Ideas?

Big ideas are those considered central or fundamental to a discipline. Some big ideas in biology, while fundamental to that discipline, may not be central to chemistry. However, other big ideas are cross-disciplinary, enabling learners to explain a broad range of phenomena both within and across disciplines. In any science discipline, students encounter a number of important ideas, but those considered "big ideas" are core to the discipline. They provide a framework for the long-term development of student understanding, allowing teachers and students to revisit ideas throughout the 7–12 curriculum and to build conceptual understanding during those years. In doing so, understanding becomes progressively more refined, developed, and elaborate. Big ideas in any discipline provide a foundation on which future, more specialized learning can build. This book focuses on the big ideas of NSE while acknowledging the current educational framework into which they must be incorporated.

The Importance of Nanoscale Science and Engineering (NSE) in 7–12 Education

Science Education in U.S. Schools Today

International comparisons reveal that students in the United States do not perform as well as those in other developed countries on tests of scientific knowledge (Schmidt, Wang, and McKnight 2005). The failure of U.S. schools to help learners understand core ideas in STEM education has led to a generation of children ill prepared to enter STEM-related fields and to secure the nation's leadership in science and technology. Without intervention, this gap is likely to increase as technologies become ubiquitous and society becomes more reliant on them. Perhaps most unfortunate is the fact that many children in the nation's rural and large urban areas are not successful in science (Lynch 2000; Grigg, Lauko, and Bockway 2006). The challenge of how to provide quality science instruction to *all* of the nation's young people is a challenge that must be taken on even if it is only improved in some schools. Some of that challenge can be addressed by the curriculum itself.

Researchers from the Third International Mathematics and Science Study (TIMSS) found that curriculum coherence is the dominant predictor of student learning (Schmidt, Wang, and McKnight 2005). When U.S. curricula are compared to those of countries whose students perform better on international benchmarks, the lack of coherence within and across years in U.S. science curricula surfaces as one important factor in this failure. Unfortunately, most of the standards documents used to guide the science curriculum are concerned with coverage of a broad set of ideas rather than with making certain that students develop deep and integrated understanding of key ideas (Wilson and Berenthal 2006). This strategy of broad coverage rather than deep understanding is supported by high-stakes tests that superficially assess science content. The trouble with covering too many concepts is that students learn neither how ideas are related to one another nor how they can be used to explain or predict phenomena. Instead, they must memorize discrete facts, and of the thousands of facts they might have memorized, they fail if they do not have the "right ones" at their disposal at test time. In addition, standards documents tend to treat all ideas as equally important. They do not identify some ideas (e.g., particle model of matter, classical mechanics, natural selection, plate tectonics) as big ideas that require greater focus in the curriculum and strategic building of understanding across time.

A Strategy for Developing a Coherent Science Curriculum

A coherent curriculum can help students build the kind of deep and meaningful understanding of big ideas that will enable them to explain phenomena within and across disciplines. Coherence refers both to alignment of instruction and assessment and to sequencing of instruction around a small set of ideas, organized to support learners in developing integrated understanding of those ideas (Schmidt, Wang, and McKnight 2005; Swartz et al. 2008). However, in attempting to address a multitude of national, state, and local standards, the U.S. science curriculum hinders the development of coherent curriculum materials and, thus, of students' coherent understanding of science.

To build coherence around a small number of critical big ideas of science, curriculum developers and educators must first know what those critical ideas are. As a first step toward that goal, in 2006 a representative group of scientists, engineers, educators, and learning specialists from across the nation worked together to determine the big ideas of NSE. (See appendixes A and B for a description of the process and a list of participants.) This book presents the group's

Introduction

consensus—not simply the authors' vision—as to what should be named a "Big Idea of NSE" and which of the big ideas should be introduced in grade 7–12 science classrooms.

NSE represents science and engineering of all disciplines at the nanoscale. The big ideas of NSE described in this book are related not only to nanoscience and nanotechnology but also to science more broadly. That is, the NSE big ideas include many concepts critical for building general science literacy (e.g., structure of matter, size and scale, models and simulations) as defined in national standards documents (AAAS 1993; NRC 1996). In fact, many people consider the big ideas of NSE to be some of the big ideas of all of science. The inherently interdisciplinary nature of NSE creates an opportunity to reorganize the way we think about traditional science content and the way we teach science content. In particular, NSE provides an opportunity to remove demarcations that currently exist between the science disciplines in order to address ideas in a multidisciplinary fashion. As such, we see the big ideas of NSE as the foundation for building coherence in the science curriculum.

Audience for This Book

We intend this book to be used primarily by grade 7–12 science teachers who wish to address NSE in their classrooms or to become more knowledgeable about NSE and its potential for engaging students in science, deepening their understanding of critical science concepts, and developing lifelong learners. This book is not meant to prescribe how NSE should be taught in the classroom or to describe activities and lessons for particular NSE topics, as can be found in other resources (e.g., Jones et al. 2007). The information in this book can help teachers to develop NSE knowledge and skills and to incorporate NSE into the science courses they are now teaching. Science resource persons and science coordinators may also find the book of value for its potential to shape curriculum decisions at the school or district level.

Organization of This Book

Section 1, "The Nine Big Ideas," is the foundation of the book. The chapters in this section introduce the reader to and define an NSE big idea, detail the content contained within the big idea, describe how the group of workshop scientists arrived at a consensus for that idea, and provide a justification for defining a concept as an NSE big idea. Each chapter also provides a number of examples that illustrate the content and that describe possible interdisciplinary connections. We also discuss how the NSE content of each big idea relates to the current 7–12 science curriculum.

In Section 2, "Integrating NSE into the 7–12 Science Curriculum," the chapters are broken down into the nine big ideas (although other big ideas are discussed in each chapter). In each, we give learning goals for that big idea and how these learning goals can be used to develop a coherent curriculum. Teachers may want to refer to the content chapters for each big idea in Section 1 if they are unsure about content information. Section 2 also identifies the prerequisite (both general and specific) knowledge necessary for each big idea, and the prior learning and misconceptions students may bring with them to the science classroom. In addition, Section 2 lists phenomena that could be used to contextualize NSE content in classrooms, as well as questions teachers could ask for discussion or for assessment. Finally, we relate the content in each big idea to the national standards (AAAS 1993; NRC 1996), highlighting both similarities and omissions in the standards with regard to NSE.

In Section 3, "Next Steps," we discuss the challenges faced by our schools in the development of an NSE-educated citizenry.

NATIONAL SCIENCE TEACHERS ASSOCIATION

References

American Association for the Advancement of Science (AAAS). 1993. *Benchmarks for science literacy*. New York: Oxford University Press.

Foley, E. T., and M. C. Hersam. 2006. Assessing the need for nanotechnology education reform in the United States. *Nanotechnology Law & Business* 3 (4): 467–484.

Grigg, W., M. Lauko, and D. Brockway. 2006. *The nation's report card: Science 2005*. Washington, DC: U. S. Department of Education, National Center for Education Statistics (U.S. Government Printing Office).

Jones, M. G., M. R. Falvo, A. R. Taylor, and B. P. Broadwell. 2007. *Nanoscale science: Activities for grades 6–12*. Arlington, VA: NSTA Press.

Lynch, S. S. 2000. *Equity and science education reform*. Hillsdale, NJ: Lawrence Erlbaum Associates.

National Research Council (NRC). 1996. *National science education standards*. Washington, DC: National Academy Press.

President's Council of Advisors on Science and Technology (PCAST). 2005. The national nano-technology initiative at five years: Assessment and recommendations of the National Nanotechnology Advisory Panel. *www.nano-and-society.org/ NELSI/entity/us_govt/NNI.html*

Roco, M. C. 2003. National nanotechnology initiative to advance broad societal goals. *MRS Bulletin* 28: 416–417.

Roco, M. C., and W. Bainbridge. 2001. *Society implications of nanoscience and nanotechnology*. Arlington, VA: National Science Foundation.

Schmidt, W. H., H. C. Wang, and C. C. McKnight. 2005. Curriculum coherence: An examination of U.S. mathematics and science content standards from an international perspective. *Journal of Curriculum Studies* 37 (5): 525–559.

Swartz, Y., A. Weizman, D. Fortus, J. Krajcik, and B. Reiser. 2008. The IQWST experience: Using coherence as a design principle for a middle school science curriculum. *Elementary School Journal* 109 (2): 199–219.

SECTION

1

The Nine Big Ideas

Introduction

The Foundational Science Content of the Nine Big Ideas in Nanoscale Science and Engineering

In Section 1, we present the big ideas of nanoscale science and engineering (NSE), discussing both the science content contained in each big idea and the justification for considering each to be foundational within NSE.

The big ideas were identified, elaborated on, and vetted in a process described in detail in Appendix A. Briefly, in 2006 and 2007, scientists from a range of disciplines, science teachers, and science educators convened in a series of workshops throughout the country to discuss, debate, and decide on the big ideas of NSE. The workshops were held for three interrelated purposes: (1) to come to a consensus about what the big ideas were, (2) to address the challenges of bringing NSE into the classroom, and (3) to create a "consensus document" (this book) that could be used by educators, researchers, and curriculum developers.

The primary workshop was held in June 2006 in Menlo Park, California. Called the Nanoscale Learning Goals Workshop and funded by the National Science Foundation (NSF), the three-day workshop was conducted jointly by the National Center for Learning and Teaching in Nanoscale Science and Engineering (NCLT) and SRI International. (See Appendix B for a list of participants.) The six big ideas that were agreed on at this workshop were presented and discussed at national and international workshops and conferences as part of the vetting process of establishing a consensus. Changes in

the list occurred, and eventually at the NSF's 2007 K–12 & Informal Nanoscale Science and Engineering Workshop in Washington, D.C., nine big ideas were agreed upon. Here are the big ideas settled on during the consensual process and examined in this book:

1. Size and Scale
2. Structure of Matter
3. Forces and Interactions
4. Quantum Effects
5. Size-Dependent Properties
6. Self-Assembly
7. Tools and Instrumentation
8. Models and Simulations
9. Science, Technology, and Society

These big ideas essentially coincide with the big ideas of NSE identified for grade 13–16 learners (Wansom et al. 2009). However, this book discusses the big ideas in a manner relevant to 7th- through 12th-grade science teachers.

A major challenge in developing a consensus about the big ideas was that much of the content related to the ideas is already present in the science curriculum. Thus, many participants in the presentations and discussions that followed the initial workshop did not necessarily see the big ideas of NSE as "new" or as needing a definition apart from that already presented in *National Science Education Standards* (NRC 1996) or *Benchmarks for Science Literacy* (AAAS

Introduction

1993). Although it is true that some big ideas are not "new," by being articulated in an NSE context they are universalized so they can be applied more clearly across disciplines. For example, the same types of forces that dominate the interactions between atoms also dominate the interactions between nanoscale objects, whether they are naturally occurring (e.g., protein, DNA) or fabricated (e.g., nanoparticles, nanowires, nanomachines). Therefore, a strong foundation in the structure of matter and how matter is held together is imperative to understanding the properties and behavior of matter at the nanoscale.

In this section of the book each big idea is examined in a clarification section (e.g., "About Size and Scale"), followed by the reasons that that big idea is important to NSE and ways that the big idea relates to current science curriculum. The discussions of the big ideas are not exhaustive but are meant to serve as introductions to the big ideas of NSE.

References

American Association for the Advancement of Science (AAAS). 1993. *Benchmarks for science literacy*. New York: Oxford University Press.

National Research Council (NRC). 1996. *National science education standards*. Washington, DC: National Academy Press.

Wansom, S., T. O. Mason, M. C. Hersam, D. Drane, G. Light, R. Cormia, S. Y. Stevens, and G. Bodner. 2009. A rubric for post-secondary degree programs in nanoscience and nanotechnology. *International Journal for Engineering Education* 25 (3): 615–627.

Chapter 1
The Foundational Science Content

Four of the big ideas represent the basic science content, and as Figure 1.1 illustrates, all four are interrelated. Concepts of size and scale connect to the other science content big ideas because size defines the nanoscale, and different physical models (i.e., classical mechanics, quantum mechanics, general relativity) are used to explain the behavior of matter at different scales. Quantum mechanics is required to explain how matter behaves at small scales. For example, a quantum mechanical model of electron behavior (Structure of Matter) is necessary to understand the interactions of matter (Forces and Interactions) at the nanoscale. The structure of matter and the way it interacts are inextricably linked.

Figure 1.1
Representation of the relationships among NSE science content big ideas

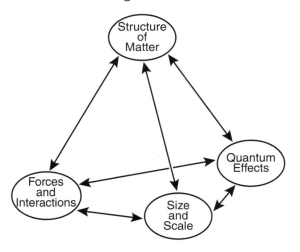

None of the science-content big ideas stands alone; each informs and is informed by the others. As authors of this book, we needed to choose how to divide the content among the big ideas. We identified connections among the big ideas, their associated content, illustrative phenomena, and learning goals.

Big Idea 1
Size and Scale
Factors relating to size and geometry (e.g., size, scale, shape, proportionality, dimensionality) help describe matter and predict its behavior.

About Size and Scale
Size is defined as the extent or bulk amount of something. Every object has a size that can be defined in either one, two, or three dimensions. Comparing an object to a reference object or reference standard (e.g., conventionally defined units) defines the size of the object by defining the scale of geometric properties such as length (e.g., meters, feet, miles), area (e.g., square inches, acres), or volume (e.g., cubic feet, liters, gallons). Each of these geometric properties can have values that differ by many orders of magnitude (AAAS 1993).

It is sometimes useful to divide this large range in sizes into scales or "worlds" (e.g., macro-, micro-, nano-, atomic), each characterized not only by the corresponding

Chapter 1

measurement units but also by (1) representative or landmark objects (Tretter et al. 2006), (2) tools that render objects in the world accessible, and (3) models that describe the behavior of matter at that scale. Figure 1.2 illustrates the approximate range of these worlds and some of their characteristics.

Although conceptually dividing the universe into these worlds can be useful as a guide, it is more accurate to consider the worlds on a continuum, in which divisions between them are somewhat blurred rather than explicitly defined. For example, the nanoscale is generally numerically defined as 1–100 nanometers (nm) (Roco 2004). In terms of matter, it is considered to represent the transition between bulk matter and individual atoms and molecules. However, protein and DNA *molecules* are often considered landmark nanoscale objects for the nanoworld. Therefore, the scales and worlds must be used as *guides* to the size landscape rather than as absolute, rigid categories.

Certain aspects of size and scale are particularly relevant to NSE. The most fundamental aspect is the definition of the nanoscale and how it relates to other scales (e.g., the macroscale, the world of cells, atoms, and molecules). In addition, the effects of changes in scale and shape also play an important role in NSE.

Scaling and Proportionality

Doubling the size of an object affects the surface area and volume disproportionately. For instance, doubling the length of the sides of a cube increases the volume eight-fold, but the surface area of the cube is only increased

Figure 1.2
Illustration of commonly used scales, with representative objects, dominant forces, relevant tools, and most useful physical laws

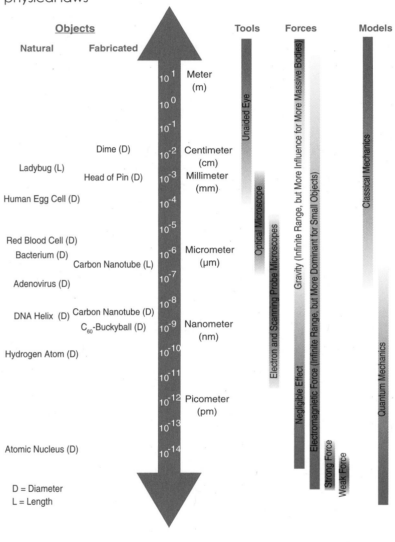

Source: Adapted from Figure 2-S9 NanoSense Size Matters Unit (*http://nanosense.org/activities/sizematters/index.html*)

four-fold. Figure 1.3 illustrates this trend. Thus, if a property is dependent on volume (e.g., heat capacity, mass), then that property will change much faster than properties dependent on area (e.g., cooling surface, porosity). People reveal an understanding of this concept when they cut up a hot potato and spread out the pieces so that it will cool more quickly. Because scale does not affect all properties equally, changes in scale usually affect the way in which a system works. For example, if a gazelle grew to the size of an elephant, its legs would break from the weight because while the mass of the gazelle is proportional to its volume, the strength of its legs increases only by the cross-sectional area of its bones (Haldane 1926).

Table 1.1
Effect of shape on the surface-to-volume ratio of a rectangular prism

Dimensions (cm)	Surface Area (cm^2)	Volume (cm^3)	S/V (cm^{-1})
10 x 10 x 10	600	1000	0.60
20 x 10 x 5	700	1000	0.70
50 x 10 x 2	1240	1000	1.24
100 x 10 x 1	2220	1000	2.22

Shape

Shape also affects the proportionality between surface area and volume. A $10 \times 10 \times 10$ cm cube may have different properties than a $1 \times 10 \times 100$ cm rectangular prism, even though both have a volume of 1000 cm^3. The surface area of the cube is only 27% of the surface area of the extended shape. Table 1.1 illustrates how different arrangements of 100 cubes change the surface area to volume ratio (S/V).* Likewise, for objects with a volume of 100 mm^3 (cubic millimeters), the surface area of a cube is ~129 mm^2, a regular tetrahedron is ~155 mm^2, and a sphere is ~104 mm^2. A sphere is *always* the shape with the minimum S/V, which is why objects like bubbles are spherically shaped.

Thus Size and Scale also includes concepts related to the measure of the geometric properties of length, area, volume, and shape, which can be represented using prefixes or scientific notation. In addition, knowledge about defining and measuring the dimensionality of each of these concepts is also important. Length (1-dimensional), area (2-D), and volume (3-D) change disproportionately with changes in size. These differences have implications for the

Figure 1.3
Comparison of the surface area (circles) and volume (triangles) of a cube vs. length of side

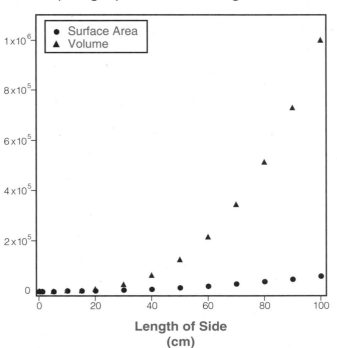

* This ratio is generally referred to as surface-to-volume ratio. We called it surface area to volume ratio here for clarity. In the rest of the book, we will use the more common terminology, surface-to-volume ratio.

Chapter 1

properties, behavior, and function of matter at all scales but more so at the nanoscale.

Why Is This a Big Idea?

Concepts of size and scale (geometry)* form part of the cognitive framework for making sense of science, and in the context of NSE, they define the nanoscale itself. Scientists tend to work in "worlds" that are defined by scale (e.g., atomic, nano-, micro-). Each world provides guidelines for types of objects that are of similar size and for how the behavior of those objects can be explained and predicted. In addition, worlds are often defined by the instrumentation necessary to observe and measure objects on the scale. For example, the world of cells is generally defined as *microscale*. Optical microscopes, or some other magnifier, are necessary to observe objects on this scale. The resolution limit of optical microscope is approximately 0.2 µm or 200 nm, meaning that they cannot be used to measure objects smaller than 200 nm. This roughly defines the lower limit of the microscale, with the upper limit being what can be seen with the unaided eye (around 0.05—0.1 mm or 50–100 µm). The nanoscale is generally defined to include any system or material with at least one dimension falling between 1 and 100 nm. In this range, other tools (e.g., scanning probe microscopes, scanning electron microscopes) are needed to observe and measure phenomena.

Scale is important when explaining phenomena. People make predictions based on macroscale experiences (those visible with the naked eye) that occur in the "world" that can be adequately explained by classical physics. But as the size or mass of an object or material transitions through the nanoscale toward the atomic scale, the ability of classical mechanics to predict the behavior of matter begins to fail. On the atomic and subatomic scales, quantum mechanics must be employed to explain the behavior of matter. As matter transitions between the bulk form and that of individual atoms and molecules, quantum effects become more important.

In addition, the forces that dominate the interactions between matter are also dependent on scale. Although all forces are present in all interactions, gravity generally dominates interactions on the macroscale; electromagnetic forces generally dominate at the nano- and atomic scales; and the strong (or nuclear) force dominates at the subatomic scale. Therefore, knowing the scale of an object helps predict how it will behave. (See "Forces and Interactions," pp. 18–24, and "Quantum Effects," pp. 24–34, for more detailed discussion of many of these ideas.)

Even small changes in size can result in large relative changes in area and even larger changes in volume. The surface-to-volume ratio (S/V) is inversely proportional to the size of the object (see Figure 1.4a and b). Changes in S/V can change the way in which objects or systems function or behave. The rate of burning a log is much slower than burning an equal mass of twigs. Inside the human body, nutrient uptake from the small intestine is more efficient due to the millions of projections (i.e., villi) that increase the absorptive surface area. Many of the special properties that matter exhibits on the nanoscale result from the effect of size on S/V. For example, adhesion properties change with increased exposed surface area. An example from everyday life is powdered sugar

---

* Recent literature has used the term *size and scale* to refer to many of the concepts included in this big idea. Like size, shape also characterizes objects and can affect S/V, and thus shape is also included in this chapter. This big idea might better be termed *size and geometry* to encompass all of these factors simultaneously, but we use *size and scale* to be consistent with terminology in the field.

sticking to the sides of a plastic measuring cup whereas larger granulated sugar does not. (This topic is discussed in greater detail in the size-dependent properties section in Chapter 2.)

Factors linked to size and scale are tied to progress and the understanding of many aspects of research and development at the nanoscale. Size and scale (and geometry) are critical for developing conceptual understanding of the behavior of matter at the nanoscale as well as the tools used to explore the nanoworld.

Relationship to the 7–12 Curriculum

Mathematics is a large part of size and scale (and geometry). In Program Standard C, the NSES state that "[t]he science program should be coordinated with the mathematics program to enhance student use and understanding of mathematics in the study of science and to improve student understanding of mathematics" (NRC 1996, p. 214). The Benchmarks (AAAS 1993) consider scale to be one of four common themes that have implications throughout all disciplines of science. Indeed, concepts related to size and scale are critical for understanding concepts in astronomy, chemistry, physics, and geology, and they extend beyond the natural sciences to geography and history.

Standard measurement units and numerical values are required to communicate in all of these subject areas. In history, geology, and astronomy, the timeline is much greater than an individual's life experience. In geography, the scales on maps indicate the size of the representation relative to the thing it represents. Because the relative magnitude of these scales is often large, scientific notation becomes a

Figure 1.4
Surface area-to-volume ratio vs. length of side of cube: (a) Linear plot (b) Semi-logarithmic plot

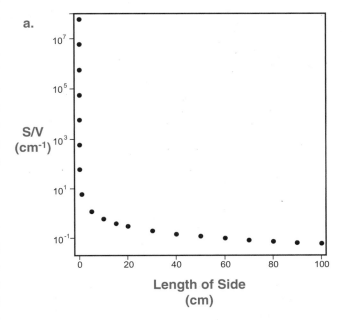

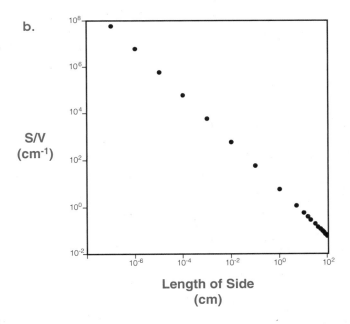

Chapter 1

useful means of communicating very large and very small numbers. Implementing scientific notation lends itself to categorizing the size of objects by orders of magnitude. This subject matter tends to fall in the domain of mathematics, but by linking it to science content, student understanding in both disciplines may benefit as one reinforces the other (NRC 1996; Judson and Sawada 2000).

However, size and scale are not simply academic constructs; they also have an impact on students' daily lives. For instance, when cooking for a larger group of people than usual, the person who prepares the food in your house should scale the recipe and increase the ingredients proportionally. It is also necessary for students and their parents to use the scale on a map to estimate the distance and time it will take to arrive at a destination. As students gain experience both in and out of school, they can begin to relate the values and units to the world around them. Doing so helps them develop skills in estimating relative quantities and sizes.

Strong support from mathematics is required in order for students to apply to science the concept of surface-to-volume ratio. Students must learn about ratios and proportions, as well as develop an understanding of what area and volume are and how to calculate them. When teachers link mathematics to scientific phenomena, they contextualize the mathematics so that students consider it in other than an algorithmic manner (NRC 1996). By using real scientific data, students gain experience applying mathematics concepts to nonidealized problems,* which connects well with the

National Council of Teachers of Mathematics standards (NCTM 1989). Linking mathematics skills for organizing and analyzing data prevents a purely descriptive study of science (NRC 1996, pp. 214–218).

Because the nanoscale lies far outside students' everyday experiences, a robust knowledge of concepts related to size and scale can be used by students and by scientists alike as they learn about this intrinsically abstract realm. Developmentally, people first learn about the size of objects in an intuitive way and in reference to their own bodies. Later they use formal and informal learning experiences to understand the meaning, for example, of measurement units, surface area, volume, and scientific notation. Extrapolating from the everyday world to the nanoscale is likely to be impossible without using such conceptual tools. Thus, concepts related to size and scale make up an important part of the cognitive framework for making sense of the nanoworld.

Big Idea 2
Structure of Matter

Materials consist of building blocks that often form a hierarchy of structures. Atoms interact with each other to form molecules. The next higher level of organization involves atoms, molecules, or nanoscale structures interacting with each other to form nanoscale assemblies and structures.

About Structure of Matter

The atomic theory describes a model in which matter is composed of discrete units called atoms. Slightly more than 100 types of atoms make up all substances. The type of atoms and their arrangements determine the identity and affect the properties of a material. For example, hydrocarbons are a class of substances consist-

---

*Nonidealized problems or data are "real" and have imperfections. Idealized math problems, on the other hand, often use data that work perfectly—for example, calculations come out with whole numbers or points fall along a perfect line.

ing of combinations of only carbon and hydrogen atoms. Because they all consist of the same type of atoms, materials in this class of compounds share many properties. However, the arrangement of the atoms also plays an important role in the properties of the material. For example, pentane and neopentane both consist of five carbon atoms and twelve hydrogen atoms, but because the atoms are arranged differently, the substances have different properties (see Table 1.2). Similarly, the identity and arrangement of the building blocks of a nanoscale structure or assembly affect its function and properties.

The type and strength of interatomic interactions are determined by the electron configuration of the atoms involved. For example, an increase in the number of electrons affects the strength of London dispersion forces and, in turn, associated properties. Table 1.3 provides an example of the melting and boiling point trends of noble gases as the atomic weight increases. Another example is the electronegativity of an atom—the tendency of an atom to accept an electron, which influences the type of interaction in which it will participate. Atoms with very different electronegativities (e.g., metals with nonmetals) tend to interact through ionic-type electrical forces, whereas atoms of nonmetals with similar electronegativities tend to interact through covalent-type electrical interactions. Likewise, the identity and properties of the building blocks of nanoscale structures and assemblies (i.e., atoms, molecules, nanoscale

Table 1.2
Comparison of some physical properties of pentane and neopentane[a]

	Chemical Formula	Boiling Point (°C)	Melting Point (°C)
Pentane	$CH_3(CH_2)_3CH_3$	36.1	-129.7
Neopentane	$C(CH_3)_4$	9.5	-16.6

[a] Weast 1976

Table 1.3
Comparison of boiling and melting points of noble gases[a]

Element		Atomic Weight	Melting Point (°C)	Boiling Point (°C)
Helium	He	4.003	< -272.2	-268.9
Neon	Ne	20.179	-248.7	-246.0
Argon	Ar	39.948	-189.2	-185.7
Krypton	Kr	83.80	-156.6	-152.3
Xenon	Xe	131.29	-111.7	-108.1
Radon	Rn	~222	-78	-61.8

[a] Weast 1976

assemblies) affect the way that they interact with one another. These ideas will be explored more fully in the Forces and Interactions section, which begins on page 18.

Electrical forces and the motion of the building blocks are essential to the formation and function of assemblies and structures at the nano-, atomic, and molecular scales. All atoms are in constant random motion that is dependent on the heat of the system and is often referred to as thermal motion. The principle that the atoms that compose all substances are in constant random motion has significant implications at the nanoscale. Because thermal motion occurs on the molecular scale, its effects are not apparent at the macroscale. For example,

Chapter 1

SCLINKS
THE WORLD'S A CLICK AWAY

Topic: Kinetic Theory

Go to: *www.scilinks.org*

Code: NSE01

as a tree log floats down a river, water molecules will be constantly colliding with it. Because the log is so large, the random collisions have no effect on its motion. If the log were a billion times smaller (i.e., nanoscale), then the random collisions with the water molecules would begin to have an effect on its trajectory or its behavior. Thus, for nanoscale phenomena, thermal motion becomes a more important factor. In addition, the number of atoms contained in a nanoscale object may be small enough that the motion of an individual atom affects the properties and behaviors of the whole. These ideas will be explored more specifically in the Forces and Interactions section in this chapter and in the Size-Dependent Properties and Self-Assembly sections in Chapter 2.

Why Is This a Big Idea?

Although scientists' understanding of the structure and behavior of matter at the bulk ($\geq 10^{-7}$ m) and atomic levels is relatively well-developed, limited knowledge exists about how matter behaves as it transitions between these two scales. Recently developed tools have provided researchers unprecedented access to this region of transition—the nanoscale—which is leading to new levels of understanding about the structure and behavior of matter.

The atomic and kinetic theories are the basis for understanding the structure and behavior of matter. In fact, renowned physicist Richard Feynman said:

If, in some cataclysm, all scientific knowledge were to be destroyed, and only one sentence passed on to the next generation of creatures, what statement would contain the most information in the fewest words? I believe it is the atomic hypothesis (or atomic fact, or whatever you wish to call it) that all things are made of atoms—little particles that move around in perpetual motion, attracting each other when they are a little distance apart, but repelling upon being squeezed into one another. (Feynman 1996, p. 4)

The atomic and kinetic theories explain an enormous number of phenomena, so that without having a thorough understanding of these concepts, it is not possible to comprehend the structure and behavior of matter at any scale, including the nanoscale.

To understand the properties and behavior of matter across scales, it is important to understand the structure and properties of its building blocks. Properties common to all atoms relate to some of the properties of matter observed at the nanoscale. In particular, (a) atoms and molecules are in constant random motion, and (b) the forces that dominate interactions between atoms and molecules are electrical in nature. Both of these properties are essential to the formation and function of assemblies at both the molecular and nanoscales.

Some of the interesting properties at the nanoscale are related to the specific properties of the constituent atoms. An example is the different forms, or allotropes, of carbon (see Figure 1.5). The forms of pure carbon traditionally taught are diamond, graphite, and charcoal.* In each form, the carbon atoms interact differently with each other, resulting in materials with very different properties (see Table 1.4, p. 14). Diamond is an extended three-

---

*Each of these forms of carbon has a nanoscale form: Adamants and diamondoids are nanoscale structures that are essentially diamond molecules; polyaromatic hydrocarbons (PAHs) are individual molecules of graphite; and carbon nanofoam is also an amorphous form of carbon.

Figure 1.5

Representations of some of the allotropes of carbon: (a) Portion of the covalent network of carbon atoms that makes up diamond (b) Portions of three sheets of carbon atoms as they are arranged in graphite (c) C_{60} buckminsterfullerene (d) Single-walled carbon nanotubes

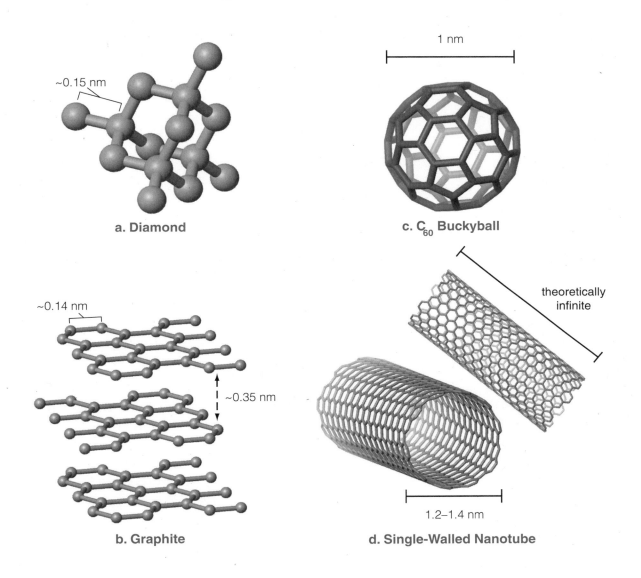

a. Diamond

c. C_{60} Buckyball

b. Graphite

d. Single-Walled Nanotube

Source: Images were created using MOLMOL (Koradi, Billeter, and Wüthrich 1996). Coordinates for (*a*) (*b*), and (*c*) were obtained from *www.nyu.edu/pages/mathmol/library*. Coordinates for the carbon nanotube were generated at *http://k.1asphost. com/tubeasp/tubeASP.asp*.

Chapter 1

Table 1.4
Comparison of some physical properties of carbon allotropes

	Diamond	Graphite	C[60] Buckyball	Carbon Nanotube
density (g/cm^3)	3.51[a]	2.25[a]	~1.65[e]	1.33–1.40[b] (depends on form)
electrical conductivity	insulator	conductor	semiconductor	semiconductor (most)
thermal conductivity (W/cm-K)	23.2[a]	(Pyrolytic graphite)[a] 19.6 (parallel to sheet) 0.0579 (perpendicular to sheet)	no data	> 2[c]
hardness (Mohs scale)	10[a]	~1[a]	individual ~10 bulk 1–2	no data
bulk modulus (G Pa)	1200[e]	207[e]	18[e]	1000–1300[d] (depends on form)

[a] Weast 1976
[b] Gao, Cagin, and Goddard 1997
[c] Che, Cagin, and Goddard 2000
[d] Dujardin et al. 1998
[e] Sussex Fullerene Group n.d.

dimensional network in which every carbon atom interacts with four other carbon atoms (Figure 1.5a, p. 13). It is an insulator and one of the hardest known substances (10 on the Mohs scale). In graphite, each carbon atom bonds to only three other atoms. The atoms form single layers of six-membered carbon atom rings that stack upon one another (Figure 1.5b, p. 13). Graphite is a relatively soft substance (2 on the Mohs scale) and is a conductor. The most recent models of charcoal suggest a structure that is an amorphous combination of these types of interactions.

There are also other allotropes of carbon, which are nanoscale structures. Buckminsterfullerenes, or buckyballs, are hollow, sphere-shaped molecules most commonly represented as structures consisting of 60 carbon atoms that look much like tiny soccer balls (Figure 1.5c, p. 13). However, structures containing 70, 76, and 84 carbon atoms have also been found in minute quantities in nature. Individual buckyballs are quite hard, perhaps harder than diamond, but as a bulk substance, they are relatively soft. Several potential applications for buckyballs are currently being investigated, including their potential use as lubricants and superconductors. Another allotrope is the carbon nanotube, which is structurally related to buckyballs. Carbon nanotubes are cylindrical fullerenes with an extended structure that looks similar to a tube of chicken-wire fencing (see Figure 1.5d, p. 13). As a material, carbon nanotubes exhibit novel properties such as high electrical conductivity and resistance to heat; they are one of the strongest and most rigid materials known. The special properties of carbon atoms allow for many different structures, each with its own unique properties.

Understanding the building blocks of a structure or material is important for understanding its function and properties. For example, proteins are nanoscale objects that carry out critical functions within all living organisms. Twenty different molecules, called amino acids, are the building blocks of proteins. Proteins consist of long chains that can be hundreds of amino acids long. Even if a protein consists of hundreds of amino acids, it is common for a single building block, or amino acid, to affect the structure and function of the whole protein.

Hemoglobin—the component of a red blood cell responsible for carrying oxygen—is a classic example of how changing a single building block of a protein can alter the function. Hemoglobin consists of four amino acid chains, which interact to form a single, functional structure (see Figure 1.6a, p. 16). Two types of amino acid chains are part of hemoglobin, alpha (α) and beta (β). There are two α-chains and two β-chains in every hemoglobin molecule. The α-chains consist of 141 amino acids; the β-chains are 146 amino acids long. Changing a single, positively charged amino acid, glutamic acid, to the neutral amino acid valine (Figure 1.6a, b, p. 16) in the β-chain changes the structure and function of the entire protein. The protein, with the mutation, maintains its structure and solubility when bound to oxygen. However, when oxygen is removed, due to changes in the way the altered amino acid interacts with other parts of the protein, the overall structure of the protein changes. The hemoglobin becomes elongated and rigid and polymerizes into long, structured fibers that give the red blood cells

a sickle shape (Finch et al. 1973). The elongated red blood cells have less flexibility and do not flow through blood vessels well, often clumping and blocking the vessels. This single change in the amino acid sequence (glutamic acid to valine) within the hemoglobin protein is the cause of sickle cell anemia. As the hemoglobin example illustrates, it is critical to understand the relationship between the building blocks and the structure and function of the whole.

Hierarchical levels of structure, which enable a single material to be multifunctional, are common in natural materials (Viney and Bell 2004). As described, amino acids and amino acid chains make up proteins; nucleic acids are organized groups of atoms that connect together to make strands that combine to form double-helical DNA or RNA structures. Figure 1.7 (p. 17) illustrates the nanoscale building blocks of bone, tooth enamel, and shell (Gao et al. 2003). The needle-like crystals that make up tooth enamel have diameters of approximately 15 to 20 nm with a length of about 1 μm. The plate-like crystals that make up dentin and bone are 2 to 4 nm thick and up to 100 nm in length and are embedded in a collagen matrix. Nacre, the substance that makes up shells, also consists of plate-like crystals that fit together like bricks. These crystals generally range from 200 to 500 nm thick and are up to a few thousand nanometers long. The nanoscale building blocks provide greater tolerance of structural flaws, thus helping maintain optimal strength (Gao et al. 2003). As scientists and engineers develop better means to fabricate and manipulate nanoscale materials, they will be able exploit this structural advantage by

Figure 1.6
(a) Representation of the peptide backbone of wild-type hemoglobin with four bound heme molecules (b) Illustration of the structure and composition of glutamic acid as compared to valine

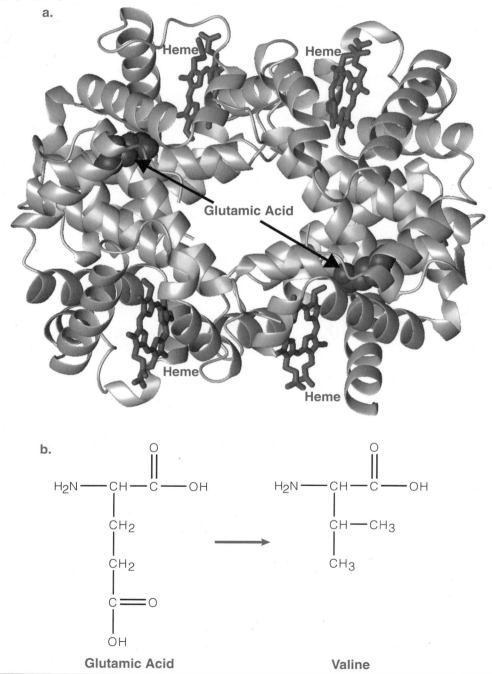

Source for (a): 1gzx (the code for the structure of the molecule in the figure) is from RCSB Protein Data Bank; image created using MOLMOL (Koradi, Billeter, and Wüthrich 1996).

using nanoscale building blocks in designed materials.

Billions of years of naturally occurring "research" have optimized an extremely broad range of natural materials, systems, and processes, often of great complexity, that form and regulate the world around us. One of the major areas of NSE research involves biomimetics, which relates to the design and fabrication of new materials by mimicking the relevant aspects of natural biological materials. Natural materials have several advantages: They are made from renewable resources; they are synthesized in aqueous environments at or near ambient temperatures; and they are biodegradable, so they have an advantage for supporting sustainability (Viney and Bell 2004). Bone (biomineralization), tooth enamel, spiders' web threads, and muscle fibers are just a few examples of materials on which research currently focuses. For instance, as a better and more permanent alternative to medical procedures such as hip replacement surgery, scientists and engineers are working to regenerate bone or to create a material similar to bone using manufactured materials as scaffolds (Jones and Hench 2003; Li 2003).

For students to understand the interesting properties of matter at the nanoscale, they must first develop a deep understanding of the structure and function of its building blocks: atoms, molecules, and other nanoscale structures or assemblies.

Figure 1.7

Images of the macroscale and nanoscale structure in biological hard tissue: (a) Tooth enamel (b) Dentin or bone (c) Nacre (shell)

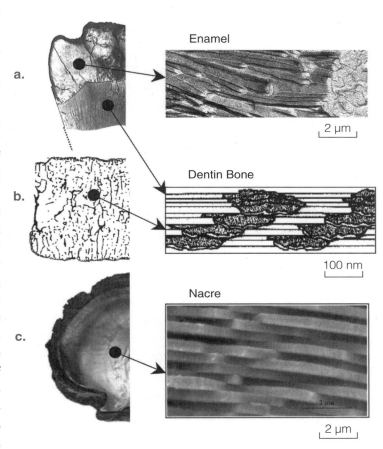

Source: Reprinted with permission from Gao, H., B. Ji, I. L. Jäger, E. Arzt, and P. Fratzel. 2003. *Proceedings of the National Academy of Sciences, USA* 100 (10): 5597–5600. Copyright 2003 National Academy of Sciences, U.S.A.

Relationship to the 7–12 Curriculum

Many of the ideas related to the structure of matter are currently in the national science standards. They provide a critical foundation for understanding the properties and behaviors of nanoscale objects and materials.

Chapter 1

Nanoscale materials themselves are made of atoms, molecules, or other nanoscale objects; therefore many of the same principles apply.

The relationship between the building blocks and the structure and function of the final product (e.g., structure, material, assembly) can be expanded beyond chemistry into other disciplines. The hemoglobin example is appropriate for a biology or biochemistry class when students learn about genetics and proteins. Ideas about hierarchical structure can also be addressed in multiple disciplines. Small, defined sets of building blocks make up proteins, RNA, and DNA, which in turn can combine with various components to form more complex structures that carry out and regulate the functions that maintain life. The process of biomineralization, which involves hierarchical structure, is relevant in chemistry, biology, geology, and engineering depending on the phenomena under study. Applying a concept to multiple phenomena can help students make sense of basic principles as they extend their understanding to include new situations.

Big Idea 3
Forces and Interactions

All interactions can be described by multiple types of forces, but the relative impact of each type of force changes with scale. On the nanoscale, a range of electrical forces with varying strengths tends to dominate the interactions between objects.

About Forces and Interactions

Four fundamental forces describe all interactions: gravitational, electromagnetic, nuclear (or strong), and weak forces. At the macroscale, the gravitational force—a force between masses that is always attractive—is usually dominant.

Forces derived from electrical charges, a subset of the electromagnetic force, generally dominate at the nano- and atomic scales. Examples include chemical bonding and biomolecular recognition. The nuclear (or strong) force is responsible for keeping the nuclei of atoms together; thus it is dominant on the subatomic scale (length scale of $\sim 10^{-15}$ m). The weak force is also involved in subatomic scale phenomena such as beta decay and other nuclear reactions.

A Continuum of Electrical Forces

Small objects of nano- and atomic length scales (e.g., atoms, molecules, nanoparticles) interact in a variety of ways, all of which are dominated by forces that are electrical in nature. These electrical forces create a continuum of forces that describe most of the interactions within matter on the nano- and atomic scales, the strength of which depends on the entities involved. Net attractive forces must bring and hold the components together in order to form a stable complex.

Many of these electrical forces occur between permanent (static) charges and are labeled as electrostatic forces, the strength of which is described by Coulomb's law. There are several types of electrostatic interactions. Ionic interactions occur between ions of integer charges. They are most commonly represented as interactions between ions in salts (i.e., ionic bonding). Other examples include interactions between charged amino acids within or between biomolecules, which are commonly referred to as "salt bridges." Dipole-dipole interactions occur between opposite partial charges that result from an uneven distribution (a separation) of positive and negative charge and are weaker

Figure 1.8

(a) The *i*, *i*+4 hydrogen bonding pattern stabilizes alpha helical polypeptides. R represents the amino acid side chains. (b) A cartoon representation of an alpha helix. Hydrogen bonds are represented by dotted lines.

a.

b.

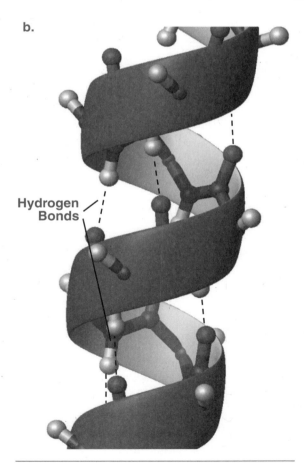

Hydrogen Bonds

Source: This image was created using MOLMOL (Koradi, Billeter, and Wüthrich 1996).

than ionic interactions. Hydrogen bonds are a type of dipole-dipole interaction that occurs between a hydrogen atom attached to a highly electronegative atom (most commonly oxygen, nitrogen, or fluorine) and another electronegative atom that has a lone pair of electrons.

Although often defined as an intermolecular force, hydrogen bonding also plays an important structural role within many large (nanoscale) molecules, such as biomolecules. For example, proteins consist of chains of amino acids that adopt structures known as alpha helices and beta sheets. As the name suggests, alpha helices consist of a spiraling amino acid chain that is stabilized by hydrogen bonds between the carbonyl (C=O) of amino acid *i* to the amide hydrogen (NH) four amino acids further along the chain (*i*+4) as shown in Figure 1.8. Beta-sheets consist of extended strands of amino acids that are held together with hydrogen bonds as illustrated in Figure 1.9 (p. 20). Hydrogen bonds between base pairs of DNA

Chapter 1

Figure 1.9
(a) Hydrogen bonds stabilize an anti-parallel beta sheet. Hydrogen bonds are represented by dotted lines. R represents the amino acid side chains. (b) Alternate representation of an anti-parallel beta sheet. Hydrogen bonds are represented by dotted lines.

a.

b.

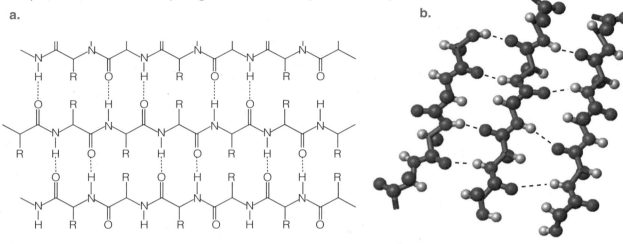

Source for (b): Created using MOLMOL (Koradi, Billeter, and Wüthrich 1996).

Figure 1.10
(a) Lewis dot representation of methane illustrates the electron sharing between the carbon and hydrogen atoms. The open circles represent the electron contributed by the hydrogen atoms and the solid dots, the electrons contributed by the carbon atom. (b) The distance between the hydrogen atoms of methane is maximized in this tetrahedral arrangement.

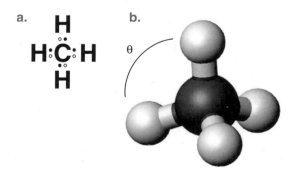

and RNA are an important part of maintaining the familiar double-helical structure.

Covalent bonds are characterized by the sharing of one or more electron pairs between atoms to balance the attraction and repulsion that occur between two atoms. This class of interactions tends to be used to describe interactions between nonmetals that have similar electronegativities. The strength of the covalent bonding depends both on the distance and the angle of the interaction between atoms. For example, methane adopts a tetragonal structure to maximize the distance between the hydrogen atoms (see Figure 1.10).

A related type of interaction is the coordinate covalent bond in which the shared pair of electrons comes from a single atom as illustrated in Figure 1.11. Coordinate covalent bonds commonly occur between transition metals and nonmetals. A large number of substances, including many minerals, are governed by this type of interaction.

Figure 1.11
An example of coordinate covalent bonding

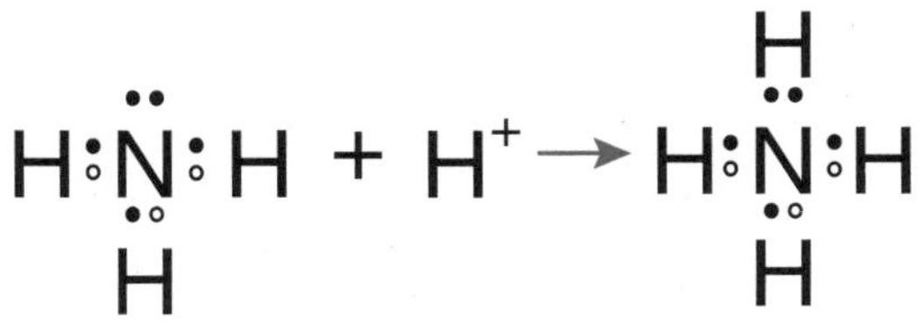

$$H:\overset{\cdot\cdot}{\underset{\cdot\cdot}{N}}:H + H^+ \rightarrow H:\overset{\overset{\textstyle H}{}}{\underset{\underset{\textstyle H}{}}{\underset{\cdot\cdot}{N}}}:H$$

In contrast to interactions governed by electrostatic forces, some types of interactions involve a dynamic behavior of electrons. The electron distribution within an atom (or molecule) may shift to create a partial charge—an induced dipole. Induced dipoles may be created when a neutral, nonpolar atom is brought into close proximity to a polar entity (see Figure 1.12) or an electric field. London forces involve two or more induced dipoles,* which result from momentary, or instantaneous, shifts in the electron distribution of neutral atoms (or molecules). Like electrostatic interactions, the strength of the interactions depends on distance but falls off more rapidly (r^6) with atomic separation. Although generally considered intermolecular, London forces also play a role in intramolecular structure.

Delocalized electrons, which are electrons that are not associated with a single atom or covalent bond, are another example of dynamic behavior of electrons. For example, in metallic bonding, electrons are delocalized and shared among a lattice of atoms, which is the source of some metallic properties. The atoms of a metal are held together by the electrostatic attraction between the positively charged metal ions and the delocalized electrons. Aromatic compounds also involve delocalized electrons.

Although categorizing forces helps characterize the range of electron behavior that mediates interactions at the atomic, molecular, and nanoscales, these forces rarely exist in pure form. Instead, they represent benchmarks along a continuum of electrical forces, the strength and character of which are defined by the partners involved in the interaction.

Specificity

Electrical forces not only are important in interactions between atoms and molecules but also dominate the interactions between structures and assemblies at the nanoscale. For example, electrical forces govern the interactions between biomolecules, many of which are nanoscale structures. Various combinations of electrical forces control the strength and specificity of the interactions between these molecules in order to perform and finely regulate the biological processes that maintain life. For example, as part of the replicating process, single-stranded DNA binding protein (SSBP) is responsible for separating the strands of the double helix to

Figure 1.12
Illustration of a dipole–induced-dipole interaction. δ+/δ- represent partial positive and negative charges respectively ($0 < \delta+ < 1; -1 < \delta- < 0$).

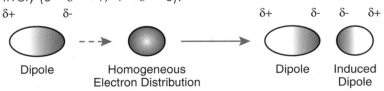

δ+   δ-

Dipole

Homogeneous
Electron Distribution

δ+   δ-   δ-   δ+

Dipole   Induced
Dipole

---

* London dispersion and induced dipoles are often grouped together as van der Waals forces, but by definition, van der Waals forces also include dipole-dipole interactions (and hydrogen bonds). To prevent confusion, when possible, we specify the individual type of interaction.

allow the DNA polymerase to create the complementary strand. To perform this function, SSBPs must be able to bind to *any* sequence of DNA. SSBPs accomplish this by binding only

Chapter 1

to the negatively charged phosphate backbone of the DNA through ionic interactions. The strength of the interaction is the same regardless of the point on the DNA strand to which the SSBP binds (Kowalczykowski, Bear, and von Hippel 1981). In contrast, the DNA-binding proteins that regulate gene expression bind to double-stranded DNA through a unique network of ionic interactions to the phosphate backbone and hydrogen bonds (dipole-dipole interactions) to the DNA bases. The interactions between this type of DNA-binding protein and DNA are quite selective. The strength of the interaction between the protein and a specific set of base-pairs along the strand is at least 1,000 times greater than the interaction at any other point along the helix. Thus, the nature of the interaction between proteins and DNA differs depending on the interacting entities (von Hippel and Berg 1986; Stevens and Glick 1997).

Strength of Interactions

Many factors play a role in the interaction between two components. For example, a polar solvent (e.g., water) will weaken electrostatic interactions. Likewise, the presence of ions in the solvent will affect the affinity of two entities interacting through electrostatic forces. For any interacting entities, the relative concentrations and temperature will affect the formation of the complex.

The same electrical forces and principles that are involved in chemical bonding—biomolecular recognition and all interactions at the nano-, molecular, and atomic scales—are important to consider in the design, fabrication, and manipulation of nanoscale materials (see Self-Assembly, p. 43, for examples). Therefore, it is necessary to understand them in order to understand and predict the function and behavior of natural and fabricated nanoscale materials.

Why Is This a Big Idea?

Nanotechnology exploits the unique interactions of matter on the nanoscale to create structures and materials with new functionality. To design and build them, it is critical to understand how they are structured, which includes understanding how they are held together. Therefore, it is necessary to have an understanding of the electrical forces that dominate the interactions between the atoms, molecules, and nanoscale structures that create nanoscale assemblies and materials.

Because the dominant forces that mediate an interaction are largely determined by scale, the same forces govern interactions between a large variety of entities. The electrical forces that bond atoms together to form molecules are also involved in interactions between nanoscale objects, both natural and fabricated. Biological molecules and molecular machines are some of the natural nanoscale objects that fall into this category, including DNA, proteins, and the ribosome. The strength and specificity of the interactions between biological molecules is extremely important as these molecules perform and regulate the biological processes that maintain life (e.g., DNA replication, protein synthesis). Likewise, interactions at the nanoscale play an important role in Earth systems, as the processes that build materials up and break them down often occur at the nanoscale (Hochella 2006). For example, many geological mineralization processes, including mineral dissolution, are mediated by electrical forces between microbes (primarily prokaryotes) and mineral surfaces (Hochella 2002).

Although the interactions dominated by electrical forces occur at a scale too small to see, the effects of those interactions can often be easily detected at the macroscale. One of the most

Figure 1.13

Nanocar on a surface of gold atoms: (a) Scanning tunneling microscope (STM) image of the nanocars on a gold surface (b) STM image of one nanocar with scale bars (scale bars based on Shirai et al. 2005) (c) Representation of the molecular structure of the nanocars

a.   **b.**   **c.**

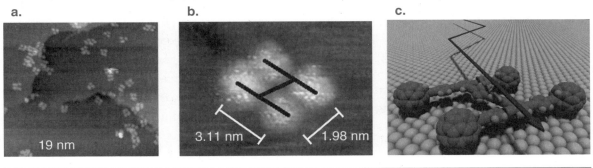

19 nm   3.11 nm   1.98 nm

Source: Figures reproduced with permission from J. M. Tour of Rice University.

familiar examples is rubbing a balloon on carpet and sticking it to the ceiling (electrostatic force). Another example is observing that flour and powdered sugar stick to a plastic measuring cup more than granulated sugar does because the attractive electrical forces between the powdered materials and the cup's surface are stronger than the gravitational forces acting on them (electrodynamic and electrostatic forces). Soap washes off oil and grease (hydrophobic/hydrophilic), but water is enough to wash off something sticky and sugary (hydrogen bonding). Our sense of touch is the result of a variety of electrical forces. Electrical forces are critical for explaining an enormous range of phenomena in the world around us.

Electrical forces also have an impact beyond the fabrication of nanoscale structures and assemblies. Once they have been created, nanoscale products are often difficult to control and manipulate. For example, researchers fabricated a nanoscale "car" with buckyballs (C_{60}) as wheels (see Figure 1.13). At room temperature, the electrical forces between the wheels and surface were so strong that the nanocar stuck to the surface. However,

at 200°C, the car was freed and able to roll across the surface. Therefore, understanding and controlling the electrical forces that can occur between two objects is important not only when building a nanoscale structure but also when determining the usefulness of the final product (Shirai et al. 2005).

Electrical forces play a critical role in nano- and atomic scale interactions crucial to all natural and living systems. As nanotechnology aims to control matter, scientists and engineers must consider electrical forces in all aspects of the process–design, fabrication, characterization, processing, and manipulation.

Relationship to the 7–12 Curriculum

High school chemistry courses typically introduce students to the bonds that keep molecules together. Chemical bonds are mediated through the electrons of the participating atoms but are rarely equated to electrical forces. In addition, curricula often represent bonds as categories of interactions (i.e., ionic, dipole-dipole, induced dipole, covalent), using algorithms (e.g., electronegativity differences) and rules (e.g., octet rule) that help students categorize interactions. While these algorithms are useful, over-reliance on them may hinder students' ability to consider electrical forces as a continuum (Taber and Coll 2002). Viewing electrical forces in terms of discrete categories may impede their conceptual understanding of phenomena (Levy Nahum et al. 2007). Students need to be reminded that the octet rule, Lewis dot structures, and other representations are models used to help explain how atoms interact, and as models, they can emphasize only a portion of any given phenomena. Relying solely on simple models and categories will hinder students' abilities to connect the electrical forces involved in chemical bonding to those that govern a range of other interactions, including those that occur at the nanoscale.

> *Sometimes it seems to me that a bond between two atoms has become so real, so tangible, so friendly, that I can almost see it. Then I awake with a little shock, for a chemical bond is not a real thing. It does not exist. No one has ever seen one. No one ever will. It is a figment of our own imagination.*
>
> —Charles A. Coulson, 1955

Connecting chemical bonds to electrical forces may help students understand that the same electrical forces dominate at the nano- and atomic scales, which include not only chemical bonding but also interactions between nanoscale structures both natural (e.g., proteins, DNA) and fabricated (e.g., nanotubes). This approach may also help remove some of the artificial barriers erected between disciplines through the traditional patterns of science instruction. In addition, curricula tend to present shape as the primary determinant of

recognition. Although shape plays an important role, complementary shape acts to align the electrical forces that govern the interaction. Focusing on electrical forces instead of chemical bonding or on shape as the primary determinant of recognition decreases emphasis on discipline-specific explanations of phenomena. In particular, the idea of electrical forces might support students in developing a broader understanding of interactions on the nano- and atomic scales.

Big Idea 4
Quantum Effects

Different models explain and predict the behavior of matter better, depending on the scale and conditions of the system. In particular, as the size or mass of an object becomes smaller and transitions through the nanoscale, quantum effects become more important.

About Quantum Effects

It is not necessary to have a deep understanding of quantum mechanics in order to develop a fundamental understanding of many nanoscale phenomena (e.g., tunneling, quantum dots). A general, qualitative understanding of these fundamental quantum mechanical concepts is adequate for the nonspecialist:

- All matter exhibits both wave-like and particle-like characters. This implies that we cannot simultaneously determine the position and momentum of a particle.
- Only discrete amounts, quanta, of energy may enter or exit certain systems (e.g., atoms, molecules, quantum dots)—energy is quantized. This is true not only for atomic

and subatomic systems but also for many nanoscale systems.

- Because of the wave-particle duality, we cannot predict exactly what did or will happen to matter at certain scales (i.e., atomic scale, subatomic scale, and often nanoscale). Instead, only the probability of a given outcome can be measured. This has implications for electron behavior within atoms, chemical bonding, and intermolecular interactions.

- An approximation of the Pauli exclusion principle for nonexperts is that two electrons cannot be in the exact same quantum state within the same system (atom). This relates to the arrangement of elements in the periodic table and the associated trends observed.

Many educators question whether ideas about quantum mechanics should be introduced in the secondary science curriculum at all. The national science standards, designed to define science literacy, contain at least some of the ideas listed above (AAAS 1993; NRC 1996). In addition, most, if not all, of these ideas are presented in a typical high school chemistry course. The vote by participants (scientists, engineers, and formal and informal science educators) at a national workshop for K–12 NSE education was nearly unanimous for the inclusion of quantum mechanics at the high school level (for more information on the workshop, see p. 3 in the Introduction and also Appendix A). Therefore, Quantum Effects is included as one of the big ideas of NSE. The challenges and some potential strategies for bringing ideas related to quantum mechanics to the secondary science classroom are discussed in Chapter 8.

Classical mechanics has its foundation in Newton's laws of motion. The model is used to describe the motion of a range of phenomena that occur over a range of scales—from the behavior of single-celled organisms to the flight of a bullet, from movement of a car to movement of planets. Yet, as matter transitions from the bulk (micro- to macroscale) to the atomic scale, classical mechanics fails in its ability to describe the behavior of matter. At this point and smaller (e.g., subatomic), it becomes necessary to use quantum mechanics to explain phenomena such as the color/spectrum of burning elements or tunneling.

It is difficult to assign an exact point at which the transition occurs. Size is relative, and as such, the point at which quantum mechanics becomes important depends on the object or system being observed as well as the act of observation. This is because any observation of an object requires an interaction between the object and a measuring device. If making a measurement or observing the object causes a negligible disturbance to the object, then the object can be considered to be "big," and classical mechanics can be used to describe its behavior. However, if the disturbance caused by the measurement or observation is significant, then the size of the object in the absolute sense is "small," and a different model, quantum mechanics, must be applied.

Werner Heisenberg (1958) used a related thought experiment to develop the idea of uncertainty. His experiment involved using a microscope to measure the path of an electron. The resolution limit of a light microscope is approximately one-half that of the wavelength of the incident light. Therefore, the uncertainty of the position of the observed object is proportional to the wavelength of the incident light. To increase the resolution (or minimize the uncertainty) such that the position of something as small as an electron could be tracked, incident light with a much shorter wavelength (higher

Chapter 1

frequency) must be used as a probe (i.e., gamma rays). However, in order to detect the electron, a gamma-ray photon must hit it. When the photon impacts with the electron, it will impart some momentum. This will change the momentum of the electron, which is the very object that was being measured. In other words, the act of measuring the position changes its momentum.

The smaller the wavelength of the incident photon, the more precisely the position of the electron can be determined. However, the smaller the wavelength of the photon, the larger the momentum it has, which will result in a larger change in the momentum of the electron after impact. Thus, although the position of the electron is known more precisely, the uncertainty of its momentum is greater, so the exact position and momentum of an electron cannot be simultaneously determined. This idea is described by the Heisenberg uncertainty principle, which is illustrated by Equation 1.1, where x denotes position, p is momentum, and h is Planck's constant. Einstein was the first to show this relationship with the photon.

Equation 1.1
Heisenberg uncertainty principle

$$\Delta x \, \Delta p \geq h$$

Several other uncertainty relationships describe pairs of complementary observables that cannot simultaneously be measured exactly (e.g., energy and time). In these cases, as one observable is measured more precisely, the other necessarily becomes less defined. Thus it is impossible to predict the *exact* behavior of matter; only predictions about the *probability* of what will happen can be calculated. This realization changed the way that we think about science and about nature itself as illustrated by Feynman and Heisenberg:

[P]hilosophers have said before that one of the fundamental requirements of science is that whenever you set up the same conditions, the same thing must happen. This is simply not true, it is not a fundamental condition of science. (Feynman 1996, p. 35)

If we want to describe what happens in an atomic event, we have to realize that the word "happens" can only apply to the observation, not to the state of affairs between two observations. (Heisenberg 1958)

Yes! Physics has given up. We do not know how to predict what would happen in a given circumstance and we believe now that it is impossible, that the only thing that can be predicted is the probability of different events. It must be recognized that this is a retrenchment in our earlier ideal of understanding nature. It may be a backward step, but no one has seen a way to avoid it. (Feynman 1996, p. 135)

The Heisenberg uncertainty principle is a consequence of matter having both a particle- and a wave-like nature. All things will exhibit either wave-like or particle-like properties depending on how they are observed. Since Newton, scientists have debated whether light should be described in terms of waves or particles. Einstein's work on blackbody radiation showed that light exhibits both wave-like and particle-like behavior. A few years earlier, J. J. Thomson's research with cathode rays provided experimental evidence for the particle-nature of electrons. First, he established that cathode rays are beams of negatively charged particles, or electrons. He then determined the mass-to-charge ratio for the negatively charged particles by measuring the amount that a magnetic field deflects the beam. He found that this ratio was independent of the cathode material, thus establishing that electrons have a particle nature.

After the realization that light could behave both as a particle and a wave, the question of whether matter would exhibit the same dual behavior became a focus of research. Louis de Broglie predicted that matter also has a wave-like nature with the relation in Equation 1.2. The momentum (p) of a particle is inversely proportional to its wavelength (λ), as described by de Broglie, where h is Planck's constant. In 1927, two independent research groups showed that a beam of electrons could create a diffraction pattern, thus illustrating the wave-like character of electrons. This provided evidence that matter can exhibit both wave-like and particle-like behavior.

Equation 1.2
The de Broglie relation

$$\lambda = h/p$$

Macroscale objects such as baseballs also exhibit wave-like behavior, but the de Broglie wavelength is so much smaller than the baseballs themselves that we only observe the average position. At these scales (e.g., macroscale), the wave-like character is not important for explaining phenomena. At smaller scales (e.g., nano-, atomic, and subatomic scales) the wavelength is on the order of the size of the objects and the wave character becomes more important.

In Latin, the word *quantum* means amount. In quantum physics, only certain discrete amounts of energy can enter or exit a system. These amounts are some multiple of $h\nu$, where h is Planck's constant and ν is the frequency of the radiation. These quanta are so small that the allowed changes in energy for macroscopic objects appear to be continuous. However, at smaller scales quantization

becomes more important. The electrons produced when metals are exposed to ultraviolet light (the photoelectric effect) provide experimental evidence for energy quantization. Electrons are not ejected from the metal unless a certain threshold frequency is met, regardless of the intensity of the incident radiation. Likewise, the kinetic energy of the ejected electrons is directly proportional to the frequency of the incident radiation but is independent of the intensity. Emission spectra of energetically excited hydrogen atoms also provide experimental evidence for energy quantization.

A full characterization, or quantum state, of a particle is defined by four quantum numbers. The particle of interest in this case is the electron. The principle quantum number n designates the state. In the case of the electron, it defines the energy level that the electron occupies within an atom. In other words, it specifies the multiple of $h\nu$, such that $E = nh\nu$.

The second quantum number, orbital angular momentum l, is associated with the orbital, or subshell, designations within each energy level. Within the classical mechanical model, an object can rotate with any angular momentum. However, according to quantum mechanics, angular momentum is quantized so only certain values are allowed. Figure 1.14 (p. 28) illustrates the probability electron densities for the hydrogen atom. For electrons, the *s*-orbitals are spherically symmetric probability distributions surrounding the nucleus of the atom that are associated with a quantum number $l = 0$. The *p*-orbitals are two-lobed distributions represented by an angular momentum quantum number of $l = 1$ (see Table 1.5, p. 29).

The magnetic quantum number m designates the energy levels available in each subshell. For example, for *s*-orbitals, $m = 0$, which

Chapter 1

Figure 1.14
Probability distribution plots for hydrogen

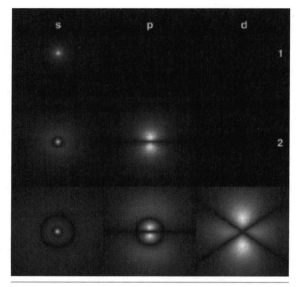

Source: Image downloaded from Wiki Commons courtesy of GNU Free Documentation License, Version 1.2.

indicates there is just one state for an *s*-orbital at each energy level. For *p*-orbitals, $m = -1$, 0, or 1, so there are three different states (i.e., p_x, p_y, p_z). Table 1.5 illustrates the relationship between the angular momentum and magnetic quantum numbers. The final quantum number *s* is the spin quantum number. While *l* defines the orbital angular momentum of the electron, *s* defines its angular momentum independent of its motion around the nucleus. Spin is the "intrinsic, characteristic and irremovable angular momentum of a particle" (Atkins 1991, p. 223). It is an intrinsic property of electrons in the same way that its rest mass and charge are intrinsic properties of electrons. The value of *s* for electrons is either +1/2 or -1/2.

To describe atoms that contain many electrons, an orbital approximation is used. According to the Pauli exclusion principle,* two electrons in the same system cannot exist in the same state (i.e., have the same set of quantum numbers). Since electrons have either spin +1/2 or -1/2, then only two electrons can occupy the same orbital—one electron with spin +1/2 and one with spin -1/2. These electrons are considered to be paired. Additional electrons must occupy higher-energy orbitals. This has a profound impact on atomic structure and molecular bonding. Pauli developed this theory to account for the periodicity of the elements.

Why Is This a Big Idea?

Quantum effects play an important role in all aspects of NSE. Classical mechanics cannot always reliably predict and explain the behavior of matter on the nanoscale, so in those cases, quantum mechanics must be applied to explain the novel properties of materials that are being exploited by nanotechnology. In addition, some of the tools that have been developed to help explore the nanoscale world require quantum mechanics to explain their function.

The quantization of energy states is apparent in many nanoscale materials and is an important factor in determining the chemical and physical properties of a material. Unbound, or unconfined, electrons can move freely and can absorb any amount of energy (see Figure 1.15). In contrast, when an electron becomes bound, or *confined* within a system like an atom or molecule, only certain types of motion are allowed. The motion and energy levels become quantized and are defined by quantum numbers *l* and *n* respectively. The more strongly the electron is confined, the larger the separation between allowed energy levels (El-Sayed 2001).

---

* Although the Pauli principle is often represented as something akin to "two electrons cannot have the same spin," the principle is actually much broader. The Pauli principle relates to a class of particles called fermions. By definition, within a single system no two fermions can be described by the same quantum state (i.e., same set of quantum numbers). An electron is an example of a fermion and the atom is the system.

Table 1.5
Relationship between the orbital angular momentum and magnetic quantum numbers

Orbital (subshell)	Orbital Angular Momentum (l)	Magnetic Quantum Number (m)
s	0	0
p	1	-1, 0, +1
d	2	-2, -1, 0, +1, +2
f	3	-3, -2, -1, 0, +1, +2, +3
g	4	-4, -3, -2, -1, 0, +1, +2, +3, +4

Conductivity of metals is due to delocalized electrons where an electron is shared among a lattice of positively charged nuclei. Band theory is a model used to describe electron behavior in metals. At 0 K, the electrons lie in the valence band, which describes the highest filled orbital, and the higher energy conduction band is empty (see Figure 1.16, p. 30). Electrons in the conduction band move in response to an applied electric field. In metals, there is no gap between the valence and conduction bands, so electrons move freely and current flows through the metal. Because the electrons are free to move within the solid, the allowed energy states are essentially continuous. However, when the size of the metal particle becomes very small, the electrons have less freedom to move and become confined. In this state, the electrons acquire kinetic energy, or confinement energy, and the energy states become discontinuous, which leads to a separation of the valence and conduction bands.

Once the separation, or band gap, approaches or is greater than kT, where k is Boltzmann's constant and T is temperature, the motion of the electrons becomes quantized and the metal becomes a semiconductor. If the separation becomes great enough, the material will transition to an insulator. At the nanoscale, materials that are conductors on the macroscale may lose their conductivity, and vice versa.

Quantum dots, which range in size from 2 nm to greater than 100 nm in diameter, are nanoscale semiconductors in which electrons are confined in all three dimensions. Their small size gives them special electrical and optical properties. Like atoms, quantum dots have quantized energy spectra because the electrons are confined. The intensity and energy of light emitted from a quantum dot is inversely proportional to its size, as summarized in Table 1.6. As the size of the quantum dot gets larger, the energy separation, or band gap, decreases, and

Figure 1.15
The energy levels in bulk metal are continuous, but become discrete when the electrons become confined.

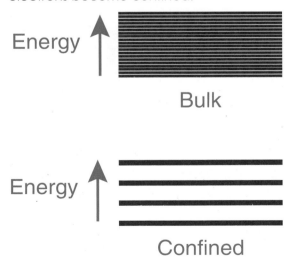

Chapter 1

Figure 1.16
The band gap between the valence and conduction bands determines the conductive properties of a material.

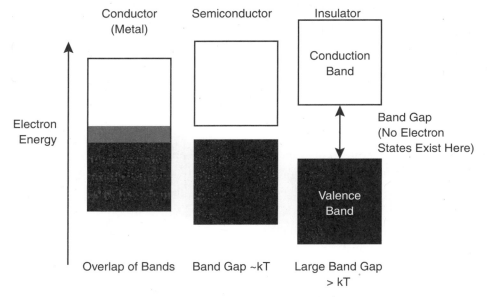

the light emitted shifts toward the red end of the spectrum (decreasing the size affords a blue shift). The special properties of quantum dots have potential applications as diverse as diode lasers, amplifiers, and biological sensors. They also have an extremely high quantum yield—the efficiency with which absorbed light produces some effect—which makes them potential candidates for more efficient solar cells.

The wave-particle duality is also an important factor in NSE. In particular, tunneling is a quantum mechanical effect that occurs when an object transitions through a classically forbidden energy state. An analogy of this phenomenon might be pushing a ball up a hill. If not provided with enough energy, the ball cannot roll over the hill to the other side. However, according to quantum mechanics, there is some nonzero probability that a particle lies anywhere described by the wave function. If the wave function predicts that the particle may

Table 1.6
Size dependence of quantum dot fluorescence emission after excitation at 365 nm

Approximate Diameter (nm)	Color	Approximate Emission Wavelength (nm)
2	blue	490
3	green	525
4	yellow	570
5	red	620

lie on the other side of the "hill," it is possible for the particle to "tunnel through" to the other side of the potential energy "hill" because of its wave-like character. This movement is energetically forbidden in classical mechanics. While the probability of this occurring on any scale is never zero, on the nanoscale and smaller, it is observed more frequently because the wave behavior of an object becomes more significant when its size or mass gets very small.

Because of the Heisenberg uncertainty principle, electrons are described not in terms of position but in terms of electron density defined by a probability distribution, which describes the *probability* of finding an electron at a distance r from the atomic nucleus. The probability density is greatest near the nucleus and falls off rapidly (exponentially) with increasing r. Thus, an electron spends a majority of its time near the nucleus. When two atoms are brought into close proximity (< 1 nm) to each other, the electron densities overlap (see Figure 1.17). At this point, an electron from atom 1 may move into the electron cloud of atom 2 without any energy added to the system. The electron has *tunneled* from atom 1 to atom 2. Classical mechanics predicts that this transfer would require an input of energy. The probability of tunneling occurring is exponentially dependent on the distance between the two atoms.

Quantum tunneling is exploited in one of the important tools of NSE, the scanning tunneling microscope (STM). STMs are nonoptical microscopes that work by scanning a sharp electrical tip across a conductive or semiconductive surface. The tip is so sharp that a single atom lies at the end (see Figure 1.18, p. 32). A constant voltage applied to the tip creates a continuous current flowing between the tip and the sample. If the tip is brought close enough to the surface (tenths of nanometers), the electron clouds of the atom on the tip interact with the electron clouds of the surface atoms and electrons may tunnel between the tip and the surface, creating an increase in current. As the tip scans at a constant height from the surface, the overlap of the electron clouds changes, and with it the probability of tunneling changes. A higher surface height affords greater overlap of the electron clouds and greater probability of

Figure 1.17
Two atoms with slightly overlapping electron densities

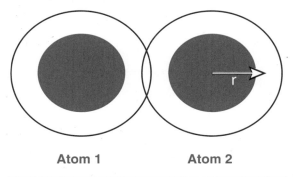

Atom 1   **Atom 2**

Source: Adapted from Ellis et al. 1993, p. 18.

tunneling, which results in an increase in current with height (see Figure 1.18, p. 32; Ellis et al. 1993). Because tunneling is so dependent on the distance between the tip and surface atoms, the STM provides an extremely sensitive measure of interatomic distance and therefore the topography of a surface. The STM can create images of surfaces to a 0.2 nm (2 Å) resolution, which is the size of some types of individual atoms (see Tools and Instrumentation in Chapter 3 for more information).

Quantum tunneling is involved in a range of phenomena. There are many biological systems—such as the porphorin in the heme/cytochrome system, β-carotene, and the chlorin in chlorophyll—that exploit quantum tunneling as part of their functions (i.e., electron transfer). The tunneling phenomenon is also used in many electronic applications. In particular, it plays a role in flash memory, which is computer memory that can be electrically erased and reprogrammed. It is currently used in digital cameras, cell phones, digital music players, and USB flash drives. Even a simple light switch relies on electrons tunneling through a layer of oxide.

Figure 1.18
Illustration of a scanning tunneling microscope probe scanning a surface. Below is a representation of the relative tunneling current as the probe moves across the surface.

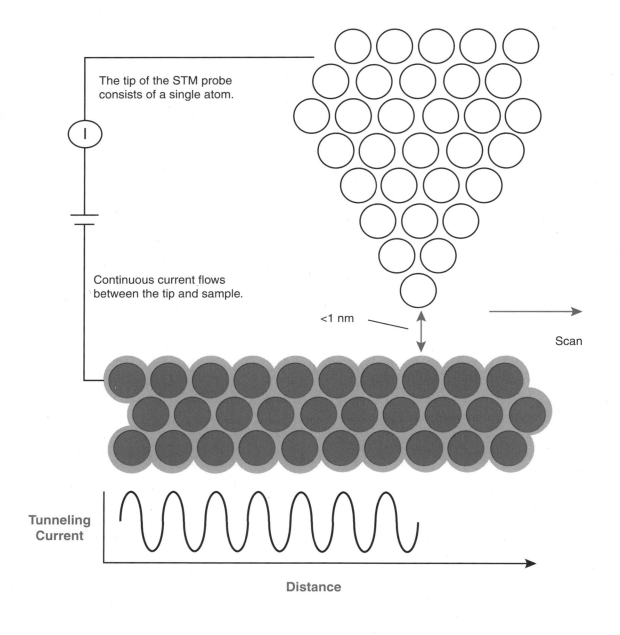

The tip of the STM probe consists of a single atom.

Continuous current flows between the tip and sample.

<1 nm

Scan

Tunneling Current

Distance

Source: Adapted from Ellis et al. 1993, p. 17.

Uncertainty and spin play a crucial role in the structure of matter and the way in which it interacts. Spintronics, or spin electronic research, aims to utilize the electron spin, as well as its charge, to carry information in solid-state devices. Already, this technology is used to increase the sensitivity of read-head sensors in hard disk drives and in magnetic random access memories (MRAMs) (McCray 2009). Ultimately, researchers hope that exploiting both electron charge and spin will decrease the power required for electronic devices.

Interactions at the nanoscale are generally dominated by electrical forces. To develop a conceptual understanding of these forces and relevant phenomena, students must have a probabilistic, or quantum mechanical model, of electron behavior rather than a solar system (classical) model of the atom.

Relationship to the 7–12 Curriculum

Our life experience is with objects and phenomena within the macroscale that can be explained with classical physics. To explain phenomena on scales too small for us to directly experience (i.e., nano-, atomic, subatomic), we must apply quantum mechanics, which is an extremely complex subject that requires extensive experience in both mathematics and science. Its counterintuitive predictions are difficult to grasp even for expert scientists. Thoughts of leading 20th century scientists may be comforting:

I think it is safe to say that no one understands quantum mechanics. (Richard Feynman 1996)

Anyone who is not shocked by quantum theory has not understood a single word. (Niels Bohr, n.d.)

I myself only came to believe in the uncertainty relations after many pangs of conscience.... (Werner Heisenberg 1958)

What I am going to tell you about is what we teach our physics students in the third or fourth year of graduate school.... It is my task to convince you not to turn away because you don't understand it. You see my physics students don't understand it.... That is because I don't understand it. Nobody does. (Richard Feynman, Nobel Lecture, 1966)

However, the difficulty of the subject matter does not preclude a qualitative introduction of quantum effects to grades 7–12 students. It is obviously inappropriate to introduce quantum mechanics in a rigorous manner using mathematical models. Reasoning about the strengths and limitations of models is in accordance with current science education standards (NRC 1996; AAAS 1993), reflecting the fact that understanding the role of models is a fundamental part of the scientific process (see Models and Simulations in Chapter 3 for more detail). As such, it is reasonable for students to begin to understand the limitations of classical mechanics as well as the advantages of some aspects of the quantum mechanical model.

In fact, a typical high school chemistry course contains many if not all of the basic quantum mechanical ideas in this section of the chapter. To understand chemical bonding, intermolecular interactions, and related ideas such as polarizability, students must hold a probabilistic model of electron behavior. They must consider electron distribution as opposed to individual electrons located in a certain place. In addition, students must understand that only certain amounts of energy are allowed in or out of atomic and molecular systems. A deeper, more mathematically rooted description

Chapter 1

of quantum effects can then be introduced in grades 13–16 and above.

However, for students to develop even a basic, qualitative understanding of quantum effects will require time in the curriculum (how *much* time is still unclear). It is not unusual to introduce these complex and nonintuitive ideas over a few days; unfortunately, there is no reason to believe that such cursory treatment of these complex ideas will lead to student learning. If this level of knowledge is desired for students, we must prioritize these ideas in the curriculum and work to develop effective instructional strategies to help students develop a useful, applicable understanding of quantum mechanical ideas.

Acknowledgments

The authors would like to thank the following people for helpful discussions and reading of this book when it was still at the manuscript stage: Nick Giordano and Nora Sabelli for comments throughout, Shanna Daly for Forces and Interactions, César Delgado for Size and Scale, Alexa Mattheyses for Quantum Effects, and Kelly Hutchinson for Structure of Matter.

References

American Association for the Advancement of Science (AAAS). 1993. *Benchmarks for science literacy.* New York: Oxford University Press.

Atkins, P. W. 1991. *Quanta: A handbook of concepts.* 2nd. ed. Oxford: Oxford University Press.

Che, J., T. Cagin, and W. A. Goddard III. 2000. Thermal conductivity of carbon nanotubes. *Nanotechnology* 11: 65–59.

Coulson, C. A. 1955. The contributions of wave mechanics to chemistry. *Journal of the American Chemical Society:* 2069–2084.

Dujardin, E., T. W. Ebbesen, A. Krishnan, P. N. Yianilos, and M. M. J. Treacy. 1998. Young's modulus of single-walled nanotubes. *Physical Review B* 58 (20): 14013–14019.

Ellis, A. B., M. J. Geselbracht, B. J. Johnson, G. C. Lisensky, and W. R. Robinson. 1993. *Teaching general chemistry: A material science companion.* Washington, DC: American Chemical Society.

El–Sayed, M. A. 2001. Some interesting properties of metals confined in time and nanometer space of different shapes. *Accounts of Chemical Research* 34 (4): 257–264.

Feynman, R. P. 1996. *Six easy pieces: Essential physics by its most brilliant teacher*, ed. R. B. Leighton and M. Sands. New York: Basic Books.

Finch, J. T., M. F. Perutz, J. F. Bertles, and J. Döbler. 1973. Structure of sickled erythrocytes and sickle-cell hemoglobin fibers. *Proceedings of the National Academy of Sciences, USA* 70 (3): 718–722.

Gao, G., T. Cagin, and W. A. Goddard III. 1997. Energetics, structure, mechanical and vibrational properties of single-walled carbon nanotubes (SWNT). *Nanotechnology* 9: 184–191.

Gao, H., B. Ji, I. L. Jäger, E. Arzt, and P. Fratzel. 2003. Materials become insensitive to flaws at nanoscale: Lessons from nature. *Proceedings of the National Academy of Sciences, USA* 100 (10): 5597–5600.

Haldane, J. B. S. 1926. *On being the right size and other essays.* Oxford: Oxford University Press.

Heisenberg, W. 1958. *Physics and philosophy.* New York: Harper.

Hochella, M. F., Jr. 2002. Sustaining Earth: Thoughts on the present and future roles of mineralogy in environmental science. *Mineralogical Magazine* 66 (5): 627–652.

Hochella, M. F., Jr. 2006. The case for nanogeoscience. *Annals of the New York Academy of Sciences* 1093: 108–122.

Jones, J. R., and L. L Hench. 2003. Regeneration of trabecular bone using porous ceramics. *Current Opinion in Solid State and Materials Science* 7: 301–307.

Judson, E., and D. Sawada. 2000. Examining the effects of a reformed junior high school science class on students' math achievement. *School Science and Mathematics* 100 (8): 19–25.

Koradi, R., M. Billeter, and K. Wüthrich. 1996. MOLMOL: A program for display and analysis of macromolecular structures. *Journal of Molecular Graphics* 14: 51–55.

Kowalczykowski, S., D. Bear, and P. von Hippel. 1981. *Single-stranded DNA binding proteins.* In *Nucleic acids, Part A*, ed. P. D. Boyer. London: Academic Press.

Levy Nahum, T., R. Mamlok–Naaman, A. Hofstein, and J. Krajcik. 2007. Developing a new teaching approach for the chemical bonding concept aligned with current scientific and pedagogical knowledge. *Science Education* 91 (4): 579–603.

Li, P. 2003. Biomimetic nano–apatite coating capable of promoting bone in growth. *Journal of Biomedical Materials Research* 66A: 79–85.

McCray, W. P. 2009. How spintronics went from the lab to the iPod. *Nature Nanotechnology* 4: 2–4.

National Council of Teachers of Mathematics (NCTM). 1989. *Principles and standards for school mathematics*. Reston, VA: NCTM.

National Research Council (NRC). 1996. *National science education standards*. Washington, DC: National Academy Press.

Roco, M. C. 2004. Nanoscale science and engineering: Unifying and transforming tools. *American Institute of Chemical Engineers Journal* 50 (5): 890–897.

Shirai, Y., A. J. Osgood, Y. Zhao, K. F. Kelly, and J. M. Tour. 2005. Directional control in thermally driven single-molecule nanocars. *Nano Letters* 5 (11): 2330–4.

Stevens, S. Y., and G. D. Glick. 1997. Evidence for sequence specific recognition by anti-single-stranded DNA autoantibodies. *Biochemistry* 38 (2): 650–658.

Sussex Fullerene Group. n.d. Some properties of carbon and C_{60}. *www.creative–science.org.uk/propc60.html*.

Taber, K. S., and R. K. Coll. 2002. Bonding. In *Chemical education: Towards research–based practice*, ed. J. K. Gilbert, O. D. Jong, R. Justi, D. F. Treagust, and J. H. Van Driel, 213–234. Dordrecht, Netherlands: Kluwer Academic Publishers.

Tretter, T. R., M. G. Jones, T. Andre, A. Negishi, and J. Minogue. 2006. Conceptual boundaries and distances: Students' and experts' concepts of the scale of scientific phenomena. *Journal of Research in Science Teaching* 43 (3): 282–319.

Viney, C., and F. I. Bell. 2004. Inspiriation versus duplication with biomolecular fibrous materials: Learning nature's lessons without copying nature's limitations. *Current Opinion in Solid State and Materials Science* 8: 165–171.

von Hippel, P., and O. G. Berg. 1986. On the specificity of DNA-protein interactions. *Proceedings of the National Academy of Sciences, USA* 83: 1608–1612.

Weast, R. C. 1976. *Handbook of chemistry and physics*. Cleveland, OH: CRC Press.

Chapter 2
Applying the Foundational Science Content

The four big ideas discussed in Chapter 1 provide the foundation for developing understanding of nanoscale phenomena. Two additional big ideas—Size-Dependent Properties and Self-Assembly—require learners to apply concepts from some or all of the four fundamental big ideas in order explain relevant phenomena.

All four big ideas discussed in Chapter 1 are connected to Size-Dependent Properties (see Figure 2.1). Size and scale define the range at which matter transitions between bulk behavior and that of individual atoms or molecules to produce the unique properties observed at the nanoscale. Aspects of the structure of

matter, the forces that govern interactions, and quantum mechanics are required to explain the unique properties that occur at the scale of this transition. In turn, these novel, size-dependent properties themselves provide new information about the structure and behavior of matter.

Self-assembly is a process that involves controlled, predictable interactions of matter. Therefore, it is closely related to the Forces and Interactions big idea (p. 18). Because the forces that generally dominate interactions are related to the scale of the phenomena, self-assembly is also linked to size and scale. In addition, modeling and simulations play an important role in the design of systems that self-assemble, and building models can help explain natural phenomena that self-assemble. Knowledge about the structure of matter helps to predict how the building blocks will assemble. Therefore, several of the science-content big ideas inform and influence the content and ideas related to Self-Assembly (see Figure 2.2, p. 38).

Big Idea 5
Size-Dependent Properties

The properties of matter can change with scale. In particular, during the transition between the bulk material and individual atoms or molecules—generally at the nanoscale—a material often exhibits unexpected properties that lead to new functionality.

Figure 2.1

Representation of the relationships between NSE science content big ideas and size-dependent properties

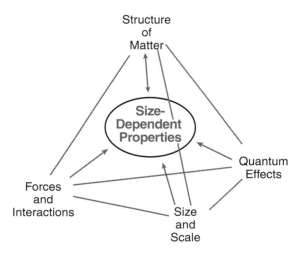

Chapter 2

Figure 2.2
Representation of the relationships between NSE science content big ideas and self-assembly

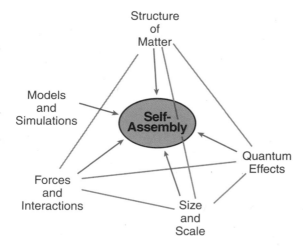

About Size-Dependent Properties

Properties are those qualities or characteristics that determine the nature of a material. They are the source of the functionality of a material—that is, they determine how it appears, how it behaves, how it interacts with and reacts to the environment, and for what applications it might be useful. The fact that all properties change with scale is at odds with the traditional concept of "intensive properties," which are defined as being independent of the amount of material (e.g., melting point, conductivity, malleability). The traditional conception of properties applies only for macroscale amounts of a material, for as the size of the material gets smaller and passes through the nanoscale, some of those intensive properties do, indeed, begin to change. Therefore, properties cannot be categorized without qualification because all properties can change depending on scale.

The properties of nanoscale materials are often different from those of the familiar macroscale material and are often unexpected (Roduner 2006; Cortie 2004). For instance, gold nanoparticles exhibit some interesting optical properties. Colloidal suspensions of gold nanoparticles exhibit different colors depending on particle size (see Table 2.1). Gold particles with a diameter of 10 to 30 nm, suspended in solution, will give rise to a red color; particles 2 to 5 nm in diameter make a yellow solution; and, as the diameter increases to 100 nm, the color shifts toward violet (Haiss et al. 2007; Link and El-Sayed 1999; Handley 1989). A Roman glass made in approximately 400 A.D. that incorporated nanoscale particles of gold into the process appears green in reflected light and red when lit from within (transmitted light) (Wagner et al. 2000). Gold nanoparticles were used in the Middle Ages to achieve some of the rich red colors found in stained glass from that period. However, it was not until the 19th century that Faraday established that gold was the source of the color.

Table 2.1
Color vs. size of gold nanoparticles

Diameter (nm)	Color of Colloidal Solution
~2	yellow
~3-5	orange, orange red
15	red
100	violet

Macroscale pieces of gold, with diameters of 1 m, 1 cm, and 1 mm, will all appear shiny and gold colored and will exhibit metallic properties including malleability and electrical conductivity. All of these pieces will exhibit melting points of 1064°C, regardless of size. However, the melting point decreases dramatically when the diameter of the gold particles falls below 100 nm. At 10 nm diameter, the melting point of a silica-encapsulated gold nanoparticle decreases approximately 100°C. As the diameter approaches 2 nm, the decrease is more significant, with a melting point of approximately half of that observed for the bulk gold (Dick et al. 2002; Lewis, Jensen, and Barrat 1997). Other properties also change at the nanoscale. For example, at sizes less than 10 nm, gold no longer conducts electricity.

The size-dependent properties observed for nanoscale materials may be categorized as either surface- or size-dominated. The dramatic increase in the surface-to-volume ratio (S/V) that occurs as the size of the material approaches the nanoscale relates to surface-dominated properties such as melting point, rate of reaction, capillary action, and adhesion. Size-dominated behaviors, such as conductivity, reactivity, and optical and magnetic properties, connect directly to the size (or the number of atoms) of the object or material.

Surface-Dominated Properties

The S/V increases dramatically as a material becomes smaller and approaches the nanoscale. (See Size and Scale in chapters 1 and 5 for more complete discussions of the surface to volume ratio.) Therefore, any phenomenon that occurs at the surface will become magnified at the nanoscale. For example, in chemical reactions, the outermost atoms of a substance react to form a new substance. This is apparent with oxidation of metals (e.g., tarnished silver, green copper oxide) where the reaction occurs on the surface of the metal. The atoms on the surface of a material experience different chemical and physical environments than the atoms in the interior, or bulk portion, of the material. In particular, they do not participate

in as many interactions (bonds). The surface atoms have excess energy, called surface energy, which is derived from unfulfilled interactions. This energy is often neglected in bulk material because it only affects the first few layers of atoms. The higher energy state of the surface atoms makes them more chemically reactive.

Cutting a material into smaller pieces results in more exposed surface area, which translates to more atoms being exposed on the surface (see Table 2.2, p. 40) and in a higher energy state. The increase in surface area is the reason that smaller pieces of material react faster than larger ones under otherwise identical conditions. At the nanoscale, a significant fraction of the atoms lies in this higher energy state relative to the bulk material. For example, many metals are coated with an oxide layer that is at least a few micrometers thick. Therefore, atoms in metals of nanoscale thickness or diameter will all behave like surface atoms and oxidize quite quickly.

The relative increase in surface area exposed at the nanoscale also affects transformations such as melting and dissolving. The melting points of metal nanoparticles are extremely sensitive to size.

The increased number of available atoms on a surface also increases the number of induced dipole interactions that can occur, affecting adhesion properties. The effect is greater as the particles get smaller. The change in adhesion properties has implications for manipulating and controlling nanoscale materials. Absorption is another surface-dependent property. The high surface area-to-volume ratio of the pores in materials made of super-absorbent polymers allows them to absorb large amounts of liquid—up to 500 times their weight—as applied in the development of disposable diapers (Kabiri et al. 2003).

Table 2.2
Relationship between cubic particle size and the fraction of atoms on the particle surface[a]

Particle Size (nm) (length of side)	Number of Atoms/ Side	Number of Atoms at Surface	Number of Atoms (total)	# Surface Atoms/ # Total Atoms (%)
0.4	2	8	8	100
0.6	3	26	27	97
0.8	4	56	64	87.5
1	5	98	125	78.5
2	10	488	1×10^3	48.8
20	100	5.9×10^4	1×10^6	5.9
200	1,000	5.9×10^6	1×10^9	0.6
2,000	10,000	5.9×10^8	1×10^{12}	0.06
20,000	100,000	5.9×10^{10}	1×10^{15}	0.006

[a] Surface defined as only the single outermost layer of atoms.

Size-Dominated Properties

Atoms in small clusters possess different electronic properties from atoms in a larger (bulk) piece of material. If a particle is large enough (~10–20 atoms deep in all directions), surface energy provides an adequate model to explain the process of chemical reactivity. When the number of atoms in a particle is very small, adding, removing, or moving a single atom may affect the electronic structure of the whole. The distinct electronic structure of particles with length scale of less than 8 to 10 nm is responsible for the changes in reactivity observed for some materials.* The number of atoms required for a substance to behave like the macroscopic substance is different for different materials; generally, the number is fewer for metals than for semiconductors.

The atoms of a material are in constant random motion. If the pieces of a material become small enough, the motion of individual atoms is no longer averaged out within the sample and can affect the properties of the material.

Many of the intrinsic properties of materials have their structural basis at nanoscale length scales. If the size of the material falls below this limit for a given property in at least one dimension, then the property for that material becomes "confined" and becomes sensitive to both size and shape (Heath 1995). For instance, the malleability of copper is derived from movement of clusters of copper atoms on a scale of 50 nanometers. Particles of copper smaller than 50 nanometers lose their malleability and ductility and are considered superhard materials (Hughes and Hansen 2003). Confinement occurs at different length scales for different properties; the same property will become confined at different length scales for different materials (Heath 1995). (See Quantum Effects in Chapter 1 for a discussion of electron confinement.)

* Often the catalytic activity of gold nanoparticles is attributed to the increase in S/V. However, that is incorrect; the catalytic activity of gold nanoparticles is due to a different reason than the increased rate of change that is a surface-dominated property.

The traditional strategy for creating desired properties is to change the composition and/or arrangement of the building blocks of the material (i.e., synthetic chemistry). However, the novel properties observed for materials at the nanoscale, and the recently developed technology to isolate, fabricate, and manipulate nanoscale materials, provide new ways to generate materials with desired properties.

Why Is This a Big Idea?

Size-dependent properties is the one truly new idea among the NSE big ideas discussed in this book. Because of the recently discovered properties of matter observed at the nanoscale, scientists are developing new models to explain the structure and behavior of matter. In addition, a large part of the nanotechnology revolution revolves around exploiting the novel properties of matter that occur at the nanoscale. The range of applications that nanotechnology may affect is extremely broad.

Already, nanoscale materials are used in a broad range of technologies and products. The cosmetic industry, for example, uses nanotechnology to address current concerns regarding sun exposure. For many years, zinc oxides have been used as sunscreens. Figure 2.3 (p. 42) illustrates the thick white paste that lifeguards used to use on their faces as sun protection. However, although zinc oxides are effective sunscreens, the white color of the final product was undesirable to consumers. As the particles of zinc oxide become smaller, however, they interact with light differently and appear increasingly colorless. When the diameter of the particles falls in the range of 10 to 100 nm, the particles maintain the chemical and physical properties of the bulk material, despite having different optical properties (Mulvaney 2001). In particular, the particles appear transparent in visible light but still scatter the harmful ultraviolet (UV) rays.

Thus, nanoparticles of zinc oxide afford effective sun protection in a way that also results in a product consumers consider desirable (see Figure 2.3, p. 42).

Some nanoscale materials also exhibit special mechanical properties. For example, carbon nanotubes, one of the strongest and stiffest materials known, with a tensile strength many times greater than that of steel, are extremely resistant to heat. Incorporating some of the raw materials used in the fabrication of automobile tires, in nanoparticle form, significantly improves tire wear without increasing rolling resistance or detrimentally affecting grip on wet surfaces.

Magnetic properties can also be size-dependent. For example, in its bulk form, aluminum is not magnetic. However, aluminum nanoparticles with a diameter of approximately 0.8 nm are magnetic (Eberhardt 2002). Magnetic susceptibility, the degree of magnetization that a substance exhibits in response to an applied magnetic field, is also dependent on size. This property is being exploited in efforts to use nanoparticles of iron oxide as an agent for water purification processes. Certain minerals exhibit greater affinity for aqueous toxic chemicals (e.g., arsenic) at length scales in the nanometer range. In particular, nanoparticles of certain forms of iron oxide exhibit a high affinity for binding arsenic, cyanides, and radionuclides and can be activated to render the bound toxins less toxic. Once bound to the nanoparticles, the toxins can be removed using magnets (Savage and Diallo 2005; Zhang 2003).

In addition to physical properties, chemical properties can also change with scale. On the macroscale, gold is considered to be less reactive than other transition metals. However, nanoscale particles of gold less than ~6 nm in diameter, embedded in certain supports, can act

Figure 2.3
Zinc oxide sunscreen on a glass slide. Similar amounts of product were applied to the slide (a, b). The micro-/nanoparticulate formula is transparent (left) and the formula with larger particles (right) is opaque.

a.

Micro- and Nanoscale
Zinc Oxide Particles

Macroscale Zinc
Oxide Particles

b.

Micro- and Nanoscale
Zinc Oxide Particles

Macroscale Zinc
Oxide Particles

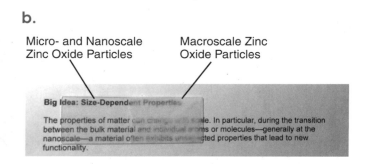

Big Idea: Size-Dependent Properties

The properties of matter can change with scale. In particular, during the transition between the bulk material and individual atoms or molecules—generally at the nanoscale—a material often exhibits unexpected properties that lead to new functionality.

as catalysts to enhance the rate of some chemical reactions (Haruta 2003). One possible application for these particles is in an automobile's catalytic converter, where harmful pollutants such as carbon monoxide react to form carbon dioxide and water. The catalysts currently used are only effective at temperatures greater than 200°C (Campbell 2004). Unfortunately, automobiles generate most of their pollution within the first five minutes after starting up. Therefore, at the time when the majority of harmful pollutants are generated, the catalytic converter is ineffective due to the low temperature of the exhaust. The use of nanoscale gold particles for this application may significantly reduce automobile-related air pollution because gold particles catalyze the oxidation of carbon monoxide even at subzero temperatures. The catalytic activity depends on the structure of the gold in contact with the environment, the support material, and particle size (Haruta 2003).

Already, nanoscale properties of matter are being utilized in applications as diverse as information storage, electronics, environmental safety, and cosmetics. As more properties are discovered and an understanding of them is developed, nanoscale properties may be applied to an even broader range of problems. The novel, often unexpected, properties that matter exhibits at the nanoscale are forcing scientists and engineers to change their models for explaining the structure and behavior of matter. Because of these unique, often unexpected properties, NSE is emerging as its own area of science.

Relationship to the 7–12 Curriculum

Identifying the properties and characteristics of materials is one of the fundamental concepts of science. As such, from their earliest experiences with science, students begin to describe the properties of objects around them. Initially, they rely on descriptions based on size, shape, color, weight, and the material of which an object is made. Many of these characteristics are unreliable because they change and are generally designated as extensive properties.

The introduction of intensive properties such as density, melting point, boiling point, and solubility—which do not change and are independent of the amount of material—helps solve the descriptive problems inherent in using extensive properties. The only exception generally mentioned in school science is that individual atoms and molecules do not share the same properties as the bulk substance. The intensive properties prove to be useful for comparing different materials and predicting their behavior within the macroscale world.

These rules, however, do not apply for the transition between bulk materials and individual atoms and molecules. Thus, with the coming of the NSE revolution, it is no longer sufficient to teach properties of matter as a dichotomy of bulk, or macroscale, properties versus atomic or molecular properties. Instead, it has become relevant to discuss the properties of matter using more refined levels. No longer can we clearly categorize properties that do change (extensive) from those that do not (intensive), because all types of properties can change depending on the scale. In particular, it is necessary to help students connect observed properties to those of the atoms and molecules that make up a substance. In addition, the use of intensive and extensive categorization must be linked to scale, as the terms are meaningful only when describing matter at the macroscale. Characterizing the transition between the macroscale and atomic scale will lead students to a much deeper and more refined understanding of the structure and behavior of matter.

Big Idea 6
Self-Assembly

Under specific conditions, some materials can spontaneously assemble into organized structures. This process provides a useful means for manipulating matter at the nanoscale.

About Self-Assembly

Recent technological advances not only provide scientists and engineers with the ability to measure and characterize properties of nanoscale materials but also allow them to control and manipulate matter at the nanoscale. One of the biggest challenges that scientists currently face is how to do so more efficiently and accurately—a requirement for large-scale fabrication of nanoscale materials.

Other approaches commonly used to manufacture extremely small objects are top-down approaches, which involve removing pieces of an object in order to reach the final product, as in creating a sculpture from a block of material. An example of a top-down manufacturing process is photolithography (see Figure 2.4, p. 44), which is currently used in the fabrication of microelectronics and micro-fluidics. In the photolithography process, the substrate, which in the case of microelectronics is a silicon surface, is coated with a photosensitive material called "photoresist." The photoresist is then exposed to radiation (e.g., UV light) through a "mask." The mask is similar to a stencil in that it ensures that only the desired patterns on the photoresist surface are exposed to radiation. The properties of the photoresist change only where it has interacted with the radiation. The surface is then exposed to a chemical that either removes the exposed portion (positive resist) or the unexposed area (negative resist) of the surface to create the designed pattern. Currently, patterns the size of tens of nanometers can be created using this methodology.

An alternate approach is to manufacture from the bottom up, combining smaller building blocks to make larger products. Again, the challenge is to purposefully manipulate the building blocks, which at the nanoscale are atoms, molecules, and other nanoscale assemblies, structures,

Chapter 2

or objects. One bottom-up process particularly useful for meeting this challenge is self-assembly. When placed in an appropriate environment, certain building blocks will assemble into organized assemblies without further external intervention. Figure 2.5 illustrates a simple model of self-assembly where the building blocks are designed such that a white triangle can only be next to an orange triangle and an orange triangle must be next to a white triangle. Self-assembly provides a means for building nanoscale materials that may possess unique and useful properties and is a strategy for synthesizing many nanostructures simultaneously.

Although there is consensus on the importance of self-assembly to NSE, the field has yet to develop a unified definition of the process. Here, we provide a general description of the process and requirements for self-assembly. Only certain components, or building blocks, are capable of self-assembling; they must possess specific characteristics (e.g., shape, charge, composition) in order to be viable (Whitesides and Grzybowski 2002). These characteristics determine how the building blocks can interact with one another. The building blocks to be assembled must be able to move readily with respect to one another, so the process is usually carried out in solution or at an interface (Whitesides and Boncheva 2002).

As with all interactions, in addition to the type and characteristics of the building blocks, the environment (e.g., concentration of components, temperature, polarity, and acidity of solvent)

Figure 2.4
Illustration of the photolithography process, an example of top-down fabrication

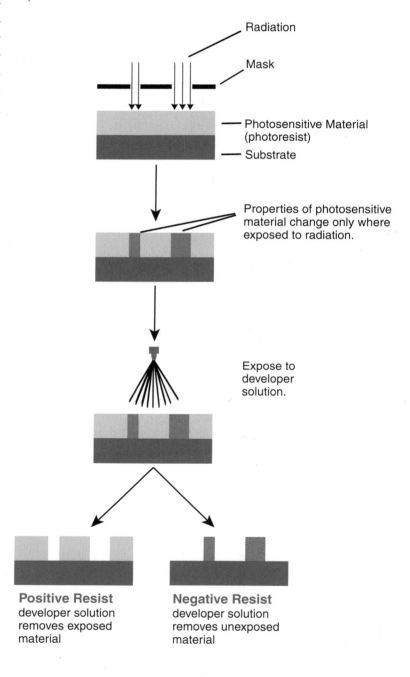

Radiation

Mask

Photosensitive Material (photoresist)

Substrate

Properties of photosensitive material change only where exposed to radiation.

Expose to developer solution.

Positive Resist
developer solution removes exposed material

Negative Resist
developer solution removes unexposed material

Figure 2.5
Illustration of a self-assembly process

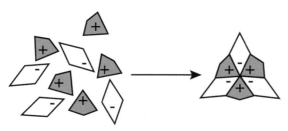

plays an important role in the process of self-assembly because attractive and repulsive forces between the building blocks and/or the building blocks and the molecules that make up the environment drive the assembly process. To form stable, assembled structures, net attractive forces must bring and hold the components together. The process of self-assembly occurs spontaneously once certain conditions are established. Thus, the free energy of the final state of the system is lower than the initial state. (See the Forces and Interactions section in Chapter 1 for a more detailed discussion of these concepts.) Templates may be used to reduce defects in the final assembled structure (see Figure 2.6).

The building blocks retain their physical identity both through and after the self-assembly process. Thus, the components can change their positions within the assembled structure, or the initial components can be isolated from the assembled structure by providing the right conditions (Whitesides and Boncheva 2002). To meet this requirement, there are certain limitations on the types of interactions that may occur between the building blocks. Generally, the interactions are relatively weak (e.g., noncovalent) or reversible (e.g., disulfide bonds). Table 2.3 (p. 46) provides a list of the more common types of interactions with some examples of their application (Whitesides, Mathias, and Seto 1991). Self-assembly is a process for accurate and controlled application of electrical forces to build higher-order, organized structures or assemblies.

Although self-assembly is a crucial technique for the advancement of nanotechnology, it is not a new process. Self-assembly occurs in nature on every scale, from astronomical to molecular. The canonical nanoscale example is the assembly of the DNA double helix. In addition, many of the molecular machines that carry out crucial functions within all living organisms

Figure 2.6
Illustration of templated self-assembly

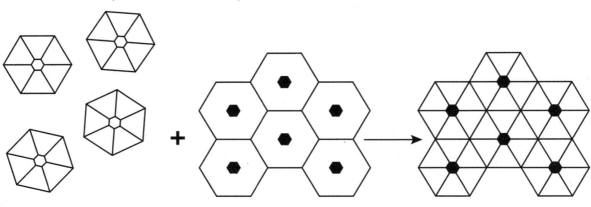

Building Blocks   Template   Assembled Structure

Chapter 2

are built through a process of self-assembly. Snowflakes too are formed by a self-assembly process. Advantages to building larger structures from a set of smaller structures include a reduction in the amount of external information that must be input and a decrease in the number of defects in the final assembled product (Kushner 1969). However, it is only recently that humans have gained the knowledge and technology to use self-assembly to make new materials.

of assembly include molecular crystals, viruses, and liquid crystals. Dynamic self-assembly, or self-organization, results in a structure that may exchange matter and energy. Examples of this type of assembly are microtubule networks (Misteli 2001) and cell division (Whitesides and Grzybowski 2002). Self-assembly is a universal process adopted and applied by engineers to nanoscale fabrication.*

Table 2.3
Types of forces and interactions that are typically involved in self-assembly

Type of Interaction	Examples
Ionic interactions	Salt bridges in and between biomolecules; LED materials
Dipole-dipole interactions	Liquid crystals
Hydrogen bonds	Stabilization of secondary structure (alpha-helices, beta-sheets) in proteins, DNA base pairing; LED materials
Reversible covalent bonds	Disulfide bonds
Metal-coordination	Zinc fingers (protein motif), organometallic complexes
Hydrophobic interactions	Lipid bilayers, monolayers, protein folding
Electrodynamic (induced-dipole)	Carbon nanotube aggregation
Aromatic π-stacking	Stabilization of nucleic acid helices; molecular tweezers; discotic liquid crystals

Source: Adapted from Whitesides, Mathias, and Seto 1991.

There are two types of self-assembly: static and dynamic (Misteli 2001; Whitesides and Grzybowski 2002). Biologists often refer to these two types as self-assembly (static) and self-organization (dynamic). The examples presented thus far are examples of static self-assembly, which occurs spontaneously and results in an aggregate structure that represents a thermodynamic minimum. Other examples of this type

Why Is This a Big Idea?

Self-assembly is a process with important implications in many disciplines of science. In biology, processes such as nucleic acid and protein

---

* Although self-assembly provides a strategy for the efficient and accurate fabrication of nanoscale structures, materials, and systems, it is not the only way or even always the best way to manufacture such products. See Appendix C for a description of some alternative manufacturing strategies.

folding, membrane formation, and organism development are examples of self-assembly. Mineral formation through crystallization is an important geological process, and galaxy and solar system formation are examples of self-assembly at astronomical scales. In chemistry, atoms or groups of atoms assemble in predictable ways to create organized structures. As such, self-assembly provides an opportunity to link fundamental concepts about the relationship between the building blocks, the forces that govern their interactions, and the energy that describes the assembly systems in many disciplines.

The explosion of new knowledge about the properties and behavior of matter at the nanoscale has afforded an extensive amount of potential new applications. However, although great strides have been made in characterizing, manipulating, and fabricating nanoscale materials, one of the greatest challenges for nanoscientists and engineers is to be able to do so more efficiently and accurately.

Self-assembly is an important process for creating nanoscale structures, materials, and systems. Although its length can reach micrometers, DNA is defined as a nanoscale structure because the diameter of the double helix is approximately 2.5 nm. The two strands of DNA come together with a controllable specificity that has yet to be duplicated on this scale. Each strand contains a certain sequence of four bases—adenine, thymine, guanine, and cytosine—that interact with a partner in another strand (adenine with thymine, guanine with cytosine). The base pairs link together through hydrogen bonds, and the planar bases "stack" above and below one another to form the familiar double helix structure of DNA (see Figure 2.7, p. 48).

Another example of nanoscale self-assembly is the formation of membranes, where the building blocks (e.g., phospholipids) have a hydrophilic end and a hydrophobic end (see Figure 2.8, p. 49). The hydrophilic ends interact with the water molecules through dipole-dipole interactions. Therefore, in an aqueous environment, the hydrophilic ends all align such that they are exposed to the water, and the hydrophobic ends are buried within. In nature, this process creates the tissues known as biological membranes, an example of which is the cell wall. These membranes are important because they create a barrier that allows cells to maintain different chemical or biochemical environments within the cell than outside of it. Phospholipids may also assemble in a single (mono-) layer on a surface. Similarly, single-walled carbon nanotube bundles, synthetically rendered hydrophilic, can be organized through self-assembly onto hydrophilic surfaces (Zhou et al. 2002). Patterns of nanotubes can be created by controlling the nature (i.e., hydrophilic or hydrophobic) of the surface.

Scientists and engineers are beginning to apply the principles observed in nature to self-assemble complex structures and machines. The processes of nucleation and crystal growth have been used to purposefully engineer crystals that have desired chemical and physical properties (Hollingsworth 2002). Nucleic acids can play a role in various aspects of the self-assembly process. Scientists have utilized the specificity of DNA strand recognition to rapidly and accurately synthesize large numbers of copies of specific sequences of DNA. This process, called PCR (polymerase chain reaction), revolutionized the field of molecular biology and was a driving force behind the biotechnology revolution. Further away from the natural function of DNA, scientists have

Chapter 2

Figure 2.7
(a) The four DNA bases interact to form two types of base pairs: A•T or G•C. (b) Two strands interact to form double-stranded DNA.

a.

Thymine — Adenine

Cytosine — Guanine

b.

When the two DNA strands interact, they form the familiar double helical structure.

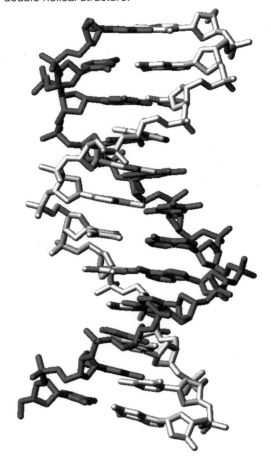

exploited the specificity of the interactions between nucleic acid strands to make scaffolds, or templates, to guide the self-assembly process. These DNA scaffolds can be in the form of specific two-dimensional (e.g., arrays and patterns) and three-dimensional shapes (e.g., polyhedra, "knots") (Seeman and Lukeman 2005). Scientists have also used DNA to direct the assembly of gold nanowires (Mbindyo et al. 2001) and nanoparticle crystallization (Park et al. 2008).

Currently, self-assembly is being used to extend the possibilities of synthetic chemistry and to build new nanoscale structures. Scientists combine large, structured groups of atoms that assemble in an ordered, symmetric

Figure 2.8
Illustration of the assembly of phospholipids into a lipid bilayer, or membrane

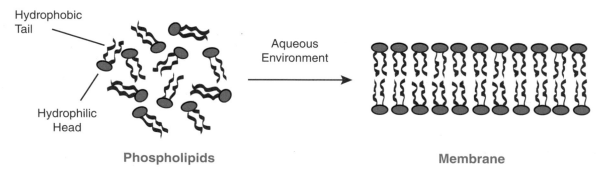

Hydrophobic
Tail

Aqueous
Environment

Hydrophilic
Head

Phospholipids

Membrane

manner through noncovalent or reversible interactions (e.g., hydrogen bonds, dipole-dipole interactions, disulfide bonds) to form ever larger (often snowflake-like) molecules called dendrimers and supramolecules (see Figure 2.9). Dendrimers are large symmetric, globular molecules that are highly branched such that they do not form linear polymeric structures. Instead, the bonds all extend out radially from a core (Fréchet 2002). These structures can be created through covalent bonding,

hydrogen bonding, or certain coordinate bonding. In general, supramolecular chemistry encompasses the processes of association and recognition that are governed by noncovalent electrical forces (e.g., hydrogen bonds, induced dipole interactions) to create large, designed molecular structures. Potential applications for dendrimers include drug delivery and as a pretreatment to enhance fabric dyes.

Scientists have learned the principles of self-assembly largely from natural processes

Figure 2.9
Illustration of the formation of a supramolecular structure. Two types of building blocks (I and II) interact through hydrogen bonds (dotted lines) to form the supramolecular structure.

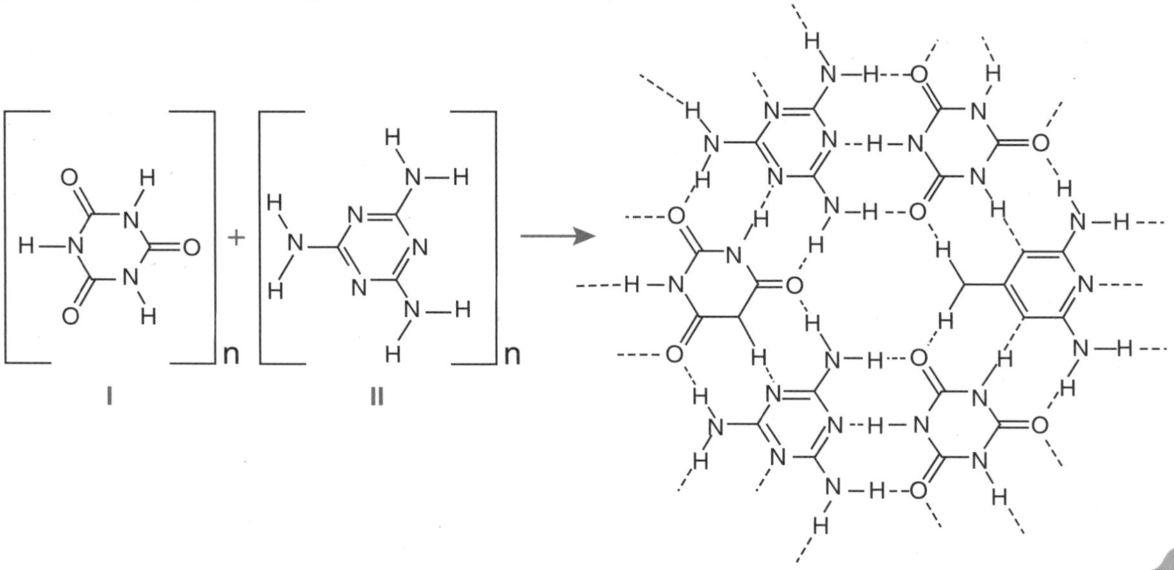

Chapter 2

and are applying them to help meet the challenges of designing and fabricating nanoscale materials. Because chemists generally focus on the molecular scale, synthesis using molecular self-assembly is perhaps the best understood process. However, chemists have little control over the building blocks, which in this case are atoms. By expanding to larger scales, where the building blocks include molecules and larger structures, scientists and engineers can begin to control the characteristics of the building blocks (Whitesides and Boncheva 2002) and have potentially more building blocks to use. Another advantage to the self-assembly process is that unlike photolithography, this bottom-up process provides a more flexible strategy for building three-dimensional structures (Seeman 2007). Thus, self-assembly promises to play an important role in the efforts to apply the novel properties of matter on this scale.

Relationship to the 7–12 Curriculum

Self-assembly is not just a process used to advance the progress of nanotechnology; self-assembly is also evident in nature as a process through which structures on every scale are built. The principles behind self-assembly are the same in both the natural and the engineered realms in that under specific conditions, components assemble into an organized structure without external intervention. As such, the process of self-assembly presents an opportunity to build a deeper understanding of the factors that influence the strength and specificity of interactions. For example, scientists and engineers use DNA to assemble nanoscale structures by exploiting its amazing specificity. In this case, the process of self-assembly can be used to support learning about the genetic code and to emphasize the tremendous specificity and power that DNA affords. In addition, those factors that are important for explaining the self-assembly process (e.g., characteristics of the building blocks, electrical forces, free energy, specificity) are all important for explaining interactions between any entities at the nano-, molecular, or atomic scale (see the Forces and Interactions section in Chapter 1 for a more detailed discussion).

Acknowledgment

The authors would like to thank Gina Ney for helpful discussions and reading of the size-dependent properties section of this chapter.

References

Campbell, C. T. 2004. The active site in nanoparticle gold catalysis. *Science* 306: 234–235.

Cortie, M. B. 2004. The weird world of nanoscale gold. *Gold Bulletin* 37 (1–2): 12–19.

Dick, K., T. Dhanasekaran, Z. Zhang, and D. Meisel. 2002. Size-dependent melting of silica-encapsulated gold nanoparticles. *Journal of the American Chemical Society* 124 (10): 2312–2317.

Eberhardt, W. 2002. Clusters as new materials. *Surface Science* 500: 242–270.

Fréchet, J. M. J. 2002. Dendrimers and supramolecular chemistry. *Proceedings of the National Academy of Sciences, U.S.A.* 99 (8): 4782–4787.

Haiss, W., N. T. K. Thanh, J. Aveyard, and D. G. Fernig. 2007. Determination of size and concentration of gold nanoparticles from UV-Vis spectra. *Analytical Chemistry* 79 (11): 4215–4221.

Handley, D. A. 1989. Methods for synthesis of colloidal gold. In *Colloidal gold: Principles, methods, and applications,* ed. A. Hayat. San Diego: Academic Press.

Haruta, M. 2003. When gold is not noble: Catalysis by nanoparticles. *The Chemical Record* 3: 75–87.

Heath, J. R. 1995. The chemistry of size and order on the nanometer scale. *Science* 270 (5240): 1315–1316.

Hollingsworth, M. D. 2002. Crystal engineering: from structure to function. *Science* 295 (5564): 2410–2413.

Hughes, D. A., and N. Hansen. 2003. Defomation structures developing on fine scales. *Philosophical Magazine* 83 (31): 3871–3893.

Kabiri, K., H. Omidian, S. A. Hashemi, and N. J. Zohuriaan-Mehr. 2003. Synthesis of fast–swelling superabsorbent hydrogels: Effect of crosslinker type and concentration on porosity and absorption rate. *European Polymer Journal* 39: 1341–1348.

Kushner, D. J. 1969. Self-assembly of biological structures. *Bacteriological Reviews* 33 (2): 302–345.

Lewis, L. J., P. Jensen, and J.-L. Barrat. 1997. Melting, freezing, and coalescence of gold nanoclusters. *Physical Review B* 56 (4): 2248–2257.

Link, S., and M. A. El-Sayed. 1999. Spectral properties and relaxation dynamics of surface plasmon electronic oscillations in gold and silver nanodots and nanorods. *Journal of Physical Chemistry, Series B* 103: 8410–8426.

Mbindyo, J. K. N., B. D. Reiss, B. R. Martin, C. D. Keating, M. J. Natan, and T. E. Mallouk. 2001. DNA-directed assembly of gold nanowires on complementary surfaces. *Advanced Materials* 13 (4): 249–254.

Misteli, T. 2001. The concept of self-organization in cellular architecture. *Journal of Cell Biology* 155 (2): 181–185.

Mulvaney, P. 2001. Not all that's gold does glitter. *MRS Bulletin*: 1009–1014.

Park, S. Y., A. K. R. Lytton-Jean, B. Lee, S. Weigand, G. C. Schatz, and C. A. Mirkin. 2008. DNA-programmable nanoparticle crystallization. *Nature* 451: 553–556.

Roduner, E. 2006. Size matters: Why nanomaterials are different. *Chemical Society Reviews* 35: 583–592.

Savage, N., and M. S. Diallo. 2005. Nanomaterials and water purification: Opportunities and challenges. *Journal of Nanoparticle Research* 7: 331–342.

Seeman, N. C. 2007. Nanotechnology and the double helix. *Scientific American, Special Edition*: 30–39.

Seeman, N. C., and P. S. Lukeman. 2005. Nucleic acid nanostructures: Bottom-up control of geometry on the nanoscale. *Reports on Progress in Physics* 68: 237–270.

Wagner, F. E., S. Haslbeck, L. Stievano, S. Calogero, Q. A. Pankhurst, and K.-P. Martinek. 2000. Before striking gold in gold-ruby glass. *Nature* 407: 691–692.

Whitesides, G. M., and M. Boncheva. 2002. Beyond molecules: Self-assembly of mesoscopic and macroscopic components. *Proceedings of the National Academy of Sciences, U.S.A.* 99 (8): 4769–4774.

Whitesides, G. M., and B. Grzybowski. 2002. Self-assembly at all scales. *Science* 295: 2418–2421.

Whitesides, G. M., J. P. Mathias, and C. T. Seto. 1991. Molecular self-assembly and nanochemistry: A chemical strategy for the synthesis of nanostructures. *Science* 254: 1312–1326.

Zhang, W.-X. 2003. Nanoscale iron particles for environmental remediation: An overview. *Journal of Nanoparticle Research* 5: 323–332.

Zhou, O., H. Shimoda, B. Gao, S. Oh, L. Fleming, and G. Z. Yue. 2002. Materials science of carbon nanotubes: Fabrication, integration, and properties of macroscopic structures of carbon nanotubes. *Accounts of Chemical Research* 35 (12): 1045–1053.

Chapter 3
Moving NSE Forward

The six big ideas of NSE discussed so far have been directly related to science content necessary for understanding nanoscale phenomena. The two big ideas in this chapter—Tools and Instrumentation and Models and Simulations—are critical for advancing the field of NSE.

Tools play an important role in NSE research and development. They enable scientists to measure, observe, study, and develop explanations of nanoscale phenomena. In addition, tools are needed to deliberately manipulate the building blocks of nanoscale products and the products themselves. Therefore, the use of tools informs content areas such as Structure of Matter and Forces and Interactions. In addition, as illustrated in Figure 3.1, each of the science content big ideas may inform the design and fabrication of new tools necessary to explore the nanoworld.

The Models and Simulations big idea connects to the four big ideas discussed in Chapter 1 and to the two discussed in Chapter 2. Building and modifying models is an inherent part of the scientific process. Simulations can help test the validity of a model and aid in the experimental, design, and fabrication processes. In addition, models and simulations play a role in the design of new tools and new materials. Thus models and simulations both inform and are informed by most of the big ideas of NSE (see Figure 3.2).

Figure 3.1
Representation of the relationships between tools and instrumentation and the other big ideas

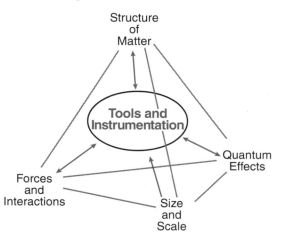

Figure 3.2
Representation of the relationships between models and simulations and the other big ideas

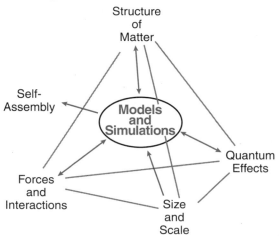

Chapter 3

Big Idea 7
Tools and Instrumentation

The development of new tools and instruments helps drive scientific progress. Recent development of specialized tools has led to new levels of understanding of matter by helping scientists detect, manipulate, isolate, measure, fabricate, and investigate nanoscale matter with unprecedented precision and accuracy.

About Tools and Instrumentation

Technology plays an important role in scientific progress, as science and technology often drive one another. The degree to which we understand the world is limited, in part, by the tools available to investigate it, and the tools and instruments available to scientists determine what is accessible for them to observe and measure. This accessibility leads scientists to new understandings and new questions—crucial parts of the scientific process—and therefore links to scientific progress. Telescopes, for example, allow for the exploration of distant portions of the universe, while optical microscopes enable the investigation of a world that is otherwise too small to see. The development of each of these tools led to enormous gains in understanding the phenomena that occur within these vastly different worlds. The development of tools and instruments such as the scanning probe microscope (SPM) and the scanning electron microscope (SEM) has rendered the nanoscale world accessible in ways impossible to imagine just a short time ago. These new instruments allow scientists and engineers to characterize and manipulate nanoscale materials and objects with relative ease. This new accessibility has led to new understandings of matter on the nanoscale and has aided in the development of new applications.

Why Is This a Big Idea?

Throughout history, the development of new instruments has provided access to previously unseen worlds. Galileo turned a new instrument, the telescope, to the skies and revealed that Earth is part of a complex planetary system. In combination with the theoretical work of Copernicus, Kepler, and Newton, Galileo's observations revolutionized astronomy. Today, a variety of telescopes orbit the Earth and examine the heavens using not just visible light but also radiation from the entire electromagnetic spectrum. The information these instruments gather provides insight into many questions, including questions about the formation of the solar system and the universe itself. New technology has sent probes to distant planets and has enabled humans to travel through space.

The development of microscopes allowed scientists to visualize and explore worlds too small to see with the unaided eye. In the 17th century, Anton van Leeuwenhoek's development of the first optical microscope opened the world of small biological organisms. He discovered that a drop of water was teeming with life and that blood was not a continuous liquid, but contained particles of some kind. This was the beginning of the biological revolution and led to a deeper understanding of the structure and function of living organisms. However, like all instruments, optical microscopes have limitations. Using visible light as a probe has a resolution limit of approximately 0.2 µm or $(2 \times 10^{-7}$ m).

The latter part of the 20th century saw tremendous advances in microscopy. SEMs use a focused beam of electrons instead of visible light to scan a sample. An image of the sample is generated from the pattern of back-scattered electrons. This technology has resolved features as small as 10 nm and has played an important role in the development of our understanding of the micro- and nanoscale worlds.

Scanning probe microscopes (SPMs) are another set of tools for investigating and working in the nanoscale world. Similar to the SEM, this class of tools creates images by scanning the sample surface. However, an SPM scans with a physical probe instead of a beam of electrons. The type of probe determines the kind of information that can be obtained. For example, an atomic force microscope (AFM) uses a probe that tapers down to a point with a radius of less than 10 nm. This probe detects the electrical inter-atomic and intermolecular forces between the tip of the probe and the surface (see Figure 3.3). A feedback loop ensures that the distance between the probe and the surface remains constant. This process is much like a finger scanning across a page to read braille (see Figure 3.3b). The amount that the probe must be adjusted in

Figure 3.3
(a) Model of an AFM creating an image of a surface (b) The tip methodically scans the surface. (c) A color-coded map of the topography of a surface (deep gray > medium gray > light gray > white

a.

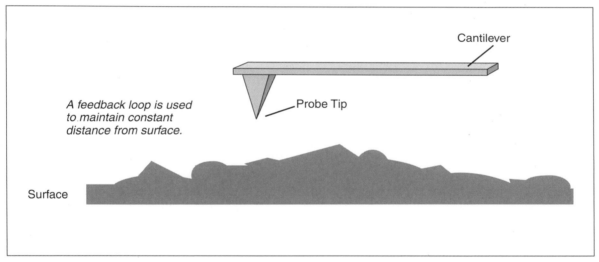

b.

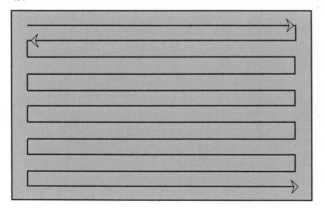

c.

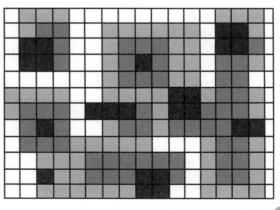

Chapter 3

order to maintain a constant distance from the surface is recorded to form the image. These distances can be depicted two-dimensionally, as illustrated in Figure 3.3c (p. 55), or translated into a three-dimensional image.

AFMs can be used to measure many types of samples besides solid surfaces. They have become useful tools for exploring the structure and function of nanoscale biological structures such as molecular machines (Müller and Dufrêne 2008). Recently, scientists were able use an AFM to identify the type of element of a single atom (Sugimoto et al. 2007). In addition, scientists have been able to use an AFM to resolve subatomic features (Giessibl et al. 2000). For example, using an AFM tip consisting of a single carbon atom, scientists were able to resolve features of less than 100 pm (10^{-10} m), detecting patterns of charge density *within* atoms. Tungsten atoms pack into a lattice in a body-centered cubic formation (Figure 3.4a). Due to this arrangement, calculations suggest that there will be four lobes of increased charge density (Figure 3.4b) in atoms on the

top layer. This pattern of electron charge density was detected with an AFM (see Figure 3.4c) (Hembacher, Giessibl, and Mannhart 2004).

Each type of SPM uses a different probe to measure certain properties of a sample. The properties that can be measured include the size and strength of magnetic features, how well the material conducts heat, and the optical or chemical properties of a surface. Although many instruments and techniques can observe and measure nanoscale structures (e.g., x-ray crystallography, nuclear magnetic resonance spectroscopy), they often have significant sample and sample preparation limitations. Like any instrument, these SPMs have limitations as to what they can image. However, the range of samples that SPMs can image and the relative ease of sample preparation have made the nanoworld much more accessible.

New tools also provide the ability to manipulate and fabricate structures on this scale. For example, SEMs can be used to create nanoscale patterns on a specially prepared surface in the photolithography process illustrated

Figure 3.4
(a) A model of atoms packed in a body-centered cubic pattern (b) The four predicted lobes of higher electron density are depicted in dark gray in the atom on the top layer (c) AFM image of tungsten reveals four lobes of local maxima of charge density (lighter color). The black circle represents the diameter of a single tungsten atom

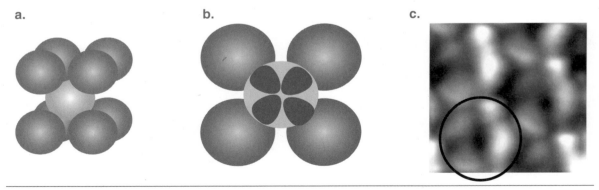

a. b. c.

Source: The image in (c) was reproduced with permission from Hembacher, S., F. J. Giessibl, and J. Mannhart. 2004. Force microscopy with light-atom probes. *Science* 305: 380–383. Copyright 2004 American Association for the Advancement of Science.

in Figure 2.4 (p. 44). This technology plays an important role in the miniaturization of electronics as engineers work to create micro- and nano-electromechanical devices (MEMs and NEMs). Another type of SPM, the scanning tunneling microscope (STM), can be used to manipulate matter atom by atom (see Quantum Effects in Chapter 1 for an explanation of tunneling and the STM). In 1990, Eigler and Schweizer produced the iconic image of xenon atoms deliberately placed on a nickel surface to form the letters IBM at the extremely low temperature of 4 K (-269°C) using an STM (see Figure 3.5). The letters were each 5 nm from top to bottom. Such new tools and instruments are critical factors in the progress of nanotechnology and the progress of the field.

Figure 3.5
Xenon atoms arranged on a nickel surface. Each letter is 5 nm from top to bottom.

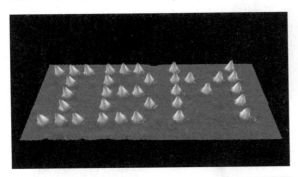

Source: Eigler and Schweizer 1990. Image originally created at IBM Corporation. Downloaded from *www.almaden. ibm.com/vis/stm/images/ibm.tif*

Relationship to the 7–12 Curriculum

Much of the grade 7–12 science curriculum in place at the time of this writing (2009) requires students to learn about objects and phenomena that cannot be seen with the naked eye. In elementary school, students learn about abstract concepts such as forces and electricity. As they learn about living organisms, students study cells and even smaller structures that govern the function of the cells (e.g., mitochondria, proteins, DNA). Using tools to observe and measure things otherwise not visible may facilitate students' conceptions of such abstract concepts— their relative size or strength or even their very existence. Optical microscopes provide access to the world of cells and small organisms, and voltmeters and ammeters allow students to measure voltage and current, respectively.

Although theory may have predicted the existence of atoms, experimental evidence provided proof of their existence. Unfortunately, the historical experiments themselves are somewhat abstract and may be less than convincing to students. Scanning probe microscopes provide new, more accessible evidence for the existence of atoms. Beyond that, the images provide evidence for the arrangement of atoms within a solid and even the electron distribution within an atom. Figure 3.6 is an AFM

Figure 3.6
Low-temperature AFM image of graphite shows the hexagonal pattern of the carbon atoms.

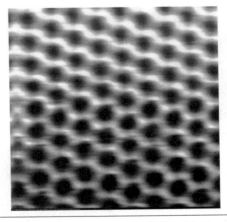

Source: Image reprinted from Hembacher, S., F. J. Giessibl, J. Mannhart, and C. F. Quate. 2003. *Proceedings of the National Academy of Sciences, USA* 100 (22): 12539-12542 with permission. Copyright (2003) National Academy of Sciences USA.

image that depicts the hexagonal arrangement of carbon atoms in graphite (Hembacher et al. 2003). In this particular image, scientists were able to finally observe a carbon atom that had previously been invisible: As shown in Figure 3.6 (p. 57), the AFM has also provided evidence for the uneven charge density due to covalent bonding in tungsten. However, students often believe that the images produced from these measurements are similar to those seen through an optical microscope (Harrison and Treagust 2002). Therefore, they often confuse the characteristics of atoms and molecules with those they see in the computer-generated images.

Available tools determine what scientists are able to observe and measure. New tools have been created in response to the desire to observe or measure a predicted phenomenon in order to better understand it. Thus, for scientists, developing new tools or instruments is often part of the experimental design. This relationship between development of tools and addressing a hypothesis is a key part of the scientific process. In addition, the tool that is used to examine a phenomenon often depends on its scale; therefore, ideas about size and scale—and tools—can be conceptually linked and explored in tandem in the classroom.

Big Idea 8
Models and Simulations

Scientists use models and simulations to help them visualize, explain, predict, and hypothesize about the structures, properties, and behaviors of phenomena (e.g., objects, materials, processes, systems). The extremely small size and complexity of nanoscale targets make models and simulations useful for the study and design of nanoscale phenomena.

About Models and Simulations

Models are alternative ways of representing a target (e.g., a phenomenon, object, material, system, or relationship); they can represent a concrete or abstract target. Models can be physical or computer-based, static or dynamic. The type of model employed depends both on its purpose and the target. It must be able to describe, explain, and/or predict certain—but not necessarily all—aspects and behaviors of a target. For example, mathematical equations are one type of model used to represent relationships and patterns. The balance between what a model can explain and cannot explain is driven by its purpose; therefore, any model is always a compromise involving the modeler's choices as to which aspects of the target to emphasize. It is possible to make multiple models of the same target that illustrate or emphasize different aspects of the target.

Throughout history, the design and manipulation of models have been essential for the advancement of science. Models are particularly useful for making predictions about and working with targets that are otherwise inaccessible. This inaccessibility may be due to the fact that targets are of an extremely small or large scale, rates of processes are either too slow or too quick to observe, phenomena or processes are potentially dangerous, or the cost of resources is too great. In the case of NSE, the targets are inaccessible due to size but at the same time often involve very complex phenomena. The processes governing the workings of the human body, micro- and nanoscale electronics, drug discovery and medical research, and the creation of highly designed and functional nanoscale materials all involve nanoscale phenomena. Progress in understanding these and other areas of NSE benefits from and depends on the application of modeling.

Models are not static entities that provide access to a "right answer," but are constantly reevaluated according to new scientific evidence, which leads to changes as the model evolves and new knowledge is incorporated. For instance, due to new discoveries regarding the structure and composition of the solar system, Pluto was recently reclassified from a planet to a dwarf planet (Vedantem 2006). New evidence suggests that at least some dinosaurs were warm-blooded, which contradicts their previous classification as reptiles (Fisher et al. 2000). Observations that even intensive properties (e.g., conductivity, melting point, magnetic properties) change at the nanoscale have changed and continue to alter the scientific model for the structure and behavior of matter (e.g., Roduner 2006; Cortie 2004; Eberhardt 2002). (See Chapter 4, "NSE and Society," for a more detailed discussion of the nature of science.)

The usefulness of a model can also depend on scale. For instance, at the macroscale, classical mechanics is a model that can generally predict the behavior of matter. However, as the scale becomes smaller and approaches the atomic and molecular scales, it becomes necessary to use quantum theory to explain the behavior of matter. When the behavior of matter in the cosmos is considered, general relativity may prove more useful. By testing real data against outcomes generated by a model, a measure of the model's usefulness is obtained.

Different models are more useful for explaining and predicting the structure, properties, and behavior for different targets. For example, many different representations may be used to illustrate an interaction between biomolecules (see Figure 3.7). Consider the interaction between a protein and a small molecule. When the purpose is to indicate the presence of an interaction, symbols or a low-

Figure 3.7
Different representations for a protein and small molecule interaction: (a) Symbolic (b) Low resolution cartoon (c) Backbone trace of protein structure (d) Interactions between atoms specified (dotted lines)

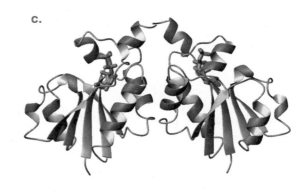

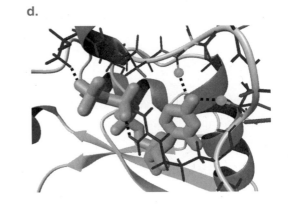

resolution cartoon provides enough information. If the location of the interaction within the protein is the question, then a higher resolution model is required and a model that traces the backbone of a protein with the small molecule bound to it would suffice. However, to characterize the forces that govern the interaction, a model in which specific atoms of the protein and small molecule are visible is necessary.

A simulation is one representation of a model in which variables are predefined, thus allowing for the exploration of a target under a single set of conditions. In particular, simulations provide access to certain aspects of the target. They can be useful for making predictions about the target but without the attendant risks or unnecessary consumption of resources. Changing variables of a model can help scientists make decisions about aspects of their work such as experimental design, process development, or the possible use of alternative materials. For example, scientists and engineers may use simulations to predict how different conditions might affect the outcome of processes such as self-assembly. They may use simulations to predict how a time-consuming and/or resource-demanding experiment may run in order to decide on the best conditions for running the actual experiment. In other instances, a phenomenon may be inaccessible to experimentation. For example, in a discussion of his theoretical studies on nucleation theory in the early 1970s, Farid Abraham, one of the pioneers of using computer simulations to study complex phenomena, said:

> As a theorist, I was at an impasse. I needed experimental information that could not be measured in the laboratory. The solution was to resort to a computer to simulate the behavior of the molecules in a droplet. (as in Finn n.d.)

His work, related to a variety of scientific phenomena, has disproved once-accepted scientific theories and helped generate new hypotheses. Abraham used simulations to further scientific progress.

Models and simulations are essential in all fields of science, helping researchers test and build their understanding of both the natural and fabricated worlds at all scales and throughout the scientific process.

Why Is This a Big Idea?

Much of the science that affects people's lives not only is extremely complex but also occurs at a scale too small to be seen (e.g., biotechnology, nanotechnology). Models provide a way for scientists to make progress in these fields, and they facilitate communication among scientists and between scientists and the general public.

Models allow scientists to visualize aspects of objects and phenomena, to predict behaviors that can be tested by experiment, to organize observations and representations of data, and to generate hypotheses and questions about the target. Likewise, modeling and simulations have always played a crucial role in the design process. Building models of potential targets, then running simulations in which a range of values for variables are tested, is a way to predict the potential efficacy of a product before fabricating it. Models and simulations of nanoscale objects and systems that cannot yet be built (e.g., Freitas and Merkle 2008) have often inspired experimentalists to attempt to build them.

Modeling plays a critical role in NSE research as scientists work to understand the novel structures and properties of matter observed at the nanoscale (Wang et al. 2006). For example, Lewis, Jensen, and Barrat (1997) used molecular dynamics simulations to predict the effect of particle size on melting point.

Scientists are also evaluating what characteristics of natural materials will be useful for creating new materials (Fratzl 2007). Models and simulations will play an important role in the development of potential new nanotechnologies such as micro- and nano-sized electronics, drug discovery and medical research, and the creation of highly designed and functional nano-related materials.

Recent advances in computer technology have greatly facilitated modeling and model building of complex structures and systems. Greater computing power provides faster calculations, which can, in turn, result in better approximations and better predictions of more complex systems. For example, molecular dynamics is a computer simulation used extensively in the study of biomolecules and materials science that helps probe the relationship among the structure, function, and motion of matter (van Gunsteren and Berendsen 1990; Karplus and McCammon 2002). The simulation describes the motion of atoms and molecules as predicted by certain laws of physics over a defined period of time. In 1977, the first molecular dynamics simulation on a protein was performed. The timescale of the original simulation was under 10 ps long (McCammon, Gelin, and Karplus 1977). In 2002, a similar simulation could be run with a timescale of 10 ns, but approximately 50 times faster (Karplus and McCammon 2002). Although nanoscale targets are small in size, they are often extremely complex when compared to noble gases or small molecules, often consisting of thousands of atoms. The ability to perform modeling and simulations on more complex systems is one of the driving factors of the nanotechnology revolution and the rapid advances made in nanoscale science. As modeling becomes a more powerful tool, the need for developing this skill becomes greater.

Building and refining models are important aspects of the scientific process, even in applied science. For example, models and simulations can play an important role in drug design (Wlodawer 2002). Scientists model biological molecules and systems in order to gain insight into their functions and the ways in which they work. Models of these targets, often enzymes or regulatory proteins, are used to make predictions about how the target works and, from that information, to design new inhibitors. Additional models and simulations are then used to generate explanations and predictions about how potential drugs bind to the target, which leads to cycles of modeling, design, synthesis, and analysis.

Many naturally occurring nanoscale objects (e.g., proteins, DNA, molecular machines) perform functions efficiently under extremely accurate control in order to maintain processes critical to life. These structures have inspired scientists and engineers to design counterparts that duplicate nature's control and efficiency but perform different desirable functions. For example, scientists and engineers have used models and simulations extensively in the effort to design, optimize, and understand the function of these new structures. Scientists have developed a helical polymer (polyphenylacetylene) that contracts and expands reversibly with changes in temperature. If the expansion and contraction of many of these polymers are coordinated, they can function similarly to an artificial "muscle" (Feringa and Browne 2008). Scientists are working to mimic the processes of

SCiLINKS
THE WORLD'S A CLICK AWAY

Topic: History of Atomic Models
Go to: www.scilinks.org
Code: NSE04

Topic: Using Models
Go to: www.scilinks.org
Code: NSE05

Chapter 3

biomineralization to improve the performance of implants (e.g., joint replacement) and hard tissue engineering (e.g., enamel, bone) (Li and Kaplan 2003; Sarikaya et al. 2003).

Scientists and engineers are also designing and fabricating nanoscale structures and assemblies that perform similarly to familiar mechanisms. An early DNA nanomechanical device (Mao et al. 1999) was designed to act as a switch. Changes in the environment induced changes in the structure of the DNA helix—the helix changed conformations from B-form (traditional) to Z-form, moving attached objects from opposite sides of the helix to being aligned on the same side of the helix. In later applications, scientists and engineers used simulations to help predict how different DNA can be used to manipulate various building blocks to create self-assembled structures (Seeman and Lukeman 2005; Mbindyo et al. 2001; Park et al. 2008). For all of these applications, building a model or simulating the phenomenon was an important first and intermediate step.

Relationship to the 7–12 Curriculum

Many educators and researchers have argued that the process of building and refining models lies at the core of the scientific process (Gilbert, Boulter, and Rutherford 1998; Schwarz and White 2005; Van Driel and Verloop 2002). Indeed, the National Science Education Standards emphasize that all students should understand that "scientists formulate and test their explanations of nature using observation, experiments, and theoretical and mathematical models" (NRC 1996, p. 171). Likewise, the Benchmarks identify models as a "common theme" and suggest that their application is critical in fields as diverse as mathematics, education, law, business and finance, and science and technology (AAAS 1993). According to Hodson (cited in Justi and

van Driel 2005) there are three goals for science education: to learn science, to learn about science, and to learn to do science. Understanding, building, and using models are essential components of all three goals. Therefore, students should use and build models to explain and make predictions about phenomena throughout the science curriculum.

Students often have difficulty in two areas: relating models to the target and understanding the many ways in which models can be used to explain various phenomena. For example, research has shown that chemistry students have difficulty moving between the target, models, and symbols (Harrison and Treagust 2002). In addition, students often believe that models in the classroom simply represent static scientific facts (Grosslight et al. 1991). In reality, models are an important part of the *process* of scientific inquiry. They are used to visualize, explain, hypothesize, and make predictions about the structure, properties, and behavior of the phenomena of interest. Therefore, students should learn more about the nature of models and how they fit into the scientific process. Students should build models and develop their own explanations about relevant targets. For students to fully understand and participate in scientific inquiry, they need to understand how to use models to generate hypotheses, make predictions, develop questions, or communicate ideas about a target. Gaining knowledge and skill in any context will help prepare students to use models in connection with NSE concepts. This skill is critical for learning NSE concepts because the nanoscale is inherently inaccessible due to both the size and complexity of the targets.

Acknowledgments

The authors would like to thank the following people for helpful discussions and reading of this chapter:

César Delgado for Tools and Instrumentation and Harry Short for Models and Simulations.

References

American Association for the Advancement of Science (AAAS). 1993. *Benchmarks for science literacy.* New York: Oxford University Press.

Cortie, M. B. 2004. The weird world of nanoscale gold. *Gold Bulletin* 37 (1–2): 12–19.

Eberhardt, W. 2002. Clusters as new materials. *Surface Science* 500: 242–270.

Eigler, D. M., and E. K. Schweizer. 1990. Positioning single atoms with a scanning tunneling microscope. *Nature* 344: 524–526.

Feringa, B. L., and W. R. Browne. 2008. Macromolecules flex their muscles. *Nature Nanotechnology* 3: 383–384.

Finn, R. n.d. Exploring materials in a simulated world. *http://domino.research.ibm.com/comm/wwwr_thinkresearch.nsf/pages/simulation196.html.*

Fisher, P. E., D. A. Russell, M. K. Stoskopf, R. E. Barrick, M. Hammer, and A. A. Kuzmitz. 2000. Cardiovascular evidence for an intermediate or higher metabolic rate in an ornithischian dinosaur. *Science* 288: 503–505.

Fratzl, P. 2007. Biomimetic materials research: What can we really learn from nature's structural materials? *Journal of the Royal Society Interface* 4: 637–642.

Freitas, R. A., Jr., and R. C. Merkle. 2008. A minimal toolset for positional diamond mechanosynthesis. *Journal of Computational and Theoretical Nanoscience* 5: 760–861.

Giessibl, F. J., S. Hembacher, H. Bielefeldt, and J. Mannhart. 2000. Subatomic features on the silicon (111)–(7×7) surface observed by atomic force microscopy. *Science* 289: 422–425.

Gilbert, J. K., C. Boulter, and M. Rutherford. 1998. Models in explanations, part 1: Horses for courses? *International Journal of Science Education* 20: 83–97.

Grosslight, L., C. Unger, E. Jay, and C. Smith. 1991. Understanding models and their use in science: Conceptions of middle and high school students and experts. *Journal of Research in Science Teaching* 28 (9): 799–822.

Harrison, A. G., and D. F. Treagust. 2002. The particulate nature of matter: Challenges in understanding the submicroscopic world. In *Chemical education: Towards research-based practice,* ed. J. K.

Gilbert, O. D. Jong, R. Justi, D. F. Treagust, and J. H. Van Driel, 271–292. Dordrecht, The Netherlands: Kluwer Academic Publishers.

Hembacher, S., F. J. Giessibl, and J. Mannhart. 2004. Force microscopy with light-atom probes. *Science* 305: 380–383.

Hembacher, S., F. J. Giessibl, J. Mannhart, and C. F. Quate. 2003. Revealing the hidden atom in graphite by low-temperature atomic force microscopy. *Proceedings of the National Academy of Sciences, USA* 100 (22): 12539–12542.

Justi, R., and J. van Driel. 2005. The development of science teachers' knowledge on models and modelling: Promoting, characterizing, and understanding the process. *International Journal of Science Education* 27 (5): 549–573.

Karplus, M., and A. McCammon. 2002. Molecular dynamics simulations of biomolecules. *Nature Structural Biology* 9 (9): 646–652.

Lewis, L. J., P. Jensen, and J.-L. Barrat. 1997. Melting, freezing, and coalescence of gold nanoclusters. *Physical Review B* 56 (4): 2248–2257.

Li, C., and D. L. Kaplan. 2003. Biomimetic composites via molecular scale self-assembly and biomineralization. *Current Opinion in Solid State and Materials Science* 7: 265–271.

Mao, C., W. Sun, Z. Shen, and N. C. Seeman. 1999. A nanomechanical device based on the B–Z transition of DNA. *Nature* 397: 144–146.

Mbindyo, J. K. N., B. D. Reiss, B. R. Martin, C. D. Keating, M. J. Natan, and T. E. Mallouk. 2001. DNA-directed assembly of gold nanowires on complementary surfaces. *Advanced Materials* 13 (4): 249–254.

McCammon, J. A., B. R. Gelin, and M. Karplus. 1977. Dynamics of folded proteins. *Nature* 267: 585–590.

Müller, D. J., and Y. F. Dufrêne. 2008. Atomic force microscopy as a multifunctional molecular toolbox in nanobiotechnology. *Nature Nanotechnology* 3: 261–269.

National Research Council (NRC). 1996. *National science education standards.* Washington, DC: National Academy Press.

Park, S. Y., A. K. R. Lytton-Jean, B. Lee, S. Weigand, G. C. Schatz, and C. A. Mirkin. 2008. DNA-programmable nanoparticle crystallization. *Nature* 451: 553–556.

Chapter 3

Roduner, E. 2006. Size matters: Why nanomaterials are different. *Chemical Society Reviews* 35: 583–592.

Sarikaya, M., C. Tamerler, A. K.-Y. Jen, K. Schulten, and F. Baneyx. 2003. Molecular biomimetics: Nanotechnology through biology. *Nature Materials* 2: 577–585.

Schwarz, C. V., and B. Y. White. 2005. Metamodeling knowledge: Developing students' understanding of scientific modeling. *Cognition and Instruction* 23 (2): 165–205.

Seeman, N. C., and P. S. Lukeman. 2005. Nucleic acid nanostructures: Bottom-up control of geometry on the nanoscale. *Reports on Progress in Physics* 68: 237–270.

Sugimoto, Y., P. Pou, M. Abe, P. Jelinek, R. Pérez, W. Morita, and Ó. Custance. 2007. Chemical identification of individual surface atoms by atomic force microscopy. *Nature* 446: 64–67.

van Driel, J. H., and N. Verloop. 2002. Experienced teachers' knowledge of teaching and learning of models and modelling in science education. *International Journal of Science Education* 24 (12): 1255–1272.

van Gunsteren, W. F., and H. J. C. Berendsen. 1990. Computer simulation of molecular dynamics: Methodology, applications, and perspectives in chemistry. *Angewante Chemie International Edition English* 29: 992–1023.

Vedantam, S. 2006. "For Pluto, a smaller world after all." *Washington Post*. August 25.

Wang, J., H. L. Duan, Z. P. Huang, and B. L. Karihaloo. 2006. A scaling law for properties of nanostructured materials. *Proceedings of the Royal Society A* 462: 1355–1363.

Wlodawer, A. 2002. Rational approach to AIDS drug design through structural biology. *Annual Reviews of Medicine* 53: 595–614.

Chapter 4
NSE and Society

The final big idea of NSE is different from the others. It describes the natures of science and technology and how society affects and is affected by scientific and technological advancement. Thus the Science, Technology, and Society big idea is linked to all of the other big ideas of NSE.

Big Idea 9
*Science, Technology, and Society**

The advancement of science involves developing explanations for how and why things work and using technology to apply that knowledge to meet objectives, solve problems, and answer questions of societal interest. Because nanotechnology is an emergent science, it provides an opportunity to witness and actively participate in scientific progress and in decision making about how to use new technologies.

About Science, Technology, and Society*

Equipped with his five senses, man explores the universe around him and calls the adventure science.

—Edwin Powell Hubble, 1954

Nature of Science

Science is a process of exploring the universe and endeavoring to explain the objects, systems, and phenomena within it. It is a dynamic process wherein scientists build upon previous knowledge, modify their understandings, make discoveries and develop new ways of thinking. Scientific progress is seldom linear. Both successful and failed investigations provide new knowledge and observations that, in turn, generate new questions to investigate. Therefore, the process of scientific inquiry is never ending, as humans will continue to develop and refine complex explanations of the world around them. Although different methods are used to study and advance physical, biological, and social domains, scientists across domains share a common goal of developing a better

* The Center for Nanotechnology in Society at Arizona State University has written "Nanotechnology & Society: Ideas for Education and Public Engagement," which discusses many of these ideas in more detail. You may obtain this document at *http://cns.asu.edu/educate/documents/Nano-SocIdeasforEd.pdf.*

Chapter 4

understanding of how the world works. NSE, as the study of all nanoscale phenomena and the fabrication of all nanoscale products (e.g., materials, devices, systems), is inherently an interdisciplinary field and as such may employ a combination of methodologies to explore the nanoscale world.

> *Science alone of all the subjects contains within itself the lesson of the danger of belief in the infallibility of the greatest teachers in the preceding generation.... Learn from science that you must doubt the experts. As a matter of fact, I can also define science another way: Science is the belief in the ignorance of experts.*
>
> —Richard Feynman, 2000

Nature of Technology

Technology involves developing tools, processes, and systems that extend human capabilities and solve problems. For example, technology helps humans control and adapt to the environment, providing easier and greater access to food, sanitation, health care, communication, and transportation. Technology is an intrinsic part of the culture that both reflects and influences societal values (AAAS 1993, p. 41). It is not just a scientific enterprise but is integrated into many facets of society, including economic structures such as manufacturing, marketing, and labor. Engineers design both automobiles and the machines required to build them. An extensive labor force helps to manufacture the necessary parts, then the whole automobile, and the finished product is marketed to consumers. For consumers to use automobiles, fuel and the infrastructure behind supplying it are required. Also tied to the system is the building and maintenance of roads. Thus technologies

often involve a large-scale and integrated organization of materials and people focused on addressing practical problems.

Technology, however, does not always improve quality of life. Many people spend hours in their automobiles during lengthy daily commutes, and the extensive use of motor vehicles has caused pollution problems that have global environmental implications. Although nanotechnology has the potential to affect our lives in many important ways, it is too soon to tell whether it will live up to its promise and whether and how new technologies will be integrated into various facets of society.

Relationship Between Science And Technology

Although scientific discoveries and new technologies can be developed independently, science and technology often drive one another. New scientific knowledge may be applied to form new technologies. The parts of the natural world that are accessible to study are often limited by available technology, and new technology can render new aspects accessible for exploration. In this way, technology helps to drive scientific progress. The tools that rendered the nanoworld accessible played this role in NSE (see Chapters 3 and 11 for further discussion).

Likewise, new technologies often create questions and problems that require new scientific knowledge. For example, the introduction of nanoscale materials into products raises many questions regarding the long-term safety and health of human beings and the environment. Without scientific breakthroughs, many technological advances would not be possible. Additionally, science and technology may progress together. Scientists currently use the Hubble Space Telescope to explore the outermost regions of the universe, but they first needed to design and develop new technologies to make the telescope into the useful instrument that it is.

As new scientific discoveries are made and new understandings about the nanoworld develop, scientists and engineers will use and apply that knowledge to a broad range of applications (e.g., electronics, pharmaceuticals, building materials, renewable energy). And new discoveries may require scientists to develop new models for explaining the world around us.

Making Decisions About Science and Technology

Scientists, engineers, government officials, and *all* citizens make decisions that affect the progress of science and technology. Priorities set by government agencies, for example, affect which scientific research efforts are pursued by determining which projects are funded. For example, the AIDS epidemic and the publicity surrounding it led to extensive funding for research directed toward understanding the disease and developing a cure. Decisions must continually be made regarding which technologies to use and how to use them, while simultaneously evaluating who stands to benefit from them (or not) and in what ways.

Benefits and Risks Associated With New Technologies

> *Technology ... is a queer thing. It brings you great gifts with one hand, and it stabs you in the back with the other.*
>
> —C.P. Snow, 1971

The technologies that humans create and use affects other living things in complex ways—both positively and negatively. The solution to one problem can create new problems, and far-reaching effects may be unanticipated. For example, ammonia coolants once used for refrigeration could leak and spoil food. To replace ammonia coolants, scientists developed chlorofluorocarbons (CFCs) and related compounds. Although these compounds were effective for the intended application, they were later linked to ozone depletion and found to be powerful greenhouse gases (Manzer 1990).

Another example is dichlorodiphenyltrichloroethane (DDT), used extensively to control the spread of insect-borne diseases such as malaria in the early 1940s and later as an agricultural pesticide. Eventually, however, scientists realized that application of DDT had a much broader effect on the ecosystem, detrimentally affecting the environment and the health of a broad range of wildlife (e.g., McLachlan and Arnold 1996). Although the use of DDT has been banned in many parts of the world, including the United States, it continues to be used in regions where malaria remains a serious health risk (Curtis and Lines 2001). In those areas of the world, the benefits are considered to outweigh the risks. It is important to evaluate and track the risks and benefits of all new technologies.

Although the goals and promises of NSE are generally positive, the resulting products and materials carry with them the risk of negative effects. Nanoscale objects are small enough to permeate biological barriers that protect living organisms. This means that any given material might present different health risks depending on whether the particles of that material are at the nanoscale or a larger scale. In addition, as with all new materials, environmental and waste

Topic: Science and Technology

Go to: *www.scilinks.org*

Code: NSE06

Chapter 4

management issues arise both from manufacturing and consumer use. New methods must be developed, for example, to protect drinking water from nanoscale materials.

The extent to which nanotechnology will ultimately affect the economic and social well-being of society remains uncertain. Will the application of nanotechnology be limited to products such as stain-free pants, sunscreens, and cosmetics, or will it be able to help solve larger societal issues such as water quality and sustainable energy? And because new technologies are not likely to benefit everyone equally, decisions must be made regarding who will benefit and at what cost. The benefits may be individual while the costs are collective. For example, automobiles provide convenient transportation for individuals, but the greenhouse gases they emit cause problems for all.

Why Is This a Big Idea?

Since the discovery of fire and the development of basic tools, humans have employed science and technology to help them adapt to and survive in their environment. Technological advances broadly influence society, including lifestyle, values, and economic and environmental systems. With the Industrial Revolution, a society driven by manual labor and agriculture shifted to one of industry and mechanization, changing not only technological conditions but socioeconomic ones as well (Freeman and Louçã 2001). More recently, computers have revolutionized the way people work and communicate. The technology generated by NSE is often touted to be the "next big thing" that will affect all aspects of life. Already it affects applications as diverse as data storage, electronics, and cosmetics, and efforts are currently under way to employ nanoscale materials to improve

healthcare and the sustainability of agriculture, energy, and the environment.

Any discussion of our technological revolution is necessarily of an abstract and historical nature. However, with NSE, students can observe and evaluate the promises that newly generated knowledge holds, then watch as scientists and engineers work toward achieving important goals. NSE provides a way for students to witness the nature of scientific progress firsthand and track the nonlinear path it follows, including both the successes and the inevitable failures along the way. Students also have an opportunity to witness how their lives and society as a whole change as people adopt new technologies.

It is difficult to determine at this time whether the advances that NSE brings will be in the form of small, incremental improvements to current technologies or in the form of broad, extensive changes (Miller et al. 2007). The media often report on scientific breakthroughs and potential applications in a manner that is flashy and attention getting, without being appropriately critical. In reality, many new applications (if not most) will not fulfill their initial promise. In the 1950s, nuclear power was touted as a solution that would provide electricity "too cheap to meter" (Pool 1997, p. 71)—one example of a promise not realized. The economic and social promises of nanotechnology may not be as extensive and far-reaching as expected—or NSE may bring widespread changes but ones unanticipated by pioneering scientists and engineers in the field.

Consider this: One of the primary global problems humans face today relates to energy demands (Smalley 2005). We are heavily dependent on fossil fuels, and demand increases despite a shared understanding that the supply is finite. The need for a reliable source of renewable energy is clear. However, despite the fact that enough energy from the Sun strikes Earth every day to meet all energy needs on the planet, we have not yet found a way to harness that energy effectively. Chemists are working to produce a nanoscale material that directly converts light to electricity by means of an array of nanoscale solar cells. The cells could be incorporated in a material that would cover a surface like plastic wrap or paint. In this way, nanoscale solar cells could be integrated with other building materials. This technology offers the promise of inexpensive production that could finally make solar power a widely used alternative to electricity. Converting to solar energy and away from nonrenewable, polluting fossil fuels could have a tremendous impact on both environmental and energy concerns. However, removing or significantly decreasing our dependence on fossil fuels, particularly oil, would also affect global political and economic balances.

In fact, scientific discoveries frequently come ahead of society's ability to fully understand what the discoveries will mean in the long term for people's lives and livelihoods (Miller et al. 2007). Scientists' ability to split the atom to control nuclear fission contributed to extensive geopolitical conflict (i.e., the Cold War), energy management, and nuclear waste. After witnessing the way this technology was being used, Albert Einstein stated succinctly, "It has become appallingly obvious that our technology has exceeded our humanity." More recently, biotechnological advances not only have brought new understandings and treatments of human diseases, but also have raised ethical questions about practices such as cloning and gene therapy.

Nanotechnology also raises critical questions. Nanoscale structures are small enough to cross the biological barriers that inherently protect all living organisms. For example, pure gold is inert in its bulk form and has long been used for a variety of applications, including filling cavities in human teeth. Although exposure to gold in this form is not harmful, the long-term effects that nanoscale particles of gold have on biological tissues remain unknown. Similarly, large particles of zinc oxide and titanium dioxide have been used for decades as sunscreens. They are approved by the Food and Drug Administration (FDA) in this form and for this application. However, while it is clear that these substances provide effective protection from the harmful UV light from the Sun in their nanoscale form, the long-term effects of exposure to nanoscale particles of the materials have not been studied extensively. Thus, the novel properties of nanoscale materials used for new applications may pose biological risks not initially understood.

Because the nanotechnology revolution is ongoing, students who study NSE can see who makes decisions and how decisions are made. They can observe who benefits from new technologies and who pays the greatest cost. Students can participate in discussions about safety concerns and other health and environmental risks and compare them with the benefits of new technology. The media are filled with reports about the promise of NSE. Citizens need good critical-thinking skills and adequate science knowledge to be able to evaluate the claims they hear and read about. Often, students do not learn these skills sufficiently in school and instead either accept as truth anything reported in the news or uniformly reject as untrustworthy anything that the media report. Neither approach is ideal. A key aspect of being scientifically literate is the ability to evaluate scientific claims based on evidence. This

Chapter 4

skill is certainly essential for making informed decisions about new nanoscale technologies.

Relationship to the 7–12 Curriculum

Recently, mass communication has focused significant attention on nanotechnology (e.g., Booker and Boysen 2005; Ratner and Ratner 2002). This attention presents an opportunity to use NSE to help motivate, interest, and engage students in learning both NSE and more traditional science. Positive student attitudes toward science correlate with higher performance on science assessments for the majority of students (Neathery 1997). Eccles and Wigfield (2002) have shown that "interest is more strongly related to indicators of deep-level learning than to surface-level learning" (p. 115), which may explain why students with low interest in science perform poorly on science exams. Researchers know that student achievement increases significantly when the science subject matter is relevant to their own lives (Schwartz-Bloom and Halpin 2003).

Because of the interrelatedness of science, technology, and society, the study of NSE does not need to be limited to the science classroom. For example, when the telescope was invented by Hans Lippershey in the 1600s, it was heralded as a revolutionary new tool for the military, allowing the Dutch fleet to track the movements of the enemy from a great distance. Within a few years, Galileo began landmark studies that changed the way that we look at ourselves within the universe by providing experimental evidence for the heliocentric solar system hypothesized by Copernicus. This discovery put Galileo in conflict with the Catholic Church and the Italian government, which ascribed to the idea of an Earth-centered solar system. Thus the invention of the telescope and Galileo's subsequent discoveries have a place not only in the science class but also in social studies, for their effect on military strategy, culture, and society.

Likewise, nanotechnology promises to influence many aspects of society. Researchers are developing nanoscale applications to solve problems in areas as diverse as, but not limited to, medicine, sustainable energy, and building materials. Efficiently harnessing the Sun's energy would impact the world's energy and environmental problems as well as shift the global economic and political power structures. Therefore, in addition to having a place in a chemistry or ecology course, the implications of new nanoscale applications are also appropriate for discussion in social studies classes.

The interdisciplinary nature of NSE allows it to suit many different contexts and to make useful cross-disciplinary connections. Yet, scientific disciplines such as chemistry, biology, geology, physics, and astronomy are often strictly demarcated in school settings. Students take classes in the disciplines, reinforcing the notion that each is a discrete entity. Rarely do students study a single scientific phenomenon by considering it from multiple perspectives (e.g., as a biologist, a chemist, and a physicist might). In reality, clear boundaries among the disciplines do not exist. Scientists often use knowledge and methodologies developed in one discipline to address problems or explain phenomena in another. This is especially true with emerging science. Enormous leaps in scientific knowledge about biological systems occurred when chemists and physicists began to apply disciplinary knowledge and methodologies to biological problems. Now, NSE, which is science and engineering of all disciplines at the nanoscale, also provides the opportunity for making new connections.

NATIONAL SCIENCE TEACHERS ASSOCIATION

As members of a society in the midst of a nanotechnology revolution, even students can be part of that revolution. NSE is "science in the making" and can be used to illustrate the dynamic nature of the scientific enterprise for students. They can witness the processes that scientists use when confronted with new phenomena. They can see how engineers create new applications not only to solve problems in the lab but also to help make everyday living easier and more enjoyable. Finally, students can debate the usefulness and the cost-benefit ratio of these applications to society, so they are prepared to participate in the critical decision-making processes in which *all* individuals within a society should play a role.

Acknowledgment

The authors would like to thank Clark Miller for helpful discussions and his reading of this chapter.

References

American Association for the Advancement of Science (AAAS). 1993. *Benchmarks for science literacy*. New York: Oxford University Press.

Booker, R. D., and E. Boysen. 2005. *Nanotechnology for dummies*. Indianapolis, IN: Wiley Publishing.

Curtis, C. F., and J. D. Lines. 2001. Should DDT be banned by international treaty? *Parasitology Today* 16 (3): 119–121.

Eccles, J. S., and A. Wigfield. 2002. Motivational beliefs, values, and goals. *Annual Review of Psychology* 53: 109–132.

Freeman, C., and F. Louça. 2001. *As time goes by: The information revolution and the industrial revolutions in historical perspective*. Oxford: Oxford University Press.

Manzer, L. E. 1990. The CFC–ozone issue: Progress on the development of alternatives to CFCs. *Science* 249 (4964): 31–35.

McLachlan, J. A., and S. F. Arnold. 1996. Environmental estrogens. *American Scientist* 84: 452–461.

Miller, C., D. Guston, D. Barben, J. Wetmore, C. Selin, and E. Fisher. 2007. *Nanotechnology & society: Ideas for education and public engagement*. Tempe, AZ: The Center for Nanotechnology in Society.

Neathery, M. F. 1997. Elementary and secondary students' perceptions toward science: Correlations with gender, ethnicity, ability, grade, and science achievement. *Electronic Journal of Science Education* 2 (1).

Pool, R. 1997. *Beyond engineering: How society shapes technology*. New York: Oxford University Press.

Ratner, M., and D. Ratner. 2002. *Nanotechnology: A gentle introduction to the next big thing*. Upper Saddle River, NJ: Prentice Hall.

Schwartz–Bloom, R. D., and M. J. Halpin. 2003. Integrating pharmacology topics in high school biology and chemistry classes improves performance. *Journal of Research in Science Teaching* 40: 922–938.

Smalley, R. E. 2005. Future global energy prosperity: The terawatt challenge. *MRS Bulletin* 30: 412–417.

SECTION

2

Integrating NSE Into the 7–12 Science Curriculum

Introduction
NSE in the Classroom

The nine big ideas of NSE outlined in Section 1 define the core principles of the discipline. Deep understanding of NSE-related concepts depends on these nine building blocks. The big ideas also provide guidance for the coordinated development and alignment of curriculum, instruction, and assessment. To successfully align these components of the educational system, however, we must follow a systematic process (Pellegrino et al. 2008), which we begin to do in this section.

Learning Goals and the Big Ideas

The scope of each big idea is necessarily broad, and as such, a thorough understanding of the concepts contained within each one must be built over an extended period of time. In this section, we present "learning goals" that define what it is that students should know and how they should know it. In other words, it is important to specify what students should be able to do with the knowledge related to specific content.

Because each big idea encompasses a vast amount of science content, multiple learning goals must be part of building an integrated understanding of each big idea. Also, due to the interdisciplinary nature of NSE and the interconnectedness of the big ideas, any given learning goal may be associated with multiple big ideas.

The first step in developing a strategy to support student learning requires explicitly defining the content contained within each big idea, a process we call unpacking. In Section I, we began the unpacking process by elaborating the content and contextualizing it within the larger scope of the discipline.

In Section 2 we continue that process: We now define the learning goals associated with the big ideas as well as the content of the learning goals at a finer "grain size." We cite the prerequisite knowledge for each learning goal, potential difficulties students might have with the content, and students' misconceptions (what some call alternative conceptions or ideas). The prerequisite knowledge, potential difficulties, and possible misconceptions can all be used for instructional and assessment purposes.

A common question related to fitting NSE into the science curriculum is, To what degree is NSE a completely new science—that is, is NSE simply a new way of looking at traditional science? In Section 1, we addressed this question in the discussions about how the content of each big idea connects to the current curriculum. This question is addressed more specifically in this section when we relate the content of each big idea of NSE to that contained in the national science standards documents—*Benchmarks for Science Literacy* (AAAS 1993) and *National Science Education Standards* (NRC 1996)—and discuss what is missing from those documents.

Introduction

Structure of the Chapters in Section 2

Each chapter presents a big idea and contains a brief summary of how the content contained within the big idea might fit into the curriculum. We then describe the prerequisite knowledge required for all the Learning Goals in that chapter. Next, we present a Learning Goal and give the prerequisite knowledge for that particular goal. (Depending on students' prior academic experiences, prerequisite knowledge may need to be taught at the same time as the content of the Learning Goal.) We discuss potential student difficulties and misconceptions. We then summarize the content of the Learning Goal and provide examples of intellectual tasks that students should be able to accomplish if the learning goal is met.

As teachers know, students in the same grade may have very different prior knowledge related to a given aspect of science content. Therefore, in many cases, we define "levels" in terms of a threshold in prerequisite knowledge (e.g., before or after students use a particle model to explain phenomena).

Finally, we present in detailed tables the national science standards that connect directly to NSE content, as well as those that help build a foundation for developing an understanding of NSE. Each chapter concludes with a discussion of what is missing from the standards documents, and perhaps from the current science curricula, in relation to the big ideas of NSE.

The individual Benchmarks are specified by the chapter (number) and section (letter); the grade level is followed by the page number.

The NSES standards are described by section heading, grade level, and page number.

Conclusion

The Learning Goals in each chapter encompass an extensive amount of science content; therefore, teachers will not be able to address all of the content contained in a single Learning Goal in a single lesson or even a single unit. Instead, teachers and curriculum developers can use this book as a guide to the process and a first step of unpacking the content and developing learning goals for NSE. We hope that this book will be used as a resource for those considering how NSE content and the big ideas might become a significant part of the grades 7–12 science curriculum.

References

American Association for the Advancement of Science (AAAS). 1993. *Benchmarks for science literacy.* New York: Oxford University Press.

National Research Council (NRC). 1996. *National science education standards.* Washington, DC: National Academy Press.

Pellegrino, J., J. Krajcik, S. Y. Stevens, N. Shin, C. Delgado, S. Geier, et al. 2008. Using Construct-Centered Design to align curriculum, instruction, and assessment development in emerging science. In *Proceedings from ICLS '08: International perspectives in the learning sciences: Creating a learning world, Vol. 3,* ed. G. Kanselaar, V. Jonker, P. A. Kirschner, and F. Prins, 314–321. Utrecht, The Netherlands: International Society of the Learning Sciences.

Chapter 5
Size and Scale*

Big Idea:

Factors relating to size and geometry (e.g. size, scale, shape, proportionality, dimensionality) help describe matter and predict its behavior.

Learning Goals

Concepts relating to size and scale (and geometry) affect students' abilities to build understanding in a variety of scientific disciplines, including developing conceptual understanding of nanoscale phenomena. Five primary learning goals are associated with Size and Scale as a big idea. Each represents different knowledge or skills that students should develop and be able to relate to discipline-specific content. (By presenting the learning goals in this order, we are not necessarily suggesting an order for their introduction into the curriculum.)

Ideally, concepts related to size and scale (and geometry) should be introduced in the context of scientific disciplines. In this chapter, we use examples from various disciplines to outline the knowledge and skills framework that students should develop related to size and scale.

---

*Recent literature has used the term *size and scale* to refer to many of the concepts included in this big idea. Like size, shape also characterizes objects and can affect S/V, and thus shape is also included in this chapter. This big idea might better be termed *size and geometry* to encompass all of these factors simultaneously, but we use *size and scale* to be consistent with terminology in the field.

> **General Prerequisite Knowledge for This Chapter**
>
> Students must be able to perform addition, subtraction, multiplication, and division and apply the functions appropriately to problems.

Learning Goal 1

Students should understand that in order to know the size of an object, it is necessary to be able to compare it to a reference.

Specific Prerequisite Knowledge

Students should be able to

- recognize that certain aspects of an object or material are measurable (NCTM 1989, p. 45);
- order familiar objects by length scale (e.g., ant < mouse < chair < table < house);
- apply the transitive property to sizes (If A < B, and B < C, then A < C); and
- define and calculate area and volume (*post-fractions and proportional reasoning*).

Potential Student Difficulties and Misconceptions

- Students may mix centimeters, inches, even invented units (NCTM 2003, 183).
- Students may not realize that relative and absolute sizes of two objects are linked (Delgado et al. 2007).

Chapter 5

Students often have difficulty

- defining the length of an object if the end (zero) of the ruler is not aligned with the edge of the object (Kenney and Kouba 1997, p. 142) and
- with measurement, especially 2-D and 3-D (Kenney and Kouba 1997, p. 151).

What Students Should Learn

People measure materials to define the size or amount of them, but different methods are used to measure different materials. Rulers are useful for measuring length of solid objects; graduated cylinders and measuring cups are useful for measuring the volume of liquids. Each of these tools contains reference marks that allow the size or amount of various things to be defined. Likewise, the unit used to define quantities is important. Three inches is not equivalent to three centimeters; 20 grams is not the same as 20 liters.

Size defined by standardized units is generally considered an absolute (quantitative) size. Estimating the relative size of two objects, often in terms of a reference object, is another important skill. The reference object may be well-known or it may be conceptually important (e.g., a hydrogen atom, the human body) rather than a standard unit (Lamon 1994; Tretter et al. 2006). "The measurement process is identical, in principle, for measuring any attribute: [C]hoose a unit, compare that unit to the object, and report the number of units" (NCTM 1989, p. 104). Comparing an object to another object instead of to a standard reference unit results in a measure of relative (qualitative) size. For example, the length of an ant may be described as approximately 200 times smaller than a human, and the diameter of a red blood cell is approximately 50,000 times larger than that of an atom.

Following are some examples of the knowledge and skills that students should develop.

Before Students Have Studied Fractions and Proportional Reasoning

Students should be able to do the following:

- Measure an object and explain why having a reference and using proper units is necessary to define the size or amount of something properly
- Describe the size of objects in multiple contexts
- Measure quantities of objects and materials (e.g., length, volume, mass)
- Estimate the size of an object relative to a standardized unit or reference object
- Explain why a scale on an image is necessary to define its size
- Use a scale to determine the size of objects in images
- Use the scale of a map to estimate distances between points

After Students Have Studied Fractions and Proportional Reasoning

Students should be able to do the following:

- Connect the relative sizes of two objects to their absolute sizes (For instance, if a pencil is 15 cm long and a table is 20 times longer, then students should be able to calculate that the table is 300 cm long.)
- Explain how the two-dimensional size (area) and three-dimensional size (volume) change with respect to changing the length scale of one dimension
- Estimate relative sizes in two and three dimensions (i.e., area and volume)

Learning Goal 2

Students should understand that some worlds are too small to be seen with the naked eye, including the micro-, nano-, and atomic and molecular worlds. Each

of these contains unique representative objects that help define the scale represented by the worlds.

Specific Prerequisite Knowledge

Students should understand

- that worlds too small or distant to observe with the naked eye cannot be measured except with special tools;
- differences in value between 10, 100, 1000, and 1,000,000 and their inverses; and
- metric units (e.g., milli-, micro-, and nano-) and understand how they relate to familiar, macroscopic measurements (e.g., meter, centimeter).

Potential Student Difficulties and Misconceptions

- Objects in the unseen world cannot be experienced and manipulated directly, which makes it difficult for students to build a robust understanding of small things (Tretter et al. 2006a).

Students may believe that

- all objects that are too small to be seen with the naked eye are roughly the same size, whereas, in fact, their relative sizes may be vastly different (Tretter, Jones, and Minogue 2006)
- small macroscopic items like ants or grains of salt are smaller than atoms and cells (Castellini et al. 2007).

Students may have difficulty developing an understanding of decimals (Cohen, Corel, and Johnson 2002), ratios and proportions (Lesh, Post, and Behr 1988), and measurement (Kenney and Kouba 1997).

What Students Should Learn

It is often conceptually useful to divide the immense range of sizes of objects studied in science into several different scales or "worlds." The tools required to observe and measure phenomena, and the models used to explain the behavior of matter, characterize each of these worlds. In addition, certain relatively familiar objects are often used as references, or landmarks, to help characterize the scale of these worlds (see Figure 1.2, p. 6). For instance, the approximate height of a human is a common reference for estimating the size of other objects in the macroworld (Tretter et al. 2006).

The macroworld is the most familiar because it is the one that people experience directly. It contains objects that humans can see without using special tools (greater than $\sim10^{-4}$ m or 100 µm). The behavior of matter in the macroworld can be predicted using classical mechanics.

The microworld is the world of individual cells; thus, cells are generally used as the representative or landmark objects to conceptually define this world. The microworld can only be observed or measured with the aid of a magnifier such as an optical microscope. Objects in this world range in size from approximately 10^{-7} to 10^{-4} m (0.1 to 100 µm; 10^2 to 10^5 nm). Classical mechanics is generally an adequate model for explaining the behavior of microscale matter.

The nanoworld is the next smaller scale and is defined as 10^{-9} to 10^{-7} meters, or 1 to 100 nm. Objects are considered part of the nanoworld if at least one dimension falls within this range. For example the diameter of the DNA double helix is approximately 2 nm, but the length of a single chromosome is approximately 5 cm. When objects have dimensions that fall in different scales, those objects are typically classified by their smallest dimension because the smallest dimension determines the tool that can render the object or material accessible for observation. Optical microscopes are not useful for the nanoscale. Instead, it is necessary

Chapter 5

to use instruments with probes smaller than the wavelength of visible light (< ~400 nm). Representative, or landmark, objects for this world include the diameter of the DNA helix (approximately 2.5 nm) or the diameter of a buckyball (approximately 1 nm). At this scale, classical mechanics begins to fail to adequately predict the behavior of matter, and quantum mechanics must be applied.

The atomic scale includes objects smaller than one nanometer. It includes individual small molecules, atoms, and subatomic particles; thus, the representative object is often a hydrogen atom, which has a diameter of approximately 0.1 nm. Quantum mechanics is the model used to explain the behavior of matter at the atomic and subatomic scales.

The divisions between the different worlds are artificial and somewhat arbitrary. They are useful in that they group things by the models useful for describing and explaining phenomena and by the tools useful for observing and measuring objects and phenomena in each of these worlds. However, the divisions between the worlds should not be considered absolute demarcations. For example, some large molecules, such as proteins, are nanoscale structures. These worlds should be used as *models* that help students to communicate and to see the relationships among the characteristics of the different worlds and the objects within them. Thinking about size in terms of worlds and metric units provides a foundation for thinking about quantities and sizes in terms of orders of magnitude and expressing sizes in scientific notation that is useful in all disciplines of science.

Examples of the knowledge and skills that students should develop follow, although the worlds in which students work will depend on their previous experiences in mathematics and science. Students should be able to

- relate the sizes of objects—between worlds—both qualitatively and quantitatively and
- name representative objects for each of the worlds.

Learning Goal 3

Students should understand that the size of an object may be represented in many ways, both qualitative and quantitative. Each representation has advantages and disadvantages depending on the purpose.

Specific Prerequisite Knowledge

Students should understand the following:

- The differences in value between 10, 100, 1000 and 1,000,000 and their inverses
- The meaning of metric prefixes (kilo-, centi-, milli-, micro-, nano-) and how they relate to each other

Potential Student Difficulties and Misconceptions

Students may

- mix features of linear and logarithmic representations (Confrey 1991) and/or
- have difficulty interpreting logarithmic graphs (Confrey 1991).

What Students Should Learn

In science, the metric system is generally used to express sizes and quantities. Prefixes distinguish fractions or multiples of a meter and can make communicating the sizes of things easier. For instance, the diameter of a hydrogen atom is approximately one-ten-billionth of a meter. This can be expressed numerically as 0.0000000001 m or 0.1 nm. Although the latter may be more convenient, the former is a more familiar unit of measure.

Alternatively, scientific notation can be especially useful when working in metric units.

In this case, the diameter of a hydrogen atom can be expressed as ~1 x 10^{-10} meters. Negative powers of 10 are the reciprocal of the powers of 10: 10^{-2} is equivalent to $(1/10^2)$. Thus, negative powers of 10 are useful for referring to numbers smaller than 1, while positive powers of 10 are used to express numbers greater than 1. A meter stick is about 10,000,000,000 times larger than the diameter of a hydrogen atom. This can be expressed more conveniently as 10^{10} times larger.

Properties and behaviors can often be predicted based on an approximate size. For instance, although eukaryotic cells can vary in diameter, because individual cells belong to the microworld, we know that an optical microscope would be an appropriate tool to observe any type of cells. It can be useful to think about values as orders of magnitude, or powers of 10. Performing approximate calculations and estimating values are facilitated using powers of 10, which also requires the ability to perform basic mathematic functions (e.g., addition, multiplication) on exponents.

Students are most familiar with using a linear scale to represent the size of objects. A logarithmic scale is useful for presenting a large range of numbers. Logarithmic scales use equal intervals for powers of 10 (i.e., 10, 100, 1000). Such a scale can easily display sizes in the nano- and macroworlds on a single number line or graph. However, intermediate numbers (e.g., 20, 500) may be difficult to estimate on a logarithmic scale.

Figure 5.1

(a) Linear plot of powers of 2 vs. exponent (b) Semilogarithmic plot of powers of 2 vs. exponent

a.

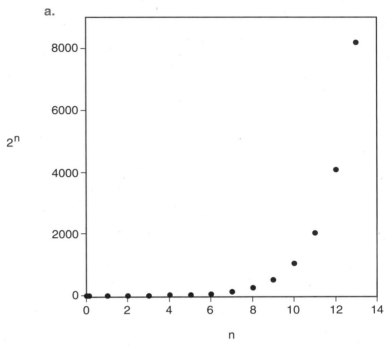

b.

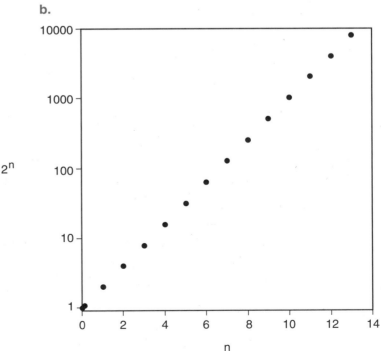

Chapter 5

In addition, logarithmic graphs are useful for representing exponential trends, but the linear nature of the representation can be difficult to interpret (see Figure 5.1, p. 81).

Examples of the knowledge and skills that students should develop follow, although the range of sizes that students work with will depend on their previous experiences in mathematics and science.

Students should be able to

- represent a single number in several ways (e.g., fraction, decimal, scientific notation) and
- evaluate and explain why various representations of size are better for different purposes.

Learning Goal 4

Students should understand that changes in scale can affect the way phenomena work and behave.

Specific Prerequisite Knowledge

- Students should be able to relate the sizes of objects both qualitatively and quantitatively.

Potential Student Difficulties and Misconceptions

- Students often have conceptual difficulties with decimals (Cohen, Corel, and Johnson 2002), ratios and proportions (Lesh, Post, and Behr 1988; Misailidou and Williams 2003), and measurement (Kenney and Kouba 1997).

What Students Should Learn

Most phenomena (i.e., objects, structures, processes, systems) have an optimal range of sizes, and most have limits on how large or small they can be. For example, if a robin were to grow to three feet long, it would not be able to fly, and if a single-celled organism (like an amoeba) had a diameter of one meter, it would not be able to

obtain enough nutrients and oxygen by means of diffusion (AAAS 1993, p. 279). A model, system, or object that functions well at one scale will not necessarily work as well, or at all, on another scale. At the nanoscale, matter often exhibits unexpected properties. For example, metals lose their metallic properties (e.g., conductivity, luster, malleability) at the nanoscale (see Learning Goals 1, 2, and 3 in Chapter 9, "Size-Dependent Properties"). Newtonian—or classical—mechanics adequately explains the behavior of matter in the macroworld, but it fails to explain the behavior of individual atoms and molecules (see Learning Goal 1 in Chapter 8, "Quantum Effects," for more detail).

Examples of knowledge and skills that students should develop follow. The phenomena they can consider and range of sizes they will work with depend on their previous mathematics and science experiences. Students should be able to do the following:

- Relate the function of a model, object, or system to its size
- Explain why there is a limit (large or small) to the size that objects, systems, or models can be
- Explain that changing the scale of a system may change how it works

Learning Goal 5

Students will understand that an object's surface-to-volume ratio depends on its size and shape.

Specific Prerequisite Knowledge

Students should be able to

- calculate the surface area and volume of familiar, regular shapes (e.g., cubes, pyramids, spheres) and
- compare quantities using ratios.

Potential Student Difficulties and Misconceptions

Students may have difficulty

- conceptualizing and calculating surface area and volume (Kordaki and Potari 1998; Zacharos 2006) and/or
- developing an understanding of ratios and proportions (Lesh, Post, and Behr 1988; Misailidou and Williams 2003).

What Students Should Learn

Surface area and volume change disproportionately when the length scale of one dimension is changed. More relevant to NSE is the idea that the surface-to-volume ratio (S/V) increases as an object of the same shape gets smaller. For example, 27 individual cubes, 1 cm to a side, have an equivalent volume (27 cm^3) to a single cube with sides 3 cm in length. However, if the surface areas are compared, the 27 cubes have a surface area of 162 cm^2, while the surface area of a single large cube is only 54 cm^2. This concept is particularly important at the nanoscale when the concept of S/V is linked with the structure of matter.

Different shapes with the same volume have different surface areas. For instance, eight cubes, 1 cm to a side, can be arranged to make a cube that is 2 cm to a side. The larger cube has a surface area of 24 cm^2. Alternatively, if the eight 1 cm^3 cubes are lined up to make a 1 cm × 1 cm × 8 cm rectangular box, then the surface area will be 34 cm^2. Different shapes with the same volume may have different surface areas. For example, if a sphere and a cube both have a volume of 1,000 mm^3, then the cube has a surface area of 600 mm^2, and the sphere a surface area of approximately 483 mm^2. At the nanoscale, both the size and shape of a material can affect its physical and chemical properties. (The relation of S/V to the properties and behavior of matter is explored in greater detail in Learning Goal 1 of Chapter 9, "Size-Dependent Properties.")

A discussion of knowledge and skills contained within this learning goal follows. The complexity of the shapes and calculations will depend on students' previous mathematics and science experiences. Students should be able to

- qualitatively explain how changes in size change the amount of surface exposed to the environment (e.g., understanding that dividing a shape exposes new surfaces) and
- quantitatively explain phenomena related to S/V as they develop more advanced mathematics and scientific knowledge.

Links to "Size and Scale" in the National Science Standards

The national science standards—the Benchmarks and the NSES (AAAS 1993; NRC 1996)—suggest that students begin to develop understanding of ideas related to size and scale from the early elementary grades. The standards related to Size and Scale are summarized in Table 5.1 (pp. 84–85). Similar content can be found in the mathematics content standards (NCTM 1989) but is not referenced here.

What's Missing From the National Science Standards?

Although concepts related to Size and Scale are well represented in the national standards, students still have difficulty learning them (Tretter et al. 2006; Castellini et al. 2007). Both standards documents discuss the value of thinking in terms of orders of magnitude, but the idea of different scales, or "worlds," is missing. The division into scales may provide direct links between the size of representative objects (e.g., eukaryotic cells and bacteria, atoms and molecules), which may help students develop an understanding of the range of sizes that occur at the submacroscopic scale. Students commonly believe that the range of magnitudes between the sizes of things too small to see is much smaller than that for larger things (Tretter, Jones, and Minogue 2006). In addition, these divisions are conceptually useful as students develop links to the physical laws that describe the behavior of matter, the dominant forces within interactions, and the appropriate tools for studying phenomena at a given scale.

The sizes, numbers, and representations presented in both the NSES and the Benchmarks pertain only to building understanding of large numbers. Numbers and measurement units smaller than macroscale are not emphasized even though a significant portion of the science content contained in the standards occurs at a scale too small to be seen with the unaided eye. The ability to communicate about submacroscopic size is important as students work to develop understanding of important NSE ideas as well.

Table 5.1
Summary of national science standards related to size and scale

DESCRIPTION OF CONTENT	STANDARD
Relationship of Mathematics, Science, and Technology	
Mathematics, science, and technology are all related.	*Benchmarks* 2B/1 6–8, p. 32 2B/3 9–12, p. 33 2B/4 9–12, p. 33 2B/5 9–12, p. 33 *NSES* SI*, 5–8, p. 145 SI, 9–12, p. 175
Representing Values With Numbers	
Numerical representations can be used to describe certain characteristics (e.g., length, weight, age). Units are helpful for standardizing and comparing measurements and defining scales.	*Benchmarks* 11D/1 K–2, p. 277 9A/1 K–2, p. 211 2A/4 K–2, p. 26 9A/3 3–5, p. 212
An understanding of the relative values of important numerical anchors (e.g., 100, 1000, 1 million) prepares students for defining "worlds" of different scale (e.g., macroworld, microworld, nanoworld) and for using scientific notation	*Benchmarks* 12B/9 6–8, p. 291 12B/6 9–12, p. 291 12B/8 9–12, p. 291 11D/1 9–12, p. 279
There are many ways to represent the numbers; which representation is most useful depends on the purpose.	*Benchmarks* 9A/3, 6–8, p. 213 12B/2 3–5, p. 290

*SI = science as inquiry

Table 5.1 continued

DESCRIPTION OF CONTENT	STANDARD
Estimation and Relative Size	
Estimation and understanding the usefulness of estimation in different circumstances are important skills.	*Benchmarks* 12B/3 K–2, p. 290 12B/5 K–2, p. 290 9A/3 K–2, p. 211 12B/3 3–5, p. 290 11D/2 3–5, p. 277 12B/10 6–8, p. 291
Powers of 10, or orders of magnitude, are useful ways for approximating values.	*Benchmarks* 9A/1 9–12, p. 214
Shapes and Geometry	
Shapes as well as numbers are useful for describing phenomena.	*Benchmarks* 2C/1 K–2, p. 36 2C/1 3–5, p. 36 9C/4 3–5, p. 223
Materials can be measured in one, two, and three dimensions. (Learning how to measure area and volume is prerequisite to developing understanding of S/V.)	*Benchmarks* 9C/1 3–5, p. 223 12B/3 6–8, p. 291 9C/1 6–8, p. 224 9C/2 9–12, p. 225
Scaling	
It is critical to understand scaling in a variety of contexts (e.g., scales on a map, choice of scale on a graph).	*Benchmarks* 9C/6 3–5, p. 223 12B/5 6–8, p. 291 9C/6 6–8, p. 224 9C/1 9–12, p. 225
Phenomena do not necessarily work the same way at all scales.	*Benchmarks* 11D/1 3–5, p. 277 11D/2 9–12, p. 279
The area and volume of an object change disproportionately; therefore, properties that depend on area or volume also change disproportionately. The immense increase in S/V at the nanoscale helps to explain many phenomena.	*Benchmarks* 11D/1 6–8, p. 278 9C/2 9–12, p. 225
Understanding ratios and proportions is a prerequisite to understanding surface–to–volume ratio	*Benchmarks* 12B/2 3–5, p. 290 12B/2 6–8, p. 291 12B/1 9–12, p. 291

Chapter 5

Acknowledgments

The authors would like to thank César Delgado for helpful discussions and reading of this chapter.

References

American Association for the Advancement of Science (AAAS). 1993. *Benchmarks for science literacy*. New York: Oxford University Press.

Castellini, O. M., G. K. Walejko, C. E. Holladay, T. J. Thiem, G. M. Zenner, and W. C. Crone. 2007. Nanotechnology and the public: Effectively communicating nanoscale science and engineering concepts. *Journal of Nanoparticle Research* 9 (2): 183–189.

Cohen, D., J. Corel, and N. Johnson. 2002. What very small numbers mean. *Journal of Experimental Psychology: General* 131 (3): 424–442.

Confrey, J. 1991. Learning to listen: A student's understanding of powers of ten. In *Radical constructivism in mathematics education*, ed. A. J. Bishop, H. Bauersfeld, J. Kilpatrick, G. Leder, S. Turnau, G. Vergnaud, and E. von Glaserfeld. Dordrecht, The Netherlands: Kluwer Academic Publishers.

Delgado, C., S. Y. Stevens, N. Shin, M. Yunker, and J. S. Krajcik. 2007. The development of students' conception of size. Paper presented at the National Association for Research in Science Teaching Conference. New Orleans, Louisiana.

Kenney, P.A., and V. L. Kouba. 1997. What do students know about measurement? In *Results from the Sixth Mathematics Assessment of the National Assessment of Educational Progress,* ed. P. A. Kenney and E. Silver. Reston, VA: National Council of Teachers of Mathematics.

Kordaki, M., and D. Potari. 1998. Children's approaches to area measurement through different contexts. *Journal of Mathematical Behavior* 17 (3): 303–316.

Lamon, S. 1994. Ratio and proportion: Cognitive foundations in unitizing and norming. In *The development of multiplicative reasoning in the learning of mathematics*, ed. G. Harel and J. Confrey. Albany: State University of New York Press.

Lesh, R., R. Post, and M. Behr. 1988. Proportional reasoning. In *Number concepts and operations in the middle grades*, ed. J. Hiebert and M. Behr. Hillsdale, NJ: Lawrence Erlbaum Associates.

Misailidou, C., and J. Williams. 2003. Diagnostic assessment of children's proportional reasoning. *Journal of Mathematical Behavior* 22 (3): 335–368.

National Council of Teachers of Mathematics (NCTM). 2003. *Principles and standards for school mathematics.* Reston, VA: NCTM.

National Research Council (NRC). 1996. *National science education standards*. Washington, DC: National Academy Press.

Tretter, T. R., M. G. Jones, T. Andre, A. Negishi, and J. Minogue. 2006. Conceptual boundaries and distances: Students' and experts' concepts of the scale of scientific phenomena. *Journal of Research in Science Teaching* 43 (3): 282–319.

Tretter, T. R., M. G. Jones, and J. Minogue. 2006. Accuracy of scale conceptions in science: Mental maneuverings across many orders of spatial magnitude. *Journal of Research in Science Teaching* 43 (10): 1061–1085.

Zacharos, K. 2006. Prevailing educational practices for area measurement and students' failure in measuring areas. *Journal of Mathematical Behavior* 25 (3): 224–239.

Chapter **6**
Structure of Matter

Big Idea:

Materials consist of building blocks that often form a hierarchy of structures. Atoms interact with each other to form molecules. The next higher level of organization involves atoms, molecules, or nanoscale structures interacting with each other to form nanoscale assemblies and structures.

The atomic and kinetic theories are the basis of understanding the structure, properties, and behavior of matter. Together, they can explain an enormous number of phenomena—ranging from chemical reactivity, to the properties of materials, to the smell of coffee spreading through a house. In addition, knowledge about the structure and motion of the building blocks of matter (atoms, molecules, and larger assemblies) will support future learning in scientific disciplines beyond chemistry (e.g., biology, physics, geology, materials science).

Although a number of learning goals can be associated with this big idea, the three learning goals in this chapter support the fundamental knowledge required to begin to understand the special properties of matter at the nanoscale. The order in which they are presented here is not meant to imply that they should be introduced in this order in a science curriculum.

General Prerequisite Knowledge for This Chapter

Each of the three learning goals in this chapter focuses on different aspects of the structure of matter. Prerequisite knowledge common to all of them includes the following:

- Everything that takes up space and has mass is considered matter.

- Matter is not a continuous material but is made of particles that are too small to see with the unaided eye.

- The particles that make up matter are in constant motion. This motion is dependent on the heat of the system and is often referred to as thermal motion. The motion of each particle is linear until it interacts with another particle; the interaction causes a change in the direction of the motion.

Learning Goal 1

Atoms are the fundamental building blocks of matter. The structure of atoms affects how they interact to form organized assemblies and structures (e.g., molecules, extended solids, nanoparticles).

Chapter 6

Specific Prerequisite Knowledge

Students should understand that

- there are two types of electrical charges—positive and negative—and
- opposite charges are attracted to each other; like charges repel each other.

Potential Student Difficulties and Misconceptions

Students may believe that

- electrons move around the nucleus in orbitals like planets around the solar system (Griffiths and Preston 1992; Unal and Zollman 1999);
- electrons move randomly within electron clouds, but in a continuous manner (i.e., have a trajectory); and/or
- atoms are made of "atoms" (Renström, Andersson, and Marton 1990).

Also, students may have difficulty adopting a model that includes particles in random motion (Kind 2004).

What Students Should Learn

Atoms are the smallest unit of every element and are therefore considered to be the fundamental building blocks of all substances. Atoms, composed of negatively charged electrons, positively charged protons, and neutral neutrons, are too small to see even with an optical microscope. An atom's positively charged nucleus contains protons and neutrons and is surrounded by electrons. The number of protons in an atom determines the type of element it is and is represented by the atomic number, which defines the place of the element on the periodic table. A neutral atom contains an equal number of electrons and protons.

Atoms and molecules are in constant motion, often called thermal motion. The thermal motion is affected by the attraction and repulsion of electrical forces between the particles. The electrical forces result from the electron distributions within the atoms.

Electrons are in constant motion and are distributed within orbitals that surround the nucleus. The orbitals take up the majority of space in an atom. Only a certain number of electrons (two) are allowed within each orbital. The description of electrons moving around the nucleus within orbitals is often connected to a solar system model of the atom, also called the Bohr model. Although a Bohr model is useful for explaining certain phenomena, the model does not accurately describe the motion of the electrons. Electrons do not behave like familiar macroscopic objects. For example, because an electron does not have a trajectory, it is impossible to know where an electron will be based just by knowing where it has been (Heisenberg uncertainty principle). Instead, the probability density is used to describe where an electron has probably been and where it is likely to be going.

A better, albeit not perfect, model of the motion is that of an "electron cloud," where the "cloud" describes the probability density of an electron. The electron cloud model provides a simplified way of visualizing the quantum mechanical behavior of an electron and is useful for intuitively understanding inter-atomic interactions and molecular bonding. (See the learning goals in Chapter 8, "Quantum Effects," for further discussion of the quantum mechanical behavior of electrons and the Heisenberg uncertainty principle.)

This learning goal contains an extensive amount of content. Examples of how students should be able to apply their knowledge of this content follow. Some of the examples require knowledge of a basic particle model of matter rather than knowledge of atomic structure.

Before and After Students Have Studied Atomic Structure

Students should be able to

- describe the motion that the particles (i.e., atoms or molecules) exhibit,
- explain the relationship between the motion of particles (i.e., atoms or molecules) and heat, and
- explain a range of phenomena (e.g., odors traveling across the room, condensation on the side of a glass) using a particle model that includes the motion of the particles and the relationship of that motion to heat.

After Students Have Studied Atomic Structure

Students should be able to

- explain the different models that describe electron behavior and
- evaluate different models for describing electron behavior and determine when each might be useful.

Learning Goal 2

Properties inherent to the building blocks affect how they combine with other building blocks, which affects the properties of a material.

Specific Prerequisite Knowledge

Before Students Have Studied Atomic Structure

To apply the ideas contained in this learning goal to particular phenomena (e.g., induced dipoles, condensation of gases to liquids, self-assembly), students should have an electron cloud model and be asked to consider electron distribution in terms of probability.

Potential Student Difficulties and Misconceptions

- Students may attribute the properties of the bulk substance to the individual atoms or molecules (Ben-Zvi, Eylon, and Silberstein 1986; Albanese and Vicentini 1997).

What Students Should Learn

All matter is composed of a combination of only about 100 types of atoms, or elements. Atoms may interact with each other in various combinations and arrangements to form molecules. Alternatively, atoms may arrange in large, extended arrays, or lattices. The type of atoms that combine, and their arrangement, determine the identity of the resulting substance. When two or more different materials combine to form a new substance, that new material has properties different from those of the original substances.

Atoms interact to form molecules or arrays through electrical forces. The manner in which these interactions form is the basis of the discipline of chemistry and can be predicted by an element's location on the periodic table. An atom's outermost electrons, called valence electrons, help determine how atoms can interact with each other.

Molecules are made of atoms and occur in a range of sizes (see Figure 6.1, p. 90). The smallest molecules consist of individual atoms (i.e., noble gases). Some molecules contain tens of thousands of atoms and are actually nanoscale structures (e.g., proteins, DNA, RNA).

The building blocks of these nanoscale structures may be atoms, as in the case of buckyballs, or groups of atoms (molecules), as is the case for proteins, DNA, and RNA. Twenty different amino acids are the building blocks that combine into chains to make proteins. Figure 6.2

Chapter 6

Figure 6.1
An illustration of the range of sizes of a single molecule

~0.1 nm

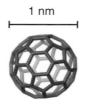

0.585 nm

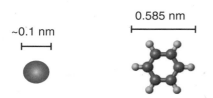

1 nm

theoretically
infinite

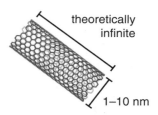

1–10 nm

Helium Atom

Benzene Molecule
6 carbon atoms +
6 hydrogen atoms
MW = 78.12

Buckyball
60 carbon atoms
MW = 720.669

Carbon Nanotube
up to millions of
carbon atoms

~1 nm

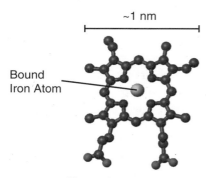

Bound
Iron Atom

~5 nm

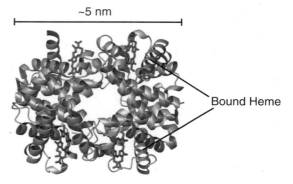

Bound Heme

Heme b
34 carbon atoms +
32 hydrogen atoms +
4 oxygen atoms +
4 nitrogen atoms +
1 iron atom
MW ~616

Protein Molecule
(hemoglobin)
thousands of atoms
(carbon, nitrogen, oxygen, sulfur, and hydrogen)
MW ~68,000

~11 nm

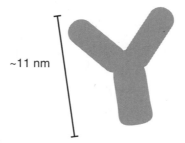

Immunoglobulin (IgG)
thousands of atoms
(carbon, nitrogen, oxygen, sulfur, and hydrogen)
MW ~150,000

Source: Images were created using MOLMOL (Koradi, Billeter, and Wüthrich 1996).

Figure 6.2

Ball-and-stick representation of an extended peptide consisting of nine amino acids

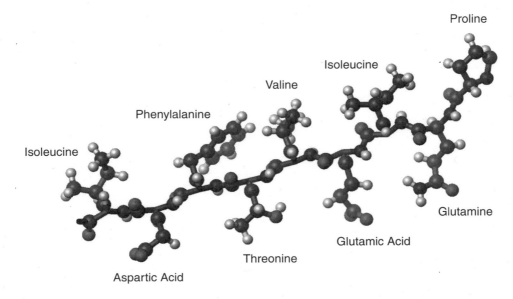

Source: Image created using MOLMOL (Koradi, Billeter, and Wüthrich 1996).

depicts a peptide chain of seven amino acids. Combinations of four different nucleotides are the building blocks that combine into chains to form DNA. RNA is composed of four slightly different nucleotides. Materials such as quantum dots are nanoscale assemblies of atoms.

Like molecules, the properties and behavior of nanoscale assemblies or structures are dependent on the arrangement of the building blocks (atoms, molecules, and/or other nanoscale structures or assemblies). Likewise, the building blocks interact through a variety of electrical forces (Chapter 7, "Forces and Interactions," will discuss the forces that govern the interactions within and between molecules and nanoscale objects and assemblies in depth). The allotropes of carbon (diamond, graphite, charcoal, buckyballs, and nanotubes) illustrate that the arrangement of the building blocks, in this case carbon atoms, affects both the identity of the substance and its properties. As shown

in Table 1.4 (p. 14), the properties of the various forms of carbon are very different despite having the same composition.

The identity of the building blocks of a whole structure or assembly is important to its structure and function. For example, changing a single nucleotide in a DNA sequence can change the affinity a protein has for it nearly 1,000-fold (Stevens and Glick 1997). Another possible effect of changing a single nucleotide is that the amino acid code changes. This results in a protein that has a different amino acid in one position. Although proteins consist of chains of amino acids that can be hundreds of amino acids long, changing just one amino acid can often have profound effects on the structure and function of the protein. (See Figure 1.6 on p. 16 and accompanying text for the example of hemoglobin and Chapter 7, "Forces and Interactions," for an in-depth discussion of the electrical forces important on the nanoscale.)

Chapter 6

The content within this learning goal can be presented in many contexts. In each, students may consider questions such as the following:

- How can the type of building blocks affect the function and properties of the whole?
- What relationship do the properties of the building blocks have to the function and properties of the whole?

Learning Goal 3

Many materials consist of hierarchical structures.

Specific Prerequisite Knowledge

- Content included in Learning Goal 1 of this chapter.

Potential Student Difficulties and Misconceptions

- Students may not consider a hierarchy of structures when they describe the structure of matter.

What Students Should Learn

Atoms make up all of the substances around us. They are the building blocks of molecules. Molecules may consist of a single atom (i.e., noble gas) or tens of thousands of atoms (e.g., large proteins, DNA strands). The next higher level of organization of matter includes nanoscale structures and assemblies. The building blocks for these structures include atoms, molecules, and other nanoscale structures and assemblies. In turn, many materials consist of nanoscale building blocks.

Buildings are examples of hierarchical structure. Bricks consist of very small particles of clay. Each brick contains millions of particles that are approximately 50 to 100 μm in diameter (see Figure 6.3). Many bricks are then used to build a wall.

Many natural materials also utilize hierarchical structuring. Figure 1.7 (p. 17) illustrates the hierarchy of structures within the hard biological tissues of bone, enamel, and shells (nacre)—all structures that consist of nanoscale building blocks. An advantage of nanoscale building blocks is that they have greater insensitivity to structural flaws than do larger building blocks (Gao et al. 2003). This means the material has greater strength and integrity than if it were made up of larger building blocks. With

Figure 6.3
Illustration of hierarchical structure. Microscale clay particles make up bricks. Bricks make up a wall.

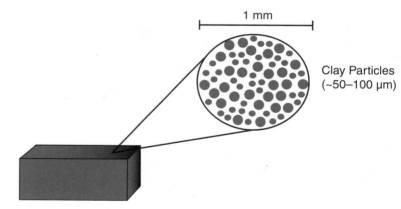

1 mm

Clay Particles
(~50–100 μm)

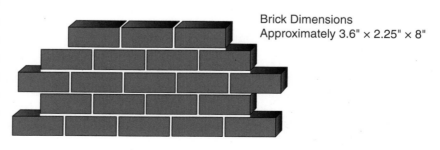

Brick Dimensions
Approximately 3.6" × 2.25" × 8"

the recent ability to fabricate and manipulate nanoscale materials, engineers are currently working to exploit this structural advantage by using nanoscale building blocks in designed materials.

As students build an understanding of the content contained within this learning goal, they may apply the ideas to many phenomena. Questions they could consider include the following:

- What are the advantages of using nanoscale building blocks?
- What are the disadvantages (or potential challenges) of using nanoscale building blocks (natural and fabricated)?
- Why is insensitivity to flaws so important? What happens when a material is sensitive to flaws?
- Are nanoscale building blocks better than building blocks of a larger scale (e.g., microscale, macroscale) for fabrication of all materials and all applications?
- How is the strength of materials measured and compared?

Links to "Structure of Matter" in the National Science Standards

Before students can begin to appreciate the novel properties of matter that are observed at the nanoscale, they must have a thorough understanding of the structure of matter. The type, arrangement, and motion of the building blocks, and the manner in which they interact, all play a role in determining the properties and behavior of a substance. Benchmarks and NSES related to these topics are summarized in Table 6.1 on pages 95–96.

What's Missing From the National Science Standards?

The traditional science curriculum supports student learning of many of the ideas in the structure of matter—generally in chemistry courses. However, study is typically limited to the organization of matter at the molecular level, focusing on atoms as the building blocks of small molecules. Little, if any, emphasis is placed on the structure and behavior of larger molecules and metals and extended solids or of nanoscale assemblies and structures.

Induced dipoles are formed by electrodynamic forces and play an important role in the structure and behavior of matter. Interactions involving induced dipoles become very important on the nanoscale. In order to understand them, students must understand how electrons are distributed and behave within atoms. In particular, they need to have a probabilistic model of electron distribution and motion. Students tend to favor a solar system model of electron behavior even after introduction to more scientifically accurate models (Cervellati and Perugini 1981; Harrison and Treagust 1996). Focusing on both the Bohr model and the electron cloud model as *models*, emphasizing the similarities and differences between them and the phenomena that they can help predict and explain, has been shown to have some pedagogical success (Kalkanis, Hadzidaki, and Stavrou 2003; McKagan, Perkins, and Wieman 2008).

The electron cloud model of the atom provides an accessible way of visualizing the behavior of electrons that will help students understand molecular bonding and interatomic and intermolecular interactions. These ideas are not emphasized in the standards documents. The electrical forces themselves will be

Chapter 6

discussed in more detail in Chapter 7, "Forces and Interactions."

Both of the standards documents introduce the model of atomic structure to students in high school. At this time, students need the knowledge of atomic structure, in particular the behavior of electrons, to develop an understanding of the ways in which atoms interact with each other. However, students are often introduced to the model as early as middle elementary school (fourth or fifth grade), but they are not likely to be asked to apply the model to explain phenomena until high school. This early introduction, then, becomes an exercise in memorization rather than an attempt to construct foundational knowledge that is built upon year after year. Perhaps it would be more useful to help younger students develop a basic particle model for matter that they can use to explain phenomena, such as the states of matter and odors traveling across the room (Smith et al. 2006), and leave the details of atomic structure for a point in the students' education when they can use that knowledge productively to build a deeper understanding of the structure and behavior of matter (Stevens, Delgado, and Krajcik, forthcoming).

Table 6.1
Summary of national science standards linked to the structure of matter

Description of Content	Standard
Materials and Objects Are Made of Parts	
Materials are generally made of smaller parts. They can be characterized by the building blocks of which they are made.	*Benchmarks* 11A/1 K–2, p. 264 4D/1 K–2, p. 76 *NSES* PS–P[a] K–4, p. 127
The building blocks of a material may be too small to be seen with the unaided eye.	*Benchmarks* 4D/3 3–5, p. 77 4D/1 6–8. p. 78
Atoms and Elements	
A few types of materials can be combined to make a multitude of materials.	*Benchmarks* 4D/4 3–5, p. 77 4D/5 6–8, p. 78 4D/6 6–8, p. 78 *NSES* PS–PC 5–8, p. 154 PS–SPM[b] 9–12, p. 179
Atoms are the building blocks of matter. They consist of protons, neutrons, and electrons. An understanding of larger structures and assemblies requires knowledge about the building blocks of which they are composed.	*Benchmarks* 4D/1 6–8, p. 78 4D/1 9–12, p. 80 4D/2 9–12, p. 80 4D/3 9–12, p. 80 *NSES* PS–SA[c] 9–12, p. 178
Structure and Composition	
Certain materials may combine to make new materials that have new properties.	*Benchmarks* 4D/4 3–5, p. 77 *NSES* PS–PC[d] 5–8, p. 154 PS–CR[e] 9–12, p. 179
Atoms can arrange in extended lattices or as discrete molecules. Electrons govern the interactions between atoms.*	*Benchmarks* 4D/1 6–8, p. 78 4D/7 9–12, p. 80 4G/2 9–12, p. 96 *NSES* PS–SPM 9–12, p. 178 PS–MF[f] 9–12, p. 179

Table 6.1 continued on page 96

Table 6.1 continued

Properties of Matter	
Changing the heat of the system can change the properties of a material.	*Benchmarks* 4D/1 3–5, p. 77 *NSES* PS–P K–4, p. 127
The properties of atoms can be predicted by the periodic table.	*Benchmarks* 4D/6 9–12, p. 80 *NSES* PS–SPM 9–12, p. 178–179
The type, arrangement, and motion of atoms and the manner in which they interact affect the properties of a material. This is true even at the nanoscale.	*Benchmarks* 4D/8 9–12, p. 80 *NSES* PS–SPM 9–12, p. 179
Kinetic Theory	
Atoms and molecules are in constant random motion (thermal motion) that is dependent on the amount of heat in the system. Thermal motion becomes more important at the nanoscale because the size of the objects approaches the scale of the motion.	*Benchmarks* 4D/3 6–8, p. 78 4E/3 9–12, p. 85 4E/4 9–12, p. 85 4D/9 9–12, p. 80 *NSES* PS–CE–ID[g] 9–12, p. 180

* These ideas are also linked closely to "Forces and Interactions," Chapter 7 in this book.
[a] Physical Science–Properties of Objects and Materials
[b] Physical Science–Structure and Properties of Matter
[c] Physical Science–Structure of Atoms
[d] Physical Science–Properties and Changes of Properties in Matter
[e] Physical Science–Chemical Reactions
[f] Physical Science–Motions and Forces
[g] Physical Science–Conservation of Energy and the Increase in Disorder

Acknowledgment

The authors would like to thank Kelly Hutchinson for helpful discussions and reading of this chapter.

References

Albanese, A., and M. Vicentini. 1997. Why do we believe that an atom is colourless? Reflections about the teaching of the particle model. *Science & Education* 6: 251–261.

American Association for the Advancement of Science (AAAS). 1993. *Benchmarks for science literacy.* New York: Oxford University Press.

Ben–Zvi, R., B.–S. Eylon, and J. Silberstein. 1986. Is an atom of copper malleable? *Journal of Chemical Education* 63 (1): 64–66.

Cervellati, R., and D. Perugini. 1981. The understanding of the atomic orbital concept by Italian high school students. *Journal of Chemical Education* 58 (7): 568–569.

Gao, H., B. Ji, I. L. Jäger, E. Arzt, and P. Fratzel. 2003. Materials become insensitive to flaws at nanoscale: Lessons from nature. *Proceedings of the National Academy of Sciences, USA* 100 (10): 5597–5600.

Griffiths, A. K., and K. R. Preston. 1992. Grade-12 students' misconceptions relating to fundamental characteristics of atoms and molecules. *Journal for Research in Science Teaching* 29 (6): 611–628.

Harrison, A. G., and D. F. Treagust. 1996. Secondary students' mental models of atoms and molecules: Implications for teaching chemistry. *Science Education* 80 (5): 509–534.

Kalkanis, G., P. Hadzidaki, and D. Stavrou. 2003. An instructional model for a radical conceptual change towards quantum mechanics concepts. *Science Education* 87: 257–280.

Kind, V. 2004. *Beyond appearances: Students' misconceptions about basic chemical ideas.* London: Royal Society of Chemistry.

Koradi, R., M. Billeter, and K. Wüthrich. 1996. MOL-MOL: A program for display and analysis of macromolecular structures. *Journal of Molecular Graphics* 14: 51–55.

McKagan, S. B., K. K. Perkins, and C. E. Wieman. 2008. Why we should teach the Bohr model and how to teach it effectively. *Physical Review Special Topics—Physics Education Research* 4 (1): 10–13.

National Research Council (NRC). 1996. *National science education standards.* Washington, DC: NRC.

Renström, L., B. Andersson, and F. Marton. 1990. Students' conceptions of matter. *Journal of Educational Psychology* 82: 555.

Smith, C. L., M. Wiser, C. W. Anderson, and J. Krajcik. 2006. Implications of research on children's learning for standards and assessment: A proposed learning progression for matter and the atomic molecular theory. *Measurement: Interdisciplinary Research and Perspectives* 4: 1–98.

Stevens, S. Y., C. Delgado, and J. S. Krajcik. Forthcoming. Developing a theoretical learning progression for atomic structure and inter-atomic interactions. *Journal of Research in Science Teaching.* (Published online August 5, 2009.)

Stevens, S. Y., and G. D. Glick. 1997. Evidence for sequence specific recognition by anti-single-stranded DNA autoantibodies. *Biochemistry* 38 (2): 650–658.

Unal, R., and D. Zollman. 1999. Students' description of an atom: A phenomenographic analysis. *http://perg.phys.ksu.edu/papers/vqm/AtomModels.pdf.*

Chapter 7
Forces and Interactions

Big Idea:

All interactions can be described by multiple types of forces, but the relative impact of each type of force changes with scale. On the nanoscale, a range of electrical forces, with varying strengths, tends to dominate the interactions between objects.

The content related to forces and interactions is important to most science disciplines. While chemistry is the most obvious place to introduce these ideas, it is important to connect aspects of this big idea to phenomena in biology, physics, and Earth science courses as well. For example, the same types of electrical forces involved in chemical bonds also govern interactions among the (nanoscale) biological molecules that regulate life processes, and they play a critical role in the process of mineral crystallization.

Five major learning goals are associated with the Forces and Interactions big idea. The order in which the learning goals are presented is not meant to suggest an order for introducing the content to students. Learning Goal 5 may be more appropriate for advanced high school science courses or lower-level undergraduate courses. The focus of each of the learning goals will differ depending on the grade level and science context (i.e., chemistry, biology, physics, or Earth science).

General Prerequisite Knowledge for This Chapter

Each learning goal represents a different aspect of the big idea, and although the focus of each learning goal is different, there is certain prerequisite knowledge common among them:

- Learning Goals 1 and 2 from Chapter 6, "Structure of Matter."

- There are two kinds of electrical charges: positive and negative.

- Opposite charges are attracted to each other; like charges repel each other.

Learning Goal 1

Small objects (e.g., atoms, molecules, nanoparticles) can interact in a variety of ways, all of which are electrical in nature. A continuum of electrical forces describes all interactions within matter on that scale.

Specific Prerequisite Knowledge

To develop an understanding of electrical forces, students must have an understanding of the following ideas:

Chapter 7

Before Students Have Studied Atomic Structure

- An ion is created when an atom or group of atoms has a net surplus (negative ion) or deficit (positive ion) of electrons. When this occurs, the atom has a net charge that is an integer value.
- Ions that are positively charged are called cations; negatively charged ions are anions.
- Certain atoms (or groups of atoms) have a greater tendency to be ionized than others. In general, for metals it is more difficult to remove an electron from the smaller atoms within a group on the periodic table than the larger ones.
- The smaller atoms within a group gain electrons more readily than the larger ones (nonmetals). The tendency of an atom to draw electrons toward it is called electronegativity.
- As atomic radius decreases, the ionization energy and electronegativity increase.
- The difference in electronegativity between the atoms participating in a bonding interaction determines the bond's polarity.
- Partial charges are charges that have less than an integer value. They are created when there is a shift in electron distribution but the electrons are not completely transferred.
- Polarizability is a measure of the potential distortion of the electron distribution. Some atoms and ions exhibit a propensity toward undergoing distortions in their electron distribution. Greater polarizability is observed for larger atoms and ions due to the decreased influence of the positively charged nucleus on the outer electrons. Anions are more polarizable than their parent atoms. The ions and atoms that cause these distortions are considered to have polarizing power, which is usually associated with small size and high charge.

- The outer shell of electrons often determines how atoms can interact with each other.

Potential Student Difficulties and Misconceptions

Students may have difficulty

- differentiating between hydrogen bonds and covalent bonds (Taber and Coll 2002) and/or
- accommodating induced dipole interactions and hydrogen bonding and the continuum of electric forces in their models of bonding and interactions, due to their heavy reliance on the octet model (Pallant and Tinker 2004).

Students often have misconceptions related to this content. They may believe that

- bond polarity is a secondary property of covalent bonds instead of thinking about a continuum between ionic and covalent bonding (Pallant and Tinker 2004);
- electrons spend most of their time equidistant between the two bonded atoms (Taber and Coll 2002);
- hydrogen bonds occur between two hydrogen atoms (Taber and Coll 2002; Pallant and Tinker 2004);
- intermolecular forces are stronger than intramolecular forces (Taber and Coll 2002);
- bonded materials must always be in the form of molecules (Pallant and Tinker 2004);
- charge-charge interaction results in neutralization, not bond formation (Boo 1998; Pallant and Tinker 2004); and/or
- intermolecular bonding describes ionic solids (Pallant and Tinker 2004; Özmen 2004).

What Students Should Learn

A range of electrical forces dominate interactions between objects on the nano- and atomic scales. Combinations of these electrical forces govern most interactions between atoms, molecules, and nanoscale objects and materials.

Figure 7.1
Coulomb's law

$$F = \frac{1}{4\pi\varepsilon_0} \frac{q_1 q_2}{r^2}$$

Electrostatic interactions are forces that occur through permanent, localized (static) separations of charges. Ionic interactions, dipole-dipole interactions, and covalent bonding are examples of electrostatic interactions. The strength of ionic and dipole-dipole interactions is described by Coulomb's law (see Figure 7.1), which states that the strength is dependent on the amount of charge (q_1, q_2), and the distance between them (r). Another factor in the equation is the permittivity of free space (ε_0), or the dielectric constant of vacuum. This physical quantity describes how the electrical field affects and is affected by the surrounding environment.

Ionic Interactions

Ionic interactions occur between ions that have opposite charges of an integer value. In chemistry, these interactions occur between ions consisting of one or more atoms and are called ionic bonds. Ionic bonds involve interactions that are based on electrostatic forces between two oppositely charged ions consisting of one or several atoms (e.g. NaCl, $MgSO_4$). In biology, ionic interactions are often called salt bridges, which can occur within or between biomolecules. Figure 7.2 shows three representations of ionic interactions: an interaction between two charged objects; a portion of an ionic solid, NaCl; and a salt bridge that occurs between the negatively charged oxygen in a phosphate group of CTP (cytidine triphosphate) and a positively charged arginine side chain in an enzyme. For ionic interactions that occur in aqueous environments (e.g.,

Figure 7.2
Ionic interactions are governed by an electrostatic force between objects with charges of integer value. (a) A simple model of ionic interaction (b) Ionic lattice of sodium chloride. Dark gray represents chlorine ion (−1), light gray represents sodium ion (+1). (c) Salt bridge occurring between the negatively charged phosphate oxygen of CTP and the positively charged arginine side chain is designated by dotted line.

a.

Ionic Interaction

b.

Ionic Lattice

c.

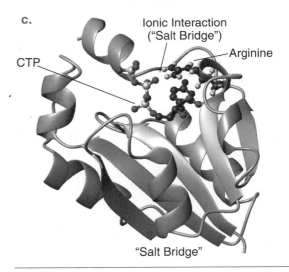

"Salt Bridge"

Source: Coordinates were obtained from the RCSB Protein Data Bank, structure 1COZ. Figures *b* and *c* were made using MOLMOL (Koradi, Billeter, and Wüthrich 1996).

Figure 7.3
Illustrations of some polar and nonpolar molecules

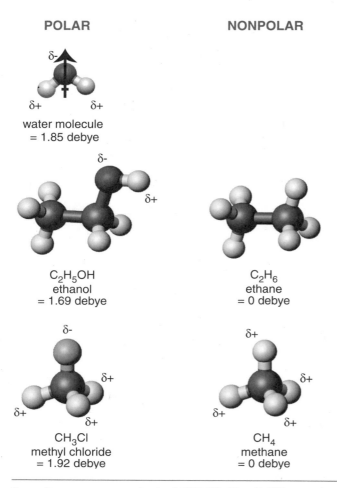

POLAR

$\delta-$
water molecule
= 1.85 debye

$\delta-$ $\delta+$
C_2H_5OH
ethanol
= 1.69 debye

$\delta-$ $\delta+$ $\delta+$ $\delta+$
CH_3Cl
methyl chloride
= 1.92 debye

NONPOLAR

C_2H_6
ethane
= 0 debye

$\delta+$ $\delta+$ $\delta+$ $\delta+$
CH_4
methane
= 0 debye

Source: Images were created using MOLMOL (Koradi, Billeter, and Wüthrich 1996). Coordinates were downloaded from *www.nyu.edu/pages/mathmol/library.*

do. The tendency to attract electrons is defined as electronegativity. A difference in electronegativity between two atoms across a bond results in a nonuniform distribution of electrons and creates partial charges. When this occurs with covalently linked atoms, a *permanent* dipole moment is formed. Carbon monoxide and ethanol are examples of this type of (polar) molecule; methane and carbon dioxide are examples of nonpolar molecules. The strength of the dipole (μ) is measured in debye. A nonpolar molecule will have a dipole moment of zero. Figure 7.3 provides examples of polar and nonpolar molecules. The partial charges are indicated by $\delta-$ and $\delta+$. Attractions and repulsions of the partial charges of polar molecules are considered dipole-dipole interactions. These electrostatic interactions are much weaker than ionic interactions.

Hydrogen bonds are among the strongest dipole-dipole interactions. They generally involve a hydrogen atom attached to a highly electron-withdrawing atom such as an oxygen, a nitrogen, or a fluorine atom, which gives the hydrogen atom a partial positive charge. This hydrogen atom interacts with a highly electronegative atom that has a lone pair of electrons in its outer shell (e.g., oxygen, nitrogen, fluorine atoms) to form a hydrogen bond. While other atoms can act as partners in the interaction, the strength of the interaction is significantly diminished. Although often regarded solely as an intermolecular interaction, as illustrated in Figure 7.4, hydrogen bonding can also mediate intramolecular interactions (see Figures 1.8 and 1.9, pp. 19–20). Hydrogen bonds are relatively weak, yet they play an important role in the

biologically relevant), the strength of the interaction is relatively weak due to the high dielectric constant of water. In contrast, the attraction between opposite charges in ionic solids is much stronger due to the vacuum surrounding the interacting atoms.

Dipole-Dipole Interactions

Within a molecule, some atoms may attract electrons more strongly than other atoms

structure and behavior of matter. For example, hydrogen bonding explains many of the special properties exhibited by water and contributes to the structure and stability of proteins, DNA, and RNA.

Figure 7.4
Hydrogen bond between two water molecules

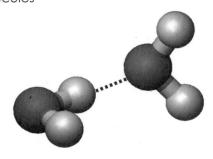

Source: Image was created using MOLMOL (Koradi, Billeter, and Wüthrich 1996). Coordinates were downloaded from *www.nyu.edu/pages/mathmol/library.*

Covalent Interactions

Covalent bonds are characterized by the sharing of one or more electron pairs between atoms and are the attraction that holds molecules together and are generally quite strong. This class of interactions tends to be used to describe interactions among nonmetals that have similar electronegativities. Although covalent bonds occur between neutral atoms, they are considered electrostatic interactions because the electrons shared between atoms act to stabilize the attractive and repulsive electrostatic forces that occur when two atoms are brought within close proximity.

Unlike ionic and dipole-dipole interactions, the strength of covalent bonds depends both on the distance (r) and the *angle* of the interaction between atoms (see Figure 1.12, p. 21). Atoms that interact through covalent bonds can form discrete molecules (e.g., O_2, H_2O), extended chains (e.g., polypeptide chains, DNA strands), or extended networks (e.g., diamond, graphite, quartz).

Electrostatic interactions involve charges that are permanent. However, not all electrical forces involve static charges. Metallic bonding and induced dipoles are examples of interactions that involve electrodynamic interactions.

Metallic Bonding

Electrons are defined as localized if they remain confined within an atom or covalent bond. Metals consist of atoms arranged in an ordered pattern in an extended lattice. The electrons in metals are delocalized, such that an electron from one atom is shared among a lattice of atoms. Metallic bonding is an attraction between positively charged metal ions and the delocalized electrons and is responsible for many of the physical properties of metals, such as conductivity, malleability, heat conduction, and luster.

Induced Dipoles

Regardless of the type of atom or molecule, an attractive force acts between the particles that make up a substance. The constant motion of electrons can momentarily create a charge imbalance that results in instantaneous, or induced, dipoles. This imbalance, or separation of charge, allows atoms to attract each other electrically even though they are neutral. The attraction due to momentary imbalances of charge is due to London dispersion forces. It is these forces that allow even noble gases to condense and freeze. London forces occur between *all* types of atoms and molecules and are weaker than all electrostatic forces. Like electrostatic interactions, the strength of the interaction is dependent on distance (d) between the charges, but for London forces, the potential energy for separating the charges is dependent on d^{-6} (instead of d^{-2} observed for electrostatic forces), so it decreases more rapidly with increased distance.

A dipole moment in a nonpolar molecule can be created in other ways. Introducing a nonpolar molecule to an electric field can create an induced dipole moment by causing distortions in the electron distribution. Ions or permanent dipoles can also induce a dipole moment in a nonpolar atom, as illustrated in Figure 1.12, on page 21.

A Continuum of Electrical Forces

These discrete categories of bonds are largely used for descriptive convenience, as none of these types of electrical interactions occur in "pure" form. For instance, molecules that are formed by covalent-type bonds between atoms are not necessarily nonpolar. Covalent bonds often have an ionic character and are called polar covalent bonds. Even a small difference in electronegativity between the bonding partners results in an uneven sharing of electrons within covalently bonded molecules. Water and methanol are examples of polar covalent molecules. Ionic bonds are never purely attractions between opposite charges; they always have some covalent character due to the polarizability of the atoms or ions involved. Thus, in reality, the electrical forces that occur between atoms should be considered as creating a continuum. The categorization of forces provides convenient benchmarks that help describe how electrons mediate interactions.

This learning goal contains an extensive amount of content. As students build an understanding of this content, they should be able to perform the followiing tasks.

Before Students Have Studied Atomic Structure

- Predict how a set of objects with a defined shape and charge interacts.

After Students Have Studied Atomic Structure

- Explain the role that electrons play in the different ways in which atoms interact.
- Explain the difference in the behavior of electrons in different types of interactions (e.g., ionic, dipole-dipole, covalent, induced dipole-induced dipole).
- Predict what types of interactions will occur between a given set of atoms or molecules.

Advanced Topics

Rather than an exhaustive description of the forces that occur and are important at the nanoscale, the forces and interactions discussed in this chapter represent only those likely to be accessible to high school students. Others, such as pi-stacking, micro-fluidic forces, and other surface forces, may be relevant and appropriate for more advanced courses.

Learning Goal 2

The characteristics of the interacting entities play a role in the formation and functioning of the assemblies.

Specific Prerequisite Knowledge

After Students Have Studied Atomic Structure

As students build an understanding of this content, they should understand these ideas:
- Learning Goal 1 of this chapter
- Learning Goal 1 from Chapter 6, "Structure of Matter"

Potential Student Difficulties and Misconceptions

Students may have several difficulties related to this content:

- They may have difficulty applying the concept of polarity (Taber and Coll 2002).
- They may confuse hydrogen bonds with covalent bonds (Özmen 2004; Taber and Coll 2002).
- They often rely on the octet model to explain interactions (Taber 1998; Taber and Coll 2002).

What Students Should Learn

Objects at the nano- and atomic scales interact through a variety of electrical forces. Two objects will be attracted to each other if they have opposite electrical charges and will repel each other if they have the same electrical charge. If the net sum of the interactions is attractive, the objects may come together to form a single assembly or complex.

Different types of electrical forces have different strengths, with the strength of an interaction defined as the energy required to separate the interacting objects. Interactions mediated by induced dipoles are always weaker than covalent or electrostatic forces. Comparing the properties of water and methane illustrates the difference in strength of hydrogen bonding compared to London forces (see Table 7.1). Because water and methane have similar molecular weights, the strength of the London forces acting between the molecules is similar. However, additional interactions (hydrogen bonds) occur between water molecules. These interactions are much stronger than London forces and are responsible for the large difference in melting and boiling points observed for water and methane.

Characteristics of the interacting entities are important for determining the type of electrical force that may occur between them. London forces occur between all types of atoms and therefore all objects. Noble gases are nonpolar and symmetric, so London forces are the only type that will occur between the atoms of noble gases. If molecules or assemblies are polar, then an electrostatic interaction may occur between them.

The relative strength of an interaction also depends on other characteristics of the atoms involved. For example, the strength of London forces increases in proportion to the size of the atom, molecule, or object (i.e., the number of electrons). The increase in melting point moving down Group VII in the periodic table illustrates this phenomenon: Fluorine and chlorine are gases, bromine is a liquid, and iodine is a solid under standard conditions. This trend is also observed for larger molecules of similar composition. Likewise, for molecules of similar molecular weight, the greater the dipole moment, the higher the boiling and melting points are. Ionic interactions tend to occur between atoms with a large difference in electronegativity—a measure of the tendency of an atom to attract electrons. The larger the difference in electronegativity between the two atoms, the stronger the ionic interaction between them is.

Shape also plays an important role in determining whether two structures will form a complex. Fitting puzzle pieces together is an example of shape complementarity (see Figure

Table 7.1
Comparison of the physical constants for water and methane

Substance	Formula	Molecular Weight (g/mol)	Melting Point (°C)	Boiling Point (°C)
Water	H_2O	18	0	100
Methane	CH_4	16	-182.5	-161.6

Chapter 7

7.5). Another way to consider this model is to recognize that fitting puzzle pieces together maximizes the amount of the surfaces that interact with each other. This approach prepares students for thinking about interactions in terms of the electrical forces (e.g., induced dipoles) that mediate them instead of by shape only.

Both shape and complementary electrical interactions are important factors for determining the likelihood that a complex will form between two structures. For instance, consider a

Figure 7.5
Puzzle model of a recognition event that depends only on complementary shape

lock and key. Many keys have the right shape to fit into a given lock, but only one key will make all of the right contacts ("interactions") such that it can unlock the lock. For nanoscale entities, those "interactions" are complementary electrical forces. Figure 7.6 illustrates a simple model for an interaction that depends on both shape and charge. Despite having complementary shapes, the interaction between the two positively charged objects is unlikely to occur, whereas the interaction between the oppositely charged ones is more likely.

Figure 7.7 illustrates that the complementarity of electrical forces is critical for a favorable interaction. Both the shape and charge are complementary between **I** and **II**. Although **I** and

Figure 7.6
Shape is not the only important factor in an interaction. The complex depicted in (a) is unlikely because the forces are not complementary. The forces in (b) are attractive so the complex is more likely.

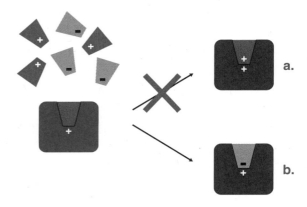

III have complementary shapes, the electrical forces are not complementary, and the repulsion is greater than the attraction as depicted in Figure 7.7b. If **III** is flipped over (see Figure 7.7c) then the formation of a complex might be favorable. The shapes of **IV** and **V** are not complementary, but the electrical forces lead to a favorable interaction (albeit not as favorable as that between **I** and **II**).

On the molecular scale, this phenomenon is illustrated by the base pairs of DNA. The bases act as a scaffold for atoms (or groups of atoms) that participate in hydrogen bonding (see Figure 2.7 on p. 48). Adenine and thymine form two hydrogen bonds when they pair, and guanine and cytosine form three hydrogen bonds upon pairing. The specificity of this simple code is such that a single-stranded sequence of 16 bases or greater can select its unique, complementary strand from a sequence of DNA that is millions of bases in length. This specificity was exploited with the polymerase chain reaction (PCR), which revolutionized molecular biology. Now

Figure 7.7
Aligning complementary charges is an important part of binding interactions: (a) Shape and charge complementarity (b) Shape, but not charge complementarity (c, d) Charge, but not shape complementarity

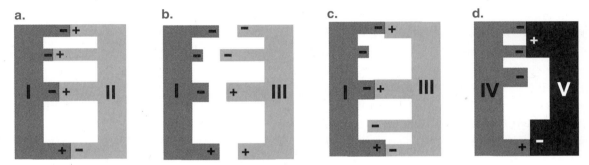

scientists use the specificity of DNA strands to help precisely assemble structures at the nanoscale (Seeman and Lukeman 2005; Mbindyo et al. 2001; Park et al. 2008).

Electrical forces also play a role in the function of assemblies of atoms or molecules. For example, hydrogen bonds play an important role in maintaining the structure of protein molecules. Albumin, the primary protein in egg white, consists of amino acid chains that form a series of alpha helices (see Figure 7.8). When the structure of albumin is intact, the egg white is liquid and clear in color. However, when the egg white is cooked, the heat breaks the hydrogen bonds that maintain the structure of the alpha helices (see Figure 1.8, p. 19). The structure is disrupted, and the amino acid chain collapses and becomes disorganized. As a result,

Figure 7.8
Ribbon representation of the backbone of albumin in its (a) active, folded state and (b) unfolded, denatured state

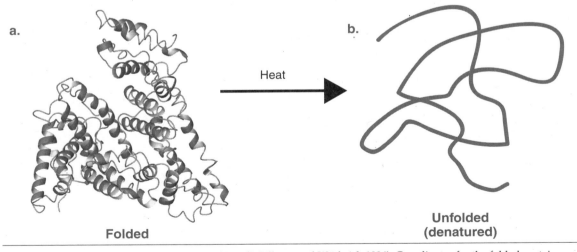

Heat

Folded

Unfolded (denatured)

Source: Images were created using MOLMOL (Koradi, Billeter, and Wüthrich 1996). Coordinates for the folded protein were obtained from the RCSB Protein Data Bank (1ao6).

the color of the egg white changes to white, and it becomes a solid.

A mutation of a single amino acid within a protein can change the structure and function by changing critical intra- or intermolecular interactions. For example, mutating the positively charged amino acid, glutamic acid, to the neutral amino acid, valine, in chain B of hemoglobin disrupts intramolecular electrical interactions that lead to a change in the structure and function of the entire protein. This single change is the cause of sickle cell anemia. (See Figure 1.6 on p. 16 and accompanying text for a more detailed discussion.)

As students build an understanding of the content contained within this learning goal, they may apply the ideas to many phenomena. Some examples of how they can apply their knowledge follow.

Before Students Have Studied Atomic Structure

- By examining the shapes of objects and their polarity, students should be able to predict how objects will interact with each other.

After Students Have Studied Atomic Structure

Students should be able to do the following:

- Apply their knowledge of electrical forces to explain why certain submacroscopic objects, structures, or assemblies interact and others do not
- Explain how electrical forces affect the properties and function of a range of structures (e.g., water molecules, noble gases, proteins, DNA)

Learning Goal 3

Many factors, including the characteristics of the interacting objects and the environment they are in, play a role in the formation (and strength) of any interaction.

Specific Prerequisite Knowledge

As students build an understanding of this content, they should understand Learning Goal 1 of this chapter.

Potential Student Difficulties and Misconceptions

Students may have several difficulties related to this content:

- Relating macroscopic phenomena with the phenomena happening at the molecular level (Treagust, Chittleborough, and Mamiala 2002)
- Applying the concept of polarity (Taber and Coll 2002)
- Considering not just the interacting entities, but also the particles in the environment

Students often have the misconception that the particles that make up a material are static (Harrison and Treagust 2002).

What Students Should Learn

Thermal motion of the building blocks is essential to the formation and functioning of an assembly. At any temperature above 0 K, atoms and molecules are in constant motion that is governed by attractions and repulsions between them. The motion of any particle is linear and continues until it interacts with another particle. The attraction or repulsion between the two particles then changes the trajectory of each of them. This motion is referred to as thermal motion; it occurs on the molecular scale and describes the random motion of atoms and molecules. In addition to random through-space motion, thermal motion also includes the rotation of atoms about chemical bonds and vibrations of atoms across chemical bonds. The scale of thermal motion is so small that it is not apparent in the macroscale world. However, thermal motion becomes an important factor in the behavior of nano- and atomic scale objects. The degree of motion of the particles that make up a substance (i.e., atoms or molecules) increases or decreases proportionally to the heat of the system.

In a chemical reaction, the rate of product formation is related to thermal motion. Changing the amount of heat in the system affects the motion of the particles. The number of collisions per unit of time changes, which affects the formation of interactions between atoms. In addition to temperature, pressure and the absolute and relative concentrations of the objects are also important factors in the formation of interactions. These three environmental variables affect how often two partners may collide, which in turn influences the formation of interactions.

Other factors also play a role in the formation and strength of interactions between atoms. The force between two opposite charges is dependent on the strength of the charges of the interacting partners and the distance between them (Figure 7.1, p. 101). Changes to

the environment also affect the strength of an electrostatic interaction. Polar solvents will weaken electrostatic interactions. However, polar solvents enhance the *hydrophobic effect*, a term that describes the behavior of nonpolar materials in a polar, usually aqueous, environment. Because the induced dipole-dipole interactions between the nonpolar molecules and the polar solvent are much weaker than the dipole-dipole interactions between the polar solvent molecules, nonpolar materials tend to cluster together when introduced into a polar environment. This explains why oil and water do not mix. Nanoscale biological examples of the hydrophobic effect include protein folding and micelles and cell membrane formation, which involve the assembly of phospholipids, which have a hydrophilic head and hydrophobic tail. When phospholipids are introduced into an aqueous environment, they assemble such that the hydrophilic heads are in contact with the water, while the hydrophobic tails all point inward, as illustrated in Figure 7.9. If the phospholipids were placed in a nonpolar environment, then the structure would be reversed,

Figure 7.9

(a) Representation of micelle formation by phospholipids (b) Cross section of micelle illustrates the arrangement of the hydrophobic and hydrophilic portions of phospholipids when they are introduced into an aqueous environment.

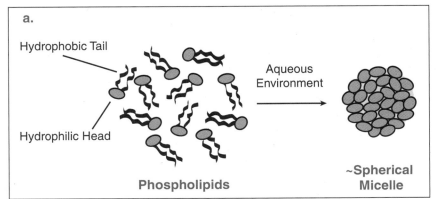
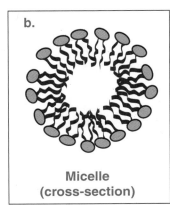

Chapter 7

with the hydrophilic heads pointed inward, and the hydrophobic tails pointed out.

The acidity of the environment can also play a role in the formation and strength of an interaction. The pH of a solvent may affect whether certain functional groups carry a charge or are neutral. For example, at a pH of 5.4, the amino acid histidine will carry a positive charge. If the pH is increased to 7.0, then the histidine is almost fully deprotonated and becomes neutral.

As students build an understanding of the content contained within this learning goal, they may apply the ideas to many phenomena. They might consider questions such as those that follow.

Before Students Have Studied Atomic Structure

- How does the environment affect the interaction of a given set of objects or structures?
- How do you know that thermal motion exists?
- How does heat affect thermal motion of particles (atoms or molecules)?
- When and how does thermal motion affect the properties of a material?

After Students Have Studied Atomic Structure

- What environmental variables affect interactions at the submicroscopic scale, and how do they affect the interactions?
- Why do different environmental variables affect the interactions in the ways that they do?

Learning Goal 4

Electrical forces are necessary for explaining a broad range of macroscopic phenomena. Students should be able to apply their knowledge of electrical forces to explain these various macroscopic (real-life) phenomena.

Specific Prerequisite Knowledge

As students build an understanding of this content, they should first understand Learning Goals 1 and 2 of this chapter.

Potential Student Difficulties and Misconceptions

- Students may have difficulty relating macroscopic phenomena with the phenomena happening at the molecular level (Pallant and Tinker 2004; Treagust, Chittleborough, and Mamiala 2002).

What Students Should Learn

A variety of electrical forces tend to dominate the interactions between objects on the nano-, molecular, and atomic scales. Students should be able to link their knowledge of electrical forces (see Learning Goal 1) and the interactions they govern with macroscale (real-life) phenomena that they observe.

After Students Have Studied Atomic Structure

Students should be able to apply their knowledge of electrical forces to answer questions such as these:

- Why do we need soap to wash off oil from our hands, but just water is adequate to wash off honey?
- Why does powdered sugar stick to a measuring cup more than granulated sugar does?
- After you rub a balloon on the carpet, you can stick it on the ceiling for a period of time. What is happening to the balloon when it is rubbed on the carpet? Why doesn't the balloon remain stuck to the ceiling indefinitely?

Learning Goal 5

A complete description of an interaction includes both the forces that govern the interaction and the change of energy for the entire system.

Specific Prerequisite Knowledge

As students build an understanding of this content, they should first understand Learning Goals 1, 2, and 3 of this chapter.

Potential Student Difficulties and Alternative Ideas

• Students often equate forces and energy (Horton et al. 2001).

What Students Should Learn

Gibbs energy, or free energy, is often used to describe the energy of a system. Often the change in free energy between two states of a system (ΔG) is used as a measure of the favorability of a system moving from one state to another (see Equation 7.1). Free energy is dependent on the enthalpy (H), entropy (S), and temperature (T) of the system. The change in enthalpy (ΔH) describes the difference in heat energy between the two states of a system. In the case of interactions, ΔH is related to the net favorable and unfavorable interactions between all entities within a system. ΔS represents the change in entropy, or disorder, between the two states of the system. Although the formation of complexes creates greater order of the parts that are being assembled, when the entire system is considered there may be greater total disorder.

Equation 7.1
Gibbs free energy

$$\Delta G = \Delta H - T\Delta S$$

When considering the energy of a system, interactions with and between the solvent and the molecules that make up the environment must be considered as well as those between the interactions of interest. For example, when in an aqueous environment, ordered shells of water molecules form around the nonpolar portions of building blocks. The ordered water molecules do not exhibit the random motion they usually have in the liquid state. If the nonpolar portions interact with each other, the ordered water molecules are released into the bulk solvent and are free to move randomly. The released water molecules are much more disordered than the organized shells that existed before the complex formed, which results in a net increase in entropy and is a significant part of the entropic contribution (ΔS) to the change in free energy between the bound and free states of the system. This effect is important in processes such as protein folding and membrane formation.

The second law of thermodynamics says that a closed system will tend to move toward maximum entropy. However, it is often energetically favorable (i.e., negative value for ΔG) for building blocks to become more ordered by combining to form organized assemblies. Although the building blocks are more ordered in the complex than in the initial state, there may be greater disorder when the whole system (including the solvent molecules) is considered.

Advanced Topic: Post-atomic Structure

The concept of free energy is probably only appropriate for advanced high school students and undergraduates. In particular, considering the energy in terms of the system is a difficult concept.

Chapter 7

Links to "Forces and Interactions" in the National Science Standards

The national science standards—the Benchmarks (AAAS 1993) and the NSES (NRC 1996)—suggest that science curriculum in the elementary and middle school years focus on the macroscopic application of forces: pushing and pulling, the behavior of magnets and electricity, and ultimately gravity. In high school, teachers should introduce electrical attractions and repulsions in terms of positive and negative charges and eventually move on to interactions at the atomic scale. Ideas related to forces are developed throughout grades K–12 in both *Benchmarks* and *NSES* and are summarized in Table 7.2 on pages 113–115.

What's Missing From the National Science Standards?

Although the importance of electromagnetic forces at the molecular level is stated in the standards documents, the focus there is on electrostatic forces. The idea that neutral atoms and molecules can still be electrically attracted to each other is difficult for students to understand, yet it is a critical concept. Electrodynamic forces play an important role in the structure and behavior of matter, especially on the nano-, molecular, and atomic scales. The following learning goal was developed at the initial Nanoscience Learning Goals Workshop (NLGW in June 2006):

> *The electrons in neutral atoms can be displaced momentarily or permanently to create a charge imbalance and become a dipole. This imbalance, or separation of charge, allows atoms to attract each other electrically even though they are*

neutral. This force is weaker than the force between permanently charged objects and is always attractive.

In addition, students typically learn about electrical forces as chemical bonds and often learn to think of the different types of interactions as discrete categories (Levy Nahum et al. 2007). This rigid categorization limits students' abilities to apply their knowledge of electrical forces beyond chemical bonding to a broader range of phenomena, such as biomolecular recognition or static electricity. Another idea generated at the workshop described the *continuum* of electrical forces that dominate interactions at the nano- and atomic scales:

> *Atoms can interact in a variety of ways, such as ionic bonding, covalent bonding, hydrogen bonding, and induced dipole interactions, which are all electrical in nature. These interactions create a continuum of electric forces that describe all interactions between atoms. The strength of the interactions depends on the atoms involved and the environment.*

Since 2001, a movement has been under way to change the traditional order of high school science courses (biology, chemistry, physics) such that biology comes later in the sequence (Lederman 2001). In this way, students would have the foundation for understanding the physical basis of biological functions. An alternative approach would be to better integrate ideas from different disciplines in all courses (Tinker and Xie 2006).

These or similar changes might help students make the necessary connections between disciplines that are required to understand the concepts and ideas of emergent science, including NSE. While students learn in biology about the different forces that are involved in interactions, they often do not connect those forces to what they learn in chemistry. For example, the hydrogen bonds that explain the behavior of water should be connected to the hydrogen bonds that keep the strands of DNA together. Too often, because biology is usually taken before chemistry, students learn the terminology without understanding its meaning (Taber and Coll 2002); therefore, they do not connect important ideas. Emphasizing connections might help students build an understanding that the forces that govern interactions on the nanoscale are the same, regardless of the objects participating in the interaction.

The concepts contained in the national science standards related to energy do not focus on nano-, atomic, or molecular scale phenomena. This could be because the standards are intended for every student; complicated concepts such as enthalpy, entropy, and free energy might be reserved for advanced learners. Unfortunately, little is known about how to help students develop an understanding of these concepts. Research toward the development of a validated learning progression for forces and interactions may help answer this question.

Table 7.2

National science standards related to developing an understanding of forces and interactions

Description of Content	Standard
Forces and Motion	
The position and motion of objects can be changed by pushing or pulling.	*Benchmarks* 4F/2 K–2, p. 89 4F/3 6–8, p. 90 *NSES* PS–M^a K–4, p. 127
The change in motion of an object is proportional to the force and inversely proportional to its mass.	*Benchmarks* 4F/1 3–5, p. 89 4F/1 9–12, p. 91 *NSES* PS–M K–4, p. 127
Magnets exert a force that acts on certain materials even without touching them.	*Benchmarks* 4G/2 K–2, p. 94 4G/2 3–5, p. 94
Gravity	
Gravitational force is an attractive force that exists between all masses. The strength of the force depends on the masses of the two bodies and their distance from each other.	*Benchmarks* 4G/1 6–8, p. 95 4G/1 9–12, p. 96 *NSES* PS–MF 9–12, p. 180
Electrical Forces	
Electrically charged objects exert a force that acts on other materials.	*Benchmarks* 4G/3 3–5, p. 94

Table 7.2 continued on page 114

Chapter 7

Table 7.2 continued

Electricity and magnetism are related.	*Benchmarks* 4G/3 6–8, p. 95 4G/5 9–12, p. 97 *NSES* PS–MF[b] 9–12, p. 180
There are two types of charges—positive and negative.	*Benchmarks* 4G/3 9–12, p. 96
The strength of electrical forces is inversely proportional to the square of the distance between the charges.	*NSES* PS–MF 9–12, p. 180
Electromagnetic forces between two small particles are stronger than the gravitational force between them.	*Benchmarks* 4G/2 9–12, p. 96 *NSES* PS–MF 9–12, p. 180
Electrical forces are the primary forces holding atoms and molecules together. They involve the outermost electrons of the atoms.	*Benchmarks* 4D/1 9–12, p. 80 4G/2 9–12, p. 96 *NSES* PS–MF 9–12, p. 180 PS–SA[c] 9–12, p. 178 PS–SPM[c] 9–12, p. 178
Properties	
The physical properties of a material are affected by the interactions among its molecules.	*NSES* PS–SPM 9–12, p. 179
Environmental Factors	
Many factors affect how atoms and molecules interact (e.g., concentration, temperature, pH, and polarity of environment).	*Benchmarks* 4D/3 6–8, p. 78 4D/4 6–8, p. 78 4D/8 9–12, p. 80 4D/9 9–12, p. 80 *NSES* PS–CR[d] 9–12, p. 179
Energy	
Energy is found in many forms.	*Benchmarks* 4E/3 6–8, p. 85 4E/4 6–8, p. 85 4E/2 9–12, p. 86 *NSES* PS–MF 5–8, p. 155 PS–CE–ID[e] 9–12, p. 180
Energy is always conserved; it cannot be created or destroyed.	*Benchmarks* 4E/1 6–8, p. 85 4E/1 9–12, p. 86

Table 7.2 continued

Kinetic Theory and Entropy	
Atoms and molecules are in constant random motion. All matter tends toward a more disordered state.	*Benchmarks* 4E/4 6–8, p. 85 4E/2 9–12, p. 86 *NSES* PS–CE–ID 9–12, p. 180 LS–MEO[f] 9–12, p. 186

[a] Physical Science—Position and Motion of Objects
[b] Physical Science—Motions and Forces
[c] Physical Science—Structure and Properties of Matter
[d] Physical Science—Chemical Reactions
[e] Physical Science—Conservation of Energy and the Increase in Disorder
[f] Life Sciences—Matter, Energy, and Organization in Living Systems

Acknowledgment

The authors would like to thank Shanna Daly for helpful discussions and reading of this chapter.

References

American Association for the Advancement of Science (AAAS). 1993. *Benchmarks for science literacy.* New York: Oxford University Press.

Boo, H. K. 1998. Students' understandings of chemical bonds and the energetics of chemical reactions. *Journal of Research in Science Teaching* 35 (5): 569–581.

Harrison, A. G., and D. F. Treagust. 2002. The particulate nature of matter: Challenges in understanding the submicroscopic world. In *Chemical education: Towards research-based practice*, ed. J. K. Gilbert, O. De Jong, R. Justi, D. F. Treagust, and J. H. van Driel. Dordrecht, The Netherlands: Kluwer Academic Publishers.

Horton, C., with other members of the Modeling Instruction in High School Chemistry Action Research Teams. June 2001, August 2002, and August 2004. Student alternative conceptions in chemistry. Tempe, AZ: Arizona State University. *www.daisley. net/hellevator/misconceptions/misconceptions.pdf*

Koradi, R., M. Billeter, and K. Wüthrich. 1996. MOL-MOL: A program for display and analysis of macromolecular structures. *Journal of Molecular Graphics* 14: 51–55.

Lederman L. 2001. Revolution in science education: Put physics first! *Physics Today* (September): 44–48.

Levy Nahum, T., R. Mamlok–Naaman, A. Hofstein, and J. Krajcik. 2007. Developing a new teaching approach for the chemical bonding concept aligned with current scientific and pedagogical knowledge. *Science Education* 91 (4): 579–603.

Mbindyo, J. K. N., B. D. Reiss, B. R. Martin, C. D. Keating, M. J. Natan, and T. E. Mallouk. 2001. DNA-directed assembly of gold nanowires on complementary surfaces. *Advanced Materials* 13 (4): 249–254.

National Research Council (NRC). 1996. *National science education standards.* Washington, DC: NRC.

Özmen, H. 2004. Some student misconceptions in chemistry: A literature review of chemical bonding. *Journal of Science Education and Technology* 13 (2): 147–159.

Pallant, A., and R. Tinker. 2004. Reasoning with atomic-scale molecular dynamic models. *Journal of Science Education and Technology* 13 (1): 51–66.

Chapter 7

Park, S. Y., A. K. R. Lytton–Jean, B. Lee, S. Weigand, G. C. Schatz, and C. A. Mirkin. 2008. DNA-programmable nanoparticle crystallization. *Nature* 451: 553–556.

Seeman, N. C., and P. S. Lukeman. 2005. Nucleic acid nanostructures: Bottom–up control of geometry on the nanoscale. *Reports on Progress in Physics* 68: 237–270.

Taber, K. S. 1998. An alternative conceptual framework from chemistry education. *International Journal of Science Education* 20 (5): 597–608.

Taber, K. S., and R. K. Coll. 2002. Bonding. In *Chemical education: Towards research–based practice*, ed. J. K. Gilbert, O. De Jong, R. Justi, D. F. Treagust, and J. J. van Driel. Dordrecht, The Netherlands: Kluwer Academic Publishers.

Tinker, R., and Q. Xie. 2006. *Nanoscience and the new secondary science curriculum.* Concord, MA: Concord Consortium.

Treagust, D. F., G. Chittleborough, and T. L. Mamiala. 2002. Students' understanding of the role of scientific models in learning science. *International Journal of Science Education* 24 (4): 357–368.

NATIONAL SCIENCE TEACHERS ASSOCIATION

Chapter **8**
Quantum Effects

Big Idea:

Different models explain and predict the behavior of matter better, depending on the scale and conditions of the system. In particular, as the size or mass of an object becomes smaller and transitions through the nanoscale, quantum effects become more important.

At the foundation of classical mechanics, Newton's laws of motion are used to describe the motion and behavior of objects in the macroscopic world. These include objects visible to the naked eye as well as astronomical objects such as planets. However, as the size or mass of an object or material transitions through the nanoscale to the atomic scale, predictions of the behavior of matter begin to fail using classical mechanics. At this point, quantum mechanics, a probabilistic model, must be applied to explain the behavior of matter.

Quantum theory is an extremely advanced and complicated model. However, some aspects are accessible and useful for building an appreciation and understanding of the novel properties exhibited by matter at the nanoscale. In this chapter, we present four learning goals that support students' understanding of the structure and behavior of matter at very small scales. The order in which they are presented is not meant to suggest an order for incorporating them into the science curriculum.

General Prerequisite Knowledge for This Chapter

Each of the learning goals in this chapter represents a different aspect of the big idea. While the focus of each learning goal is different, some prerequisite knowledge is required for developing an understanding of all of them. Students should understand the following:

- Newton's laws of motion predict the behavior of matter at the macroscale and are the foundation of classical mechanics. One of the principles of classical mechanics is that by knowing the position and the momentum of an object at a given time, it is possible to predict the trajectory that it has and will follow.

- Atoms consist of a dense nucleus that contains protons and neutrons; the nucleus is surrounded by negatively charged electrons. The electrons are distributed into shells. The periodic table predicts how many electrons are in the shells of atoms of each element.

In addition, students should understand

- the measurement of lengths on the macro-, micro-, nano-, and atomic scales and

- how to relate the sizes of objects in the macroworld to objects in other worlds (i.e., micro-, nano-, and sub-nano-) both qualitatively and quantitatively.

Chapter 8

Learning Goal 1

All matter behaves with both particle-like and wave-like character. As a material gets smaller and transitions through the nanoscale, the importance of the wave-like character increases, and quantum mechanics is needed to predict and explain its behavior.

Specific Prerequisite Knowledge

Students must have some experience with waves and how they behave, including

- the relationship between wavelength and frequency and
- diffraction and interference.

Potential Student Difficulties and Misconceptions

- Students will likely struggle with conceptualizing how a single entity can behave like both a wave *and* a particle (Olsen 2002).

What Students Should Learn

All things exhibit either wave-like or particle-like properties depending on the method used to observe them. Experimental evidence for the particle-nature of electrons was initially observed using cathode rays (i.e., beams of electrons). In the late 19th century, J. J. Thomson calculated a mass-to-charge ratio for electrons by measuring the effect of a magnetic field on the path of the beam. He found that the ratio is independent of the cathode material used. The wave-like character of electrons was illustrated by the diffraction and interference patterns created by a beam of electrons. Similarly, light (photons) also exhibit both particle- and wave-like character, as do all atomic and subatomic-sized particles. Actually, all objects exhibit wave-like behavior, but the wavelengths are too small to be measured for larger objects like bullets or baseballs, so we observe only the average position. As the size of an object gets smaller, moving through the nanoscale toward the atomic scale, the wavelength becomes more significant relative to the size of the object, and the wave character becomes more important.

As students build understanding of this fundamental quantum mechanical principle, they should consider both experimental and theoretical evidence for the quantum mechanical behavior of matter. Students could consider the following:

- What does wave-particle duality mean? What is the evidence for it?
- What are the implications of matter exhibiting both wave-like and particle-like behavior?
- If classical mechanics cannot predict behavior _____ (e.g., at the nanoscale, of individual atoms), then is it wrong? Why do we continue to learn about and use Newton's laws?
- What is tunneling? When is it likely to occur? Why?
- What are some phenomena that involve tunneling?

Learning Goal 2

Only discrete amounts of energy can enter or exit atomic and subatomic systems. This is also true for many nanoscale systems.

Specific Prerequisite Knowledge

- Students should understand basic concepts about energy.

Potential Student Difficulties and Misconceptions

- Students may believe that classical mechanics effectively and accurately predicts and describes the behavior of matter under all conditions and scales (Kalkanis, Hadzidaki, and Stavrou 2003).

What Students Should Learn

Many systems can absorb any amount of energy, but for some systems, energy is only allowed in or out in certain discrete amounts. When this occurs, the energy levels are considered to be quantized. These systems are traditionally found at the atomic and subatomic scales, but the phenomenon is also observed for some nanoscale systems (e.g., quantum dots). The photoelectric effect, a phenomenon in which ejection of electrons from the surface of a metal is dependent on the frequency of the incident light rather than on its intensity, illustrates the quantization phenomenon (see Figure 8.1). The energies that generate electron ejection are integer multiples of $h\nu$ where h is Planck's constant and ν is the threshold frequency of the incident light (radiation). This is counter to daily experience in which if greater force is applied, a greater or faster response results.

The quantization of energy levels is related to the transition of conductors to semiconductors at the nanoscale (see Size-Dependent Properties in Chapter 2, pp. 37–43, and Figures 1.15 and 1.16, pp. 29–30, and accompanying text for further discussion of this phenomenon). Quantum dots are nanoscale semiconductors that also have quantized energy levels.

Students could address questions such as the following:

- When should the quantum or classical models be applied to a system?

Figure 8.1
Representation of the photoelectric effect

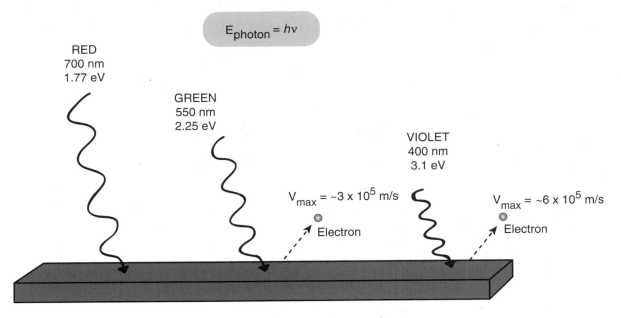

$E_{photon} = h\nu$

RED
700 nm
1.77 eV

GREEN
550 nm
2.25 eV

VIOLET
400 nm
3.1 eV

$V_{max} = {\sim}3 \times 10^5$ m/s

$V_{max} = {\sim}6 \times 10^5$ m/s

Electron

Electron

2.0 eV required to eject an electron from potassium

Chapter 8

- What is different between quantum mechanical and classical mechanical predictions of the behavior of _____ (e.g., matter, electrons, photons)?
- How can a conductive metal turn into a semiconductor? What happens? Why does it happen?
- How do quantum dots work? Why does their size affect the color they emit?

Learning Goal 3

It is impossible to know exactly what did or will happen to matter at the nano-, atomic, and subatomic scales.

Specific Prerequisite Knowledge

Students should know the following:

- Any event can be described as certain, impossible, or somewhere in between.
- Probabilities are generally expressed as fractions, ratios, or percentages. Some events are easier to predict than others.
- Often predictions can be made based on what is known about the past, assuming that conditions are the same in both instances.
- In order to make predictions about the likelihood of an event occurring, a mathematical model may be useful.

Potential Student Difficulties and Misconceptions

Students may have difficulty

- conceptualizing and working with a probabilistic model (Kalkanis, Hadzidaki, and Stavrou 2003) and
- considering the probability of an event occurring in relation to other events that have already occurred (e.g., if a coin lands heads up several times in a row, they often believe that the probability of tails for the next toss is higher than for earlier tosses) (AAAS 1993).

What Students Should Learn

The wave-particle duality brings certain limitations. Within the realm of classical mechanics, the ability to determine the exact position and momentum of an object at any given instant enables one to predict the path the object will take. However, when the wave-like character of something (e.g., a particle) becomes important, it is impossible to define its exact position. Instead only the probability of its location can be defined. This transition generally occurs when the object is very small (i.e., at the lower end of the nanoscale, the atomic and subatomic scales).

There are several pairs of observables that cannot simultaneously be measured exactly (e.g., position and momentum; energy and time); as one observable is measured more precisely, the other necessarily becomes less defined. For instance, it is impossible to predict the exact path of a particle such as an electron or photon because the act of measuring its position precisely alters its path and therefore its momentum. It is impossible to predict the exact behavior of matter; one can only state the probability of what will happen. This is one of the fundamental concepts of quantum mechanics.

Before Learning About Atomic Structure

Students should be able to

- explain what probability means and consider the probability of the occurrence of events, and
- provide examples of probability being used to make predictions for familiar phenomena (e.g., weather, odds of rolling dice).

After Learning About Atomic Structure

Students should be able to

- describe the uncertainty principle and explain what it means and under what conditions it is especially important,
- describe and use a model of atomic structure that includes a probabilistic model of electron distribution within an atom (see Learning Goal 1 in Chapter 6, "Structure of Matter," for more detail), and
- apply the idea of electron densities to explain induced-dipole interactions.

Learning Goal 4

The quantum mechanical behavior of electrons helps to explain the arrangement of the elements in the periodic table.

Specific Prerequisite Knowledge

- Protons, neutrons, electrons, and photons are each defined by particular characteristics.

Potential Student Difficulties and Misconceptions

- Although it may be a useful analogy, the angular momentum (or spin) of an electron is not the same sort of "spinning on its axis" that describes angular momentum on the macroscale (classical mechanics).

What Students Should Learn

Spin is an important characteristic of fundamental particles (e.g., electrons, photons). It is defined as the *intrinsic* angular momentum of the particle. Within the classical mechanical model, an object can rotate with any angular momentum (continuous). However, according to quantum mechanics, angular momentum is quantized.

Spin plays an important role in atomic structure and molecular bonding. In 1925, Wolfgang Pauli developed the exclusion principle to account for the periodicity of the elements. Within the orbital approximation, each electron within the system (i.e., atom) must be unique. There are only two allowed spin states for electrons, +1/2 or -1/2. Therefore, only two electrons can occupy the same orbital—one electron with spin +1/2 and one with spin -1/2. The two electrons within an orbital are considered paired. Additional electrons must occupy different orbitals because all electrons within an atom must have different quantum states. (See the Quantum Effects section, pp. 24–28, of Chapter 1 for an explanation of quantum states.)

Students should be able to explain what the Pauli exclusion principle is and how it relates to the characteristics of the elements and their arrangement in the periodic table.

Links to "Quantum Effects" in the National Science Standards

Although quantum mechanics is complex and difficult subject matter, some ideas are appropriate for qualitative introduction at the high school level. Table 8.1 on pages 122–123 presents the ideas related to quantum mechanics represented in the national standards.

What's Missing From the National Science Standards?

In order to illustrate the limitations of Newton's laws, the Benchmarks discuss Einstein's theory of relativity in the historical perspectives section (AAAS 1993, pp. 244–245). The parallel failure of classical mechanics at small scales and the need for quantum mechanics is not discussed in either the Benchmarks or the National

Chapter 8

Science Education Standards, despite the fact that some quantum mechanical ideas are necessary for developing an understanding of many concepts introduced in high school science curricula. Although high school chemistry curricula generally cover atomic structure, the trends in the periodic table, and chemical bonding, the Pauli exclusion principle is not explicitly stated in either set of standards. In addition, developing an understanding of induced dipole interactions requires a probabilistic electron cloud model of an atom.

The absence of many quantum mechanical ideas in the national science standards may be because they were written for *all* students and quantum mechanical ideas are difficult,

nonintuitive concepts that not all students can grasp. We must decide to what degree these complex ideas should be introduced into secondary classrooms. In this chapter, we have discussed a few fundamental ideas that educators and researchers have suggested to be appropriate for high school learners. However it will take more than a few days of instruction for students to develop an understanding of these quantum mechanical ideas. Because little is known about how students learn these concepts, stronger efforts must be made by researchers and curriculum developers to support the learning of the abstract concepts of quantum mechanics so we can determine how aspects of the discipline can be introduced into the classroom.

Table 8.1
National science standards related to developing an understanding of quantum effects

Description of Content	Standard
Energy Levels	
Different energy levels are associated with different configurations of atoms and molecules.	*Benchmarks* 4E/4 9–12, p. 86 4E/5 9–12, p. 86 *NSES* PS–EIM[a] 9–12, p. 179
Waves	
Light interacts with matter in three ways: absorption, transmission, and scattering. The human eye sees only a small range of the wavelengths of the electromagnetic spectrum.	*Benchmarks* 4F/2 6–8, p. 90 4F/5 6–8, p. 90 *NSES* PS–TE[b] 5–8, p. 155
The wavelength of light is related to energy in the context of light from the Sun.	*NSES* PS–TE 5–8, p. 155
Waves come in many forms (e.g., light, sound, seismic, in water), all exhibiting similar behavior.	*Benchmarks* 4F/4 6–8, p. 90 4F/6 9–12, p. 92 *NSES* PS–EIM 9–12, p. 180

Table 8.1 continued

The acceleration of charged particles produces electromagnetic waves.	*Benchmarks* 4F/3 9–12, p. 92 *NSES* PS–EIM 9–12, p. 180
Uncertainty	
The behavior of matter at the nano-, atomic, and subatomic scales cannot be predicted exactly. Only the probability of an event occurring can be determined.	*Benchmarks* 11C/7 9–12, p. 275 11A/4 9–12, p. 266
Many factors determine how accurate a prediction might be.	*Benchmarks* 9D/1 K–2, p. 227 9D/2 K–2, p. 227 9D/1 3–5, p. 228 9D/2 3–5, p. 228 9D/3 3–5, p. 228 9D/6 3–5, p. 228 9D/1 6–8, p. 229 9D/2 6–8, p. 229 9D/1 9–12, p. 230 9D/8 9–12, p. 230

[a] Physical Science—Interactions of Energy and Matter
[b] Physical Science—Transfer of Energy

Acknowledgment

The authors would like to thank Alexa Mattheyses for helpful discussions and reading of this chapter.

References

American Association for the Advancement of Science (AAAS). 1993. *Benchmarks for science literacy*. New York: Oxford University Press.

Kalkanis, G., P. Hadzidaki, and D. Stavrou. 2003. An instructional model for a radical conceptual change towards quantum mechanics concepts. *Science Education* 87: 257–280.

National Research Council (NRC). 1996. *National Science Education Standards*. Washington, DC: NRC.

Olsen, R. V. 2002. Introducing quantum mechanics in the upper secondary school: A study in Norway. *International Journal of Science Education* 24 (6): 565–574.

Chapter 9
Size-Dependent Properties

Big Idea:

The properties of matter can change with scale. In particular, during the transition between the bulk material and individual atoms or molecules, a material often exhibits unexpected properties that lead to new functionality. This transition generally occurs at the nanoscale.

The unique, often unexpected properties observed at the nanoscale represent phenomena that are truly novel and therefore not included in the traditional science curriculum. Because the properties and applications of nanoscale objects and phenomena are so diverse, these ideas can fit into the curriculum in a multitude of places in physics, chemistry, biology, and Earth science. An advantage to exploring these properties is that students must focus on the source of the properties and therefore develop a better understanding of the structure and behavior of matter in general.

General Prerequisite Knowledge for This Chapter

Each of the five learning goals in this chapter represents a different aspect of the big idea: Size-Dependent Properties. While the focus of each learning goal is different, students need some common prerequisite knowledge for developing understanding of the goals. Students should understand the following:

- The qualities or characteristics that determine the nature of a material are the properties of the material.

- Properties determine how a material looks and behaves, how it interacts with and reacts to the environment, and for which applications it might be useful.

- Matter is made up of particles too small to see. The particles (atoms or molecules) within a substance are in constant random motion, which is also known as thermal energy.

- The type of building blocks, their motion, and how they are arranged give a substance its properties. The building blocks for molecules are atoms. Atoms, molecules, and other nanoscale structures and assemblies can be building blocks for nanoscale structures and assemblies.

- Individual atoms and molecules do not exhibit the same properties as the bulk (macroscale) substance.

- Certain types of properties (intensive) are generally more reliable for distinguishing between two materials.

- Learning Goal 2 in Chapter 5, "Size and Scale."

Chapter 9

Learning Goal 1

The surface-to-volume ratio increases as the size of an object becomes smaller. As a result, as the size of an object approaches the nanoscale, the fraction of the atoms on the surface increases dramatically, and surface-related properties become more important.

Specific Prerequisite Knowledge

Understanding how size affects surface-related properties may involve knowledge about these topics:

- The surface area is the total number of square units (un^2) that are required to cover the surface of an object.
- The volume of an object is a measure of the space that it occupies in cubic units (un^3).
- The relative value of two quantities can be described by a ratio.
- Substances can react chemically (in characteristic ways) with other substances to form new substances (compounds) with different characteristic properties.
- The nature of the interactions among a substance's atoms and/or molecules and their arrangement affect the characteristic properties.
- Changing characteristics of the environment can affect chemical reactivity.

Potential Difficulties and Misconceptions

Students may believe that all atoms or molecules in a material (both surface and interior) behave in the same way. They may have difficulty

- conceptualizing and calculating surface area and volume (Kordaki and Potari 1998; Zacharos 2006) and/or

- developing an understanding of ratios and proportions (Lesh, Post, and Behr 1988; Misailidou and Williams 2003).

What Students Should Learn

Changing the length scale of one dimension of an object changes its area and volume disproportionately; thus, properties dependent on area and volume will also change disproportionately. One of the consequences of decreasing size in all dimensions is an increase in the surface-to-volume ratio (S/V). These changes manifest in an increase in the relative number of atoms on the surface. Unlike the inner atoms of a solid, surface atoms are not fully bonded, so they possess higher energy (known as surface energy) than the inner atoms. In addition, the chemical environment of atoms on the surface is different from that of the atoms contained within the bulk of the material.

Chemical reactions involve the interaction between atoms or molecules in the surrounding environment and the atoms at the surface of a material. Changes in the amount of exposed surface area affect the *rate* of chemical reactions. Likewise, physical changes such as melting and dissolving are surface-dependent—the processes of these transformations involve atoms and molecules on the surface of the material interacting with atoms or molecules in the environment.

Because the proportion of atoms that lie at the surface increases dramatically for nanoscale entities, interactions involving surface forces (e.g., London dispersion forces) can dramatically affect the behavior of materials at the nanoscale. Even on the macroscale, the effect of increased surface area by decreasing size can be observed. For example, by crushing a tablet into smaller pieces, its rate of dissolution is increased.

There are some ideas related to size-dependent properties that students should explore and explain.

Before Students Have Studied Atomic Structure

- What is the relationship between the *rate* of transformation (i.e., chemical or physical transformations) and the surface-to-volume ratio?
- Categorize surface- and volume-dependent properties.

After Students Have Studied Atomic Structure

- What is happening at the molecular or atomic level during a chemical or physical transformation?
- Why does an increase in surface area change the way materials interact with each other on a molecular or atomic level.

Learning Goal 2

Some of the characteristic properties of matter change with size, particularly as the length scale of the sample decreases and approaches the atomic scale.

Specific Prerequisite Knowledge

Some of the size-related properties relevant to NSE are electrical, optical, mechanical, and magnetic in nature. Discussion of these types of materials may occur in a number of science contexts, and understanding each type requires different prerequisite knowledge.

Potential Student Difficulties and Misconceptions

Students may believe the following:

- The individual atoms or molecules of a substance have the same properties as the bulk substance. For example, students may believe that gold atoms have gold color (Ben-

Zvi, Eylon, and Silberstein 1986; Albanese and Vicentini 1997).

- Intensive properties are always the same regardless of the amount of material.

What Students Should Learn

In addition to an increase in S/V, other factors contribute to the change in properties observed at the nanoscale. Different substances have different characteristic properties, which depend on the composition of the substance—the type of atoms, their arrangement, their movement, and how they interact with each other. The size-dependent properties discussed below illustrate how classical intensive properties change with scale. These examples relate to important ideas already in the science curriculum, but students could also explore myriad other examples.

Many different size-dependent properties have been characterized for the noble metals (e.g., silver, gold, copper). Some of the nanoscale properties of gold were discussed in the size-dependent properties section of Chapter 2. The size dependence of the optical properties of gold nanoparticles can easily be demonstrated in the classroom. A monodispersed colloidal gold solution, containing nanoparticles approximately 13 nm in diameter, can be easily synthesized (Handley 1989a). Figure 9.1a on page 128 illustrates the composition of the gold nanoparticles. The gold particles are sheathed with negative charge. Addition of a few drops of concentrated sodium chloride solution changes the charge of the nanoparticles, resulting in some aggregation. The increased size of the particles changes the way that light interacts with them, resulting in a violet color (see Figure 9.1b, p. 128).

This size-dependent phenomenon has been used to create a biosensor (Elghanian et al. 1997). Scientists have exploited the specificity of complementary DNA strands in combination

Figure 9.1

(a) A representation of a gold nanoparticle prepared with hydrochloroauric acid and sodium citrate. Negatively charged citrate (-3) will lie on the surface (Handley 1989b). (b) Representation of a monodispersed colloidal solution of 13 nm gold nanoparticles. When the electrolyte content (salt concentration) is changed, the gold nanoparticles aggregate (McFarland et al. 2004).

a.

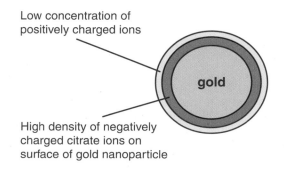

Low concentration of positively charged ions

gold

High density of negatively charged citrate ions on surface of gold nanoparticle

b.

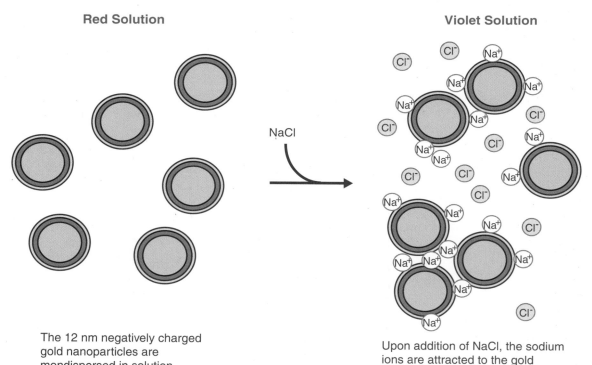

Red Solution

Violet Solution

NaCl

The 12 nm negatively charged gold nanoparticles are mondispersed in solution.

Upon addition of NaCl, the sodium ions are attracted to the gold nanoparticles, which decreases the surface charge and leads to particle aggregation.

Figure 9.2
(a) Gold nanoparticles are attached to strands of single-stranded DNA that are complementary to the sequence to be detected. The solution of monodispersed modified gold nanoparticles is red. (b) The modified gold nanoparticles aggregate along the detected DNA sequence and the solution changes to violet.

a.   Red Colloidal Solution

b.   Violet Colloidal Solution

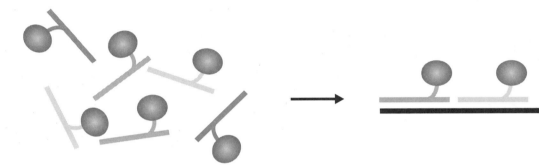

The gold nanoparticles attached to single-stranded DNA form a monodispersed colloidal solution.

When the DNA strands hybridize to their complementary sequences on the target sequence, the gold nanoparticles "aggregate."

with gold nanoparticles to detect certain DNA sequences. Gold nanoparticles are attached to parts of one of the DNA strands of interest. A solution of these assemblies is red in color. When a DNA strand with a sequence complementary to that attached to the nanoparticles is added, an interaction between complementary DNA strands occurs, as illustrated in Figure 9.2. The assemblies of DNA and nanoparticles act like a larger "particle," and the solution turns from red to violet, allowing the detection of the desired DNA sequence. Other examples of nanoscale optical properties include the iridescence of butterfly wings, opals, and soap bubbles.

The physical properties typically used to characterize a material also apply to a "bulk" substance (e.g., conductivity, magnetic properties). In other words, the properties describe the average behavior of the atoms and/or molecules of the substance. However on the nanoscale, the number of particles involved may be small enough that the behavior of individual particles affects the properties of the whole. An example of this is magnets. When a magnet is cut into small enough pieces, its magnetic moment becomes increasingly sensitive to the random motion of particles that is always present in matter (also known as thermal energy). At a certain point, known as the superparamagnetic limit, the inherent thermal energy of the material is similar to that of the energy required to change the direction of the magnetic moment. This critical particle size occurs at the nanoscale. Hard-disk drives and data recording tapes are among the applications that depend on magnetic materials. The superparamagnetic limit defines the limit for using magnetic materials for data storage.

Chapter 9

At the nanoscale, electrical properties are not necessarily the same as they are on the macroscale. Materials that are conductors on the macroscale may become semiconductors or may completely lose their conductivity at the nanoscale and vice versa. This phenomenon occurs when the electrons in the material become confined. (See the Quantum Effects section of Chapter 1 for an explanation of this phenomenon.)

Students can explore a broad range of size-dependent properties. Questions they might address include the following:

- How does the size of a material affect its optical properties?
- Why is there a size limit to the use of magnetic materials for data storage?
- What characteristics at the atomic or molecular scale make a material a conductor or insulator?

Students should be able to do the following:

- Explain the effect of thermal motion on the observed properties of a material
- Explain how the same material can change from conductor to semiconductor to insulator and explain what is happening during the transition

Students should include molecular, atomic, or subatomic phenomena in their explanations.

Learning Goal 3

The shape of nanoscale structures can lead to unique properties.

Specific Prerequisite Knowledge

- Students need to know about different shapes, both two- and three-dimensional, and how to calculate area and volume of those shapes.

Potential Student Difficulties and Misconceptions

Students may believe that

- the characteristic properties of a material are independent of its shape and/or
- properties are always the same in all three directions in a given material.

What Students Should Learn

In general, there is a causal relationship between structure and properties; at the nanoscale, shape also sometimes plays a role in determining the properties of a material. For example, a colloidal suspension of spherical silver nanoparticles is blue, while suspensions of tetragonal particles of similar size make a red solution, and pentagonal particles are a green solution (Mock et al. 2002). In fact, when the tetragonal particles are heated, the vertices become rounded and the particles shift to an orange color, and after extended heating they appear yellow-green. It is thus obvious that small changes in shape have a dramatic effect on the optical properties of the silver nanoparticles.

Although the colors of nanoparticles provide a vivid example of the effects of size and shape on properties of matter, the source of the color, plasmon resonance, is an advanced and complex topic. Students can also explore more accessible phenomena. For example, at the nanoscale, the properties of a material can be different in different directions (dimensions). One example of this is carbon nanotubes, which have special properties that are different from other forms of carbon. In particular, they can be either semiconductors or conductors. However, as either conductors or semiconductors, they conduct electricity in only two dimensions.

Changing shape can change the surface area and volume disproportionately. Thus, the properties that are dependent on area and volume will also change disproportionately. (See Learning Goal 1 of this chapter and Learning Goal 5 of Chapter 5, " Size and Scale," for more detailed discussion.)

Atoms in a crystalline solid arrange in an ordered, repeating manner. Depending on the face of the crystal that is exposed to the environment, a different number of unfulfilled bonds will lie at the surface. For example, as represented in Figure 9.3, in a body-centered cubic packing, depending on how the surface is cut, there will be either four or five atoms at the surface. In addition, there may be different types of atoms at the surface depending on which plane is exposed. For rough surfaces of bulk material, the variation of surfaces means that the differences are averaged out. However, for precisely manufactured materials, such as those used in the semiconductor industry, the effect of different surface energy can be important.

This learning goal is probably best suited for advanced high school courses or undergraduates because it requires students to integrate knowledge of many difficult concepts.

Figure 9.3
(a) Atoms packed in body-centered cubic form
(b) Alternative surfaces have different numbers and perhaps different types of atoms at the surface.

a.

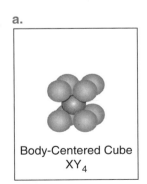

Body-Centered Cube
XY_4

b.

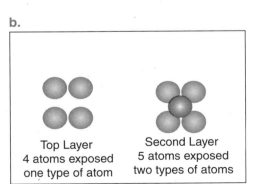

Top Layer
4 atoms exposed
one type of atom

Second Layer
5 atoms exposed
two types of atoms

Links to "Size-Dependent Properties" in the National Science Standards

To fully appreciate the special properties of matter that occur at the nanoscale, students must already understand the types of properties that exist and the source of those properties. Both the Benchmarks and the NSES introduce the concept of properties in the early elementary grades. The standards related to the properties of matter are summarized in Table 9.1 on page 133.

What's Missing From the National Science Standards?

Although the NSES and Benchmarks develop ideas related to the properties of matter in grades K–12, some ideas are not explained in terms of current views of science. The NSES state that intensive properties do not change with respect to the amount of substance (NRC 1996, p. 154). However, we can no longer speak of intensive properties as being independent of the amount of substance because we now know that intensive properties do change at the nanoscale. Instead, we must think of them as limited descriptors that apply only to bulk properties, where the variations in amount occur within the macroscale. Because the property changes occur at a scale too small to be directly experienced, this is a challenging concept.

The Benchmarks explicitly discuss the implications that scale may have on properties (in

Chapter 9

Table 9.1
Table 9.1
National science standards related to developing an understanding of size-dependent properties

Description of Content	Standard
General Properties	
Objects can be described by their characteristics and the materials of which they are made.	*Benchmarks* 4D/1 K–2, p. 76 *NSES* PS–P[a] K–4, p. 127
Substances react with each other in characteristic ways. The periodic table predicts certain properties of the elements	*Benchmarks,* 4D/6, 6–8, p. 78–79 4D/6, 9–12, p. 80 *NSES* PS–PC[b] 5–8, p. 154 PS–SPM[c] 9–12, p. 178
Intensive properties are more reliable for distinguishing between two substances than extensive properties.	*NSES* PS–PC 5–8, p. 154
Factors That Affect Properties	
The arrangement of atoms affects the properties of a material.	*Benchmarks* 11C/5 6–8, p. 274 4D/8, 9–12, p. 80 *NSES* 9–12 PS–SPM 9–12, p. 178
The environment may play a role in the physical properties that are exhibited by a given substance or object.	*Benchmarks* 4D/2, K–2, p. 76 4D/1 3–5, p. 77 4D/4 6–8, p. 78 *NSES* PS–P K–4, p. 127
Surface- and Volume-Dependent Properties	
Some properties depend on the surface area of the material, others depend on the volume.	*Benchmarks* 11D/1, 6–8, p. 278 9C/2, 9–12, p. 225
Miscellaneous	
Standards related to miscellaneous properties of materials	*Benchmarks* 4G/4, 9–12, p. 97 9C/1, 6–8, p. 224 *NSES* E&SS–PEM[d] K–4, p. 134 PS–CR[e] 9–12, p. 179

[a] Physical Science—Properties of Objects and Materials
[b] Physical Science—Properties and Changes of Properties in Matter
[c] Physical Science—Structure and Properties of Matter
[d] Earth and Space Science—Properties of Earth Materials
[e] Physical Science—Chemical Reactions

Benchmarks, see 11D/2 6–8, p. 278; 11D/2 9–12, p. 279; and 9C/2 9–12) (AAAS 1993, p. 225), but the NSES do not. The Benchmarks focus on the difference between surface-dependent and volume-dependent properties. However, because these Benchmarks are not listed in sections related to the structure of matter, it is unlikely that they will be connected to studies of the properties of matter. For students to conceptually link relevant mathematics and science concepts, the connections must be made explicit.

In the second volume of *Atlas of Science Literacy*, two benchmarks were added that relate to the change in properties observed at the nanoscale:

> *Objects made up of a small number of atoms may exhibit different properties than macroscopic objects made up of the same kinds of atoms.* (AAAS 2007, p. 55, 8B/H5)

> *Groups of atoms and molecules can form structures that can be measured in billionths of a meter. The properties of structures at this scale (known as the nanoscale), and materials composed of such structures, can be very different than the properties at the macroscopic scale because of the increase in the ratio of surface area to volume and changes in the relative strengths of different forces at different scales. Increased knowledge of the properties of materials at the nanoscale provides a basis for the development of new materials and new uses of existing materials.* (AAAS 2007, p. 55, 8B/H6)

These new benchmarks have been incorporated into the new strand map for materials science (AAAS 2007, pp. 54–55).

Acknowledgment

The authors would like to thank Gina Ney for helpful discussions and reading of this chapter.

References

Albanese, A., and M. Vicentini. 1997. Why do we believe that an atom is colourless? Reflections about the teaching of the particle model. *Science & Education* 6: 251–261.

American Association for the Advancement of Science (AAAS). 1993. *Benchmarks for science literacy.* New York: Oxford University Press.

American Association for the Advancement of Science (AAAS). 2007. *Atlas of science literacy. Vol. 2.* Washington, DC: AAAS

Ben–Zvi, R., B.–S. Eylon, and J. Silberstein. 1986. Is an atom of copper malleable? *Journal of Chemical Education* 63 (1): 64–66.

Elghanian, R., J. J. Storhoff, R. C. Mucic, R. L. Letsinger, and C. A. Mirkin. 1997. Selective colorimetric detection of polynucleotides based on the distance-dependent optical properties of gold nanoparticles. *Science* 277: 1078–1081.

Handley, D. A. 1989a. Methods for synthesis of colloidal gold. In *Colloidal gold: Principles, methods, and applications*, ed. M. A. Hayat. San Diego: Academic Press.

Handley, D. A. 1989b. The development and application of colloidal gold as a microscopic probe. In *Colloidal gold: Principles, methods, and applications*, ed. M. A. Hayat. San Diego: Academic Press.

Kordaki, M., and D. Potari. 1998. Children's approaches to area measurement through different contexts. *Journal of Mathematical Behavior* 17 (3): 303–316.

Lesh, R., R. Post, and M. Behr. 1988. Proportional reasoning. In *Number concepts and operations in the middle grades*, ed. J. Hiebert and M. Behr. Hillsdale, NJ: Lawrence Erlbaum Associates.

McFarland, A. D., C. L. Haynes, C. A. Mirkin, R. P. Van Duyne, and H. A. Godwin. 2004. Color my nanoworld. *Journal of Chemical Education* 81 (4): 544A–544B.

Misailidou, C., and J. Williams. 2003. Diagnostic assessment of children's proportional reasoning. *Journal of Mathematical Behavior* 22 (3): 335–368.

Mock, J. J., M. Barbic, D. R. Smith, D. A. Schultz, and S. Schultz. 2002. Shape effects in plasmon resonance of individual colloidal silver nanoparticles. *Journal of Chemical Physics* 116 (15): 6755–6759.

National Research Council (NRC). 1996. *National science education standards.* Washington, DC: National Academy Press.

Zacharos, K. 2006. Prevailing educational practices for area measurement and students' failure in measuring areas. *Journal of Mathematical Behavior* 25 (3): 224–239.

Chapter **10**
Self-Assembly

Big Idea:

Under specific conditions, some materials can spontaneously assemble into organized structures. This process provides a useful means for manipulating matter at the nanoscale.

Self-assembly is the process of matter organizing autonomously and without human intervention (Whitesides, Mathias, and Seto 1991; Whitesides and Boncheva 2002). The process of self-assembly can be introduced in a range of contexts in the natural and applied sciences. In particular, it can be used to support the development of student understanding of the content described in Chapter 7, "Forces and Interactions." In this chapter, we discuss three learning goals associated with self-assembly. The order in which they are presented is not meant to suggest an order of incorporation into the curriculum.

General Prerequisite Knowledge for This Chapter

Each of the learning goals in this chapter represents a different aspect of the big idea: Self-Assembly. Although the focus of each learning goal is different, students need common prerequisite knowledge in order to develop conceptual understanding of all of them. Students must understand the following:

- Assembled structures can have different properties from their individual parts, which can lead to new and useful materials.

- In order to assemble, objects must be capable of selectively interacting with each other.

- The same set of parts may be able to assemble into different structures depending on the conditions and the processes used.

- When objects interact to create stable bound structures, net attractive forces must bring and hold them together.

- On the nanoscale, electromagnetic forces will generally dominate interactions.

Chapter 10

Learning Goal 1

Students should be able to define and describe the process of self-assembly and provide examples of the process.

Specific Prerequisite Knowledge

- Students should know that matter interacts through different types of forces.

What Students Should Learn

Self-assembly occurs when building blocks, placed in the proper environment, spontaneously assemble into a predictable, organized structure. This process occurs on every scale, from galaxy formation to DNA replication. The forces that tend to dominate the interactions depend on the scale of the assembly. Astronomical scale assemblies, such as solar systems and galaxies, are governed by gravity. At the nanoscale, electrical forces predominate, although magnetic forces can also be useful.

Before Learning About Atomic Structure

Students should be able to predict or explain the interactions between the building blocks to be self-assembled using the appropriate "rules" for the materials involved. The rules are as follows:

- Electromagnetic forces: Like charges repel and opposite charges attract.
- Hydrophobic interactions: Like substances attract and opposite substances repel.

Students should be able to apply the rules to do the following:

- Explain why flour clumps in water (hydrophobic interactions)
- Explain the mechanism for soap washing off greasy dishes (hydrophobic interactions)

- Predict how a set of electrically charged or magnetic objects of various shapes will assemble

After Learning About Atomic Structure

- Describe the phenomenon of self-assembly at the molecular level using electrical forces.

Learning Goal 2

Students should understand that many factors affect the process of self-assembly. These include the structure, composition, motion, and properties of the components to be assembled and the environment in which the assembly will take place.

Specific Prerequisite Knowledge

- Students should be able to define self-assembly and provide examples of the process (see Learning Goal 1).

Before Learning About Atomic Structure

Students must understand that

- magnets either push or pull as they interact with other magnets,
- magnets make certain things move without actually touching them, and
- shape plays a role in how objects interact. However, instead of thinking about shape as in puzzle pieces, students should think about maximizing the surfaces that interact.

After Learning About Atomic Structure

Students must understand that

- several different types of electrical forces occur between objects on the nano- and molecular scales (see Learning Goal 1 in Chapter 7, "Forces and Interactions");

- atoms consist of a positive nucleus surrounded by negatively charged electrons; and
- electrons are involved in inter-atomic interactions (See Learning Goal 1 in Chapter 6, "Structure of Matter").

Potential Student Difficulties and Misconceptions

See Learning Goals 2, 3, and 4 in Chapter 7, "Forces and Interactions," and Learning Goal 1 in Chapter 6, "Structure of Matter."

What Students Should Learn

The choice of materials, or parts, is important to the success of making something. When evaluating the materials to be assembled, several characteristics must be considered. The composition and structure will determine how the parts may interact with each other, and certain materials will be more amenable than others to interacting under a given set of conditions. In order to self-assemble into predictable, organized structures, objects must interact with each other in a specific way. The characteristics of the building blocks ensure that this can happen. (See Learning Goals 1 and 2 in Chapter 7, "Forces and Interactions.")

The environment also plays an important role in whether the building blocks will self-assemble. Components must be able to move with respect to one another in order to assemble. Therefore, characteristics such as temperature, pressure, and concentration of the different components affect how and whether the assembly will proceed spontaneously. At the nanoscale, thermal motion plays a particularly important role. In addition, the polarity and pH of the solution may also play a role. For example, ionic interactions are much weaker in water than in air, or in a vacuum, and even weaker if the solution contains ionized salts. (This is Learning Goal 3 from Chapter 7, "Forces and Interactions," applied to self-assembly.)

> *It may happen that small differences in the initial conditions produce very great ones in the final phenomena.*
>
> —Henri Poincaré, 1908

Students should be able to do the following:
- Identify and evaluate characteristics of the building blocks and environment (1) to predict how the building blocks will organize and assemble or (2) to explain why the building blocks organized themselves in the manner that they did in the final assembly.

The level at which they can do this will depend on students' previous knowledge and experiences.

Before Learning About Particle Model and Molecules

Students should be able to develop a puzzle model of interactions and explain why only certain puzzle pieces fit together.

In the classroom, self-assembly can be illustrated with these phenomena:
- The specificity of interactions with and between magnets. Elementary students learn that magnets have specificity; they are only attracted to certain materials and have directionality to their interactions with each other (AAAS 1993).
- Soap bubbles, and oil trapped in soap bubbles

Students should be able to explain qualitatively how these phenomena occur and on what variables the assembly process depends.

Chapter 10

After Learning About Particle Model and Molecules

Once students are introduced to the structure of matter at the molecular level, they can begin to consider the self-assembly of submacroscopic materials. For example, students should be able to

- explain why snowflakes are almost always hexagonal (see Figure 10.1) and
- predict how the hydrophobic and hydrophilic ends of the molecules that make up soap will behave in water, ethanol, or hexane.

Learning Goal 3

Students should understand that the process of self-assembly can be described in terms of forces and energy.

Specific Prerequisite Knowledge

Students should understand

- the content contained in Learning Goals 1 and 2;
- the concepts covered in Learning Goal 1 in Chapter 6, "Structure of Matter"; and
- the content within Learning Goals 1, 2, and 3 in Chapter 7, "Forces and Interactions."

Potential Student Difficulties and Misconceptions

- See Learning Goals 1 and 2 in Chapter 7, "Forces and Interactions," and Learning Goal 1 in Chapter 6, "Structure of Matter."

What Students Should Learn

The process of self-assembly involves the coordinated interaction of many building blocks. For the process to proceed spontaneously, the change in free energy (ΔG) between the initial and final states must be negative. It is important to consider not just the entities that are combining to form the final assembly but the whole system, including the molecules in the environment surrounding the building blocks. (This is Learning Goal 5 in Chapter 7, "Forces and Interactions," applied to the phenomenon of self-assembly.)

Note: Analyzing systems in terms of energy is an advanced concept that might be more appropriate for the second year of chemistry or physics in high school or the college undergraduate level.

Links to "Self-Assembly" in the National Science Standards

Most of the scientific concepts behind self-assembly are contained within the Forces and Interactions big idea. In addition, a thorough understanding of the building blocks to be assembled is important for explaining the process of self-assembly, thus links to concepts within the Structure of Matter are also important. However, there are some ideas that are unique to self-assembly. Table 10.1, on pages 140–141, summarizes the standards from the Benchmarks and the NSES that are not tabulated under other big ideas.

What's Missing From the National Science Standards?

Although no standards or benchmarks directly relate to self-assembly, many of the concepts related to the process (e.g., electrical forces, interactions, systems) are already found in the standards documents. Despite being represented in the standards, concepts specifically related to engineering and technology are often lacking in the current science curriculum. Self-assembly provides an opportunity for students to learn to critically evaluate and design

Figure 10.1
(a) Within the typical pressure and temperature range experienced in clouds, water molecules crystallize into a hexagonal pattern when water freezes. Dotted lines represent hydrogen bonds. (b) Therefore, snowflakes are almost always hexagonal.

a.

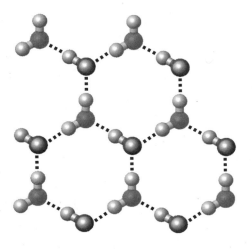

b.

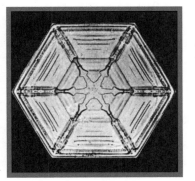

Source: Images of the ice were created using MOLMOL (Koradi, Billeter, and Wüthrich 1996). Coordinates were obtained from the *www.nyu.edu/pages/mathmol/library.* The snowflake images are from the NOAA Photo Library. The photos were taken by Wilson Bentley in 1902 for the *Monthly Weather Review.*

Chapter 10

materials and aspects of the environment in order to explain or fabricate organized, higher-order structures.

Self-assembly is a universal process that has important implications in many disciplines of science (e.g., biology, astrophysics, geology, chemistry). As such, it provides an opportunity to link fundamental concepts (e.g., forces and interactions, energy) among disciplines.

Table 10.1
National science standards containing concepts related to understanding self-assembly

Description of Content	Standard
Parts vs. Whole	
Materials are made up of parts. The function and properties of the whole may be different from those of the parts.	*Benchmarks* 11A/1 K–2, p. 264 11A/3 K–2, p. 264
The relationship of the parts affects the workings of the whole.	*Benchmarks* 11A/2 K–2, p. 264 11A/1 3–5, p. 265 11A/2 K–5, p. 264 11A/2 6–8, p. 265 11A/1 9–12, p. 266 *NSES* UCP[a] p .116
The configuration and behavior of atoms determines the properties of a larger structure (also in Chapter 6, "Structure of Matter").	*Benchmarks* 4D/7 9–12, p. 80 4D/8 9–12, p. 80 *NSES* PS–SPM[b] 9–12, p. 179
Fabrication	
Objects can be categorized as natural or fabricated.	*Benchmarks* 8B/2 3–5, p. 188 *NSES* ST[c] K–4, p. 138
The choice of materials, or components, is important to the success of making the final product.	*Benchmarks* 8B/1 K–2, p. 188
Mass production is a more efficient way of making products.	*Benchmarks* 8B/4 3–5, p. 189
Design	
Many factors must be considered in the design process.	*Benchmarks* 8B/1 6–8, p. 190 8B/4 9–12, p.191 *NSES* ST 5–8, p. 166

Table 10.1 continued

Systems	
Systems may be organized in different ways.	*Benchmarks* 11C/3 9–12, p. 275 *NSES* UCP, p. 116–117
The whole system must be considered in order to explain phenomena.	*Benchmarks* 11A/2 6–8, p. 265 11A/3 6–8, p. 265
Equilibrium	
The idea of equilibrium can help explain many phenomena.	*Benchmarks* 11C/1 6–8, p. 274 11C/2 6–8, p. 274 11C/3 6–8, p. 274 11C/1 9–12, p. 275 11C/5 9–12, p. 275 *NSES* UCP p. 118

[a] Unifying Concepts and Processes
[b] Physical Science—Structure and Properties of Matter
[c] Science and Technology

References

American Association for the Advancement of Science (AAAS). 1993. *Benchmarks for science literacy.* New York: Oxford University Press.

Koradi, R., M. Billeter, and K. Wüthrich. 1996. MOL-MOL: A program for display and analysis of macromolecular structures. *Journal of Molecular Graphics* 14: 51–55.

National Research Council (NRC). 1996. *National science education standards.* Washington, DC: NRC.

Whitesides, G. M., and M. Boncheva. 2002. Beyond molecules: Self-assembly of mesoscopic and macroscopic components. *Proceedings of the National Academy of Sciences, U.S.A.* 99 (8): 4769–4774.

Whitesides, G. M., J. P. Mathias, and C. T. Seto. 1991. Molecular self-assembly and nanochemistry: A chemical strategy for the synthesis of nanostructures. *Science* 254: 1312–1326.

Chapter **11**
Tools and Instrumentation

Big Idea:

Development of new tools and instruments helps drive scientific progress. Recent development of specialized tools has led to new levels of understanding of matter by helping scientists detect, manipulate, isolate, measure, fabricate, and investigate nanoscale matter with unprecedented precision and accuracy.

The tools that are available to scientists determine what is accessible for them to study; therefore, when new tools and instruments are developed, new worlds may become open to exploration and investigation. This accessibility leads to the types of new questions and new understandings that are essential to the scientific process. The rapid progress of the field of NSE is due, in large part, to the development of tools such as the atomic force microscope (AFM) and scanning tunneling microscope (STM) that have rendered the nanoscale world more accessible.

Four major learning goals are associated with the Tools and Instrumentation big idea. Focus can be placed on different aspects of the learning goals depending on the grade level and science context (chemistry, physics, Earth science, or biology). The order of presentation is not meant to imply an order of introduction into the curriculum.

General Prerequisite Knowledge for This Chapter

This set of learning goals requires that students have a certain amount of knowledge common to all. Students must first understand the following:

- Tools allow scientists to explore and investigate the world.

- Often, the system under study is inaccessible in some way (e.g., too far away, too small, too fast) so that scientists cannot study it using their unaided senses.

- Throughout history, tools and instruments have been developed to enhance the user's senses. For example, telescopes and light microscopes enhance vision. With these tools and instruments, scientists can better describe, characterize, and ultimately understand the universe.

- Tools may provide more reliable and reproducible ways of observing and measuring phenomena (e.g., rulers, balances).

Chapter 11

- All tools have limitations, the source of which may be due to technical considerations or to aspects of the system under investigation. Therefore, different tools are better for different purposes.

- Choosing the correct tool to investigate a given phenomenon is an important part of scientific practice.

- To choose the appropriate tool, one must consider the size of the phenomenon. To do so requires understanding the relative sizes of objects—in particular, to be able to define the "worlds" constituted by a range of sizes (e.g., macro-, micro-, nano-, and atomic worlds) and how they relate to one another (see Learning Goal 2 in Chapter 5, " Size and Scale").

- Different tools are used at different scales to visualize and manipulate matter.

Learning Goal 1

Specialized tools are required to detect, measure, and investigate the nanoscale because structures on this scale are too small to be seen with optical microscopes.

Specific Prerequisite Knowledge

Students should understand the following:

- The electromagnetic spectrum represents a broad range of wavelengths of radiation (or light). The range of wavelengths in the electromagnetic spectrum spans from gamma rays (less than 10^{-12} m) to radio waves (1–10^4 m) in length. Visible light is only a small portion of the spectrum (400–700 nm, or 4×10^{-7} to 7×10^{-7} m). Other types of radiation (or light) can be used to study otherwise inaccessible objects.

- In order to observe an object, the wavelength of the radiation must be approximately the same size or smaller than the object itself.

Potential Student Difficulties and Misconceptions

- Students may believe that it is possible to see atoms and molecules with a light microscope (Griffiths and Preston 1992; Harrison and Treagust 2002).

What Students Should Learn

Nanoscale objects are too small to see with the naked eye. A logical approach for observing something too small to see is to magnify it using a magnifying glass or optical (light) microscope. However, optical microscopes are only useful for observing objects larger than 0.2 µm (2×10^{-7} m). Diffraction limits the resolution of light microscopes to about one-half the length of wavelength of the probing radiation. In this case, the radiation is visible light. The wavelength of visible light falls between about 400 nm (4×10^{-7} m) and 700 nm (7×10^{-7} m); therefore, the smallest object that a visible light microscope can resolve is about 200 nm (2×10^{-7} m). The nanoscale is defined to be 1–100 nm (10^{-9} – 10^{-7} m) so visible light microscopes are not useful for studying the nanoscale world.

To investigate materials on the nanoscale, scientists must use different tools, some of which use radiation, or light, with a smaller wavelength, that enable smaller phenomena to be studied. Scientists use x-rays to determine the structure of molecules and other small structures. Given that atoms are about 10^{-10} m in diameter, and x-rays have a wavelength of approximately 10^{-12}–10^{-9} m, x-rays can provide atomic resolution.

Other tools include scanning electron microscopes, which use a focused beam of electrons to scan the surface of a sample. A high resolution, three-dimensional image is produced from analyzing the electrons that are back scattered. The resolution of these microscopes can reach 1 nm. Scanning probe microscopes (SPMs) use a physical probe to scan the sample. These instruments enhance the sense of touch using a very fine tip that scans over the surface of the sample, much like a finger reading a page of braille (see Figure 3.3, p. 55). In this way, the SPMs produce an image of the sample surface. These microscopes have resolved subatomic features. Different types of probes can be used to obtain information on different properties of the sample. The most common examples of SPMs are atomic force microscopes and scanning tunneling microscopes. Atomic force microscopes (AFMs) detect inter-atomic or intermolecular forces; scanning tunneling microscopes* (STMs) detect tunneling current in a sample. (See Quantum Effects in Chapter 1 for a description of the STM mechanism.) Other probes measure characteristics such as the strength and direction of magnetic forces and thermal conductivity.

The content in this learning goal will differ depending on the context in which it is introduced. Some possible learning performances follow. Students should be able to

- describe the uses and limitations of commonly used measurement tools (e.g., balance, graduated cylinder, ruler);
- describe the limitations of tools commonly used to observe and measure phenomena

that are too small to see (e.g., magnifying glass, optical microscope); and
- design a probe to create an image with high resolution.

Students should be able to answer questions such as
- How does the size of the probe affect the precision and accuracy of the measurement?

Learning Goal 2

Scientists and engineers have developed specialized tools and techniques to manipulate, isolate, and fabricate nanoscale structures.

Specific Prerequisite Knowledge
- See Learning Goal 1 of this chapter.

Potential Student Difficulties and Misconceptions
- Students may believe that tools do not exist that are small enough to work with things that are too small to see.

What Students Should Learn
People can easily use their hands to build a structure using bricks. If the building blocks are too large (e.g., steel beams, concrete blocks), special tools or machines are required to manipulate them. Likewise, when the building blocks are too small, special tools are required to manipulate them in a controlled manner. For instance, tweezers facilitate the task of lining up grains of sand in a precise pattern.

The challenge is even greater for nanoscale objects. New instruments and techniques allow scientists and engineers to work productively and efficiently at the nanoscale, and new tools provide unprecedented control over the

---

* The quantum mechanical concepts behind the function of the STM are likely more appropriate for advanced high school students or grades 13–16.

Chapter 11

building blocks of matter. Figure 11.1, page 146, illustrates how, under certain conditions, scientists were able to use an STM to arrange iron atoms in a ring configuration they call a "quantum corral." This was one of the first examples of using tools to isolate, analyze, and manipulate individual atoms in a controlled manner. Scientists and engineers also use STMs and other tools to analyze and manipulate nanoscale materials.

Figure 11.1
The process of forming a ring, or "quantum corral,"of iron atoms on a copper surface

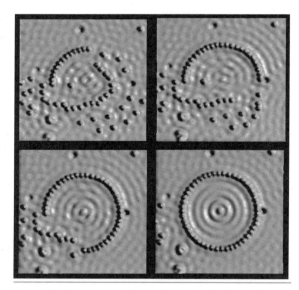

Source: Last image reprinted with permission from Crommie, M. F., C. P. Lutz, and D. M. Eigler. 1993. *Science* 262 (5131): 218–220. Copyright 1993. American Association for the Advancement of Science. All images originally created at IBM Corporation.

Eventually, students should be able to
- explain why special tools are needed to work with small objects and
- describe the challenges of working with (e.g., designing, fabricating, manipulating) nanoscale materials and provide examples

of tools that help scientists, engineers, and manufacturers overcome these challenges.

Learning Goal 3

Although the nanoscale world has always existed in nature, scientists and engineers were unable to study it, or to manufacture new nanoscale structures, until advances in technology allowed the development of highly specialized and sensitive tools.

Specific Prerequisite Knowledge
- See Learning Goal 1 in this chapter.

Potential Student Difficulties and Misconceptions
- Students may believe that an optical microscope can be used to observe and measure nanoscale objects and atoms (Griffiths and Preston 1992; Harrison and Treagust 2002).

What Students Should Learn
Throughout history, the development of tools has initiated huge leaps in scientific knowledge. The telescope opened up the universe beyond Earth, and the optical microscope led to profound changes in the understanding of the structure and function of living organisms. As with these examples, the nanoworld has always existed, but little was known about it before tools were developed that made it accessible to study.

One example is proteins, which are nanoscale objects that perform an enormous number of functions necessary for the survival of all organisms. In the late 18th century, protein was known as a biological substance with particular characteristics. By the mid–19th century, scientists determined that proteins are made primarily of carbon, nitrogen, hydrogen, oxygen, and small amounts of phosphorus and sulfur. It was not until the mid–20th century that it was conclusively shown that proteins consist of chains of amino acids. In the 1960s, the first high (atomic) resolution protein structure was determined using x-ray crystallography. Determining these structures has provided great insight into how proteins function. Today, new tools such as cryo-electron microscopy and atomic force microscopy are pushing the understanding of the relationship between protein structure and function forward by giving near atomic resolution in certain environments. Through their studies of the structure and function of proteins, scientists have developed a better understanding of the important biochemical processes that maintain life.

The development of scanning probe microscopes, especially AFMs and STMs, has rendered the nanoscale more accessible than ever before and has helped scientists and engineers observe, measure, manipulate, and fabricate nanoscale materials. These tools and others are a driving force behind the scientific progress of the nanotechnology revolution.

By the end of the lessons, students should be able to

- evaluate the advantages and disadvantages of observing or measuring phenomena using a particular tool or technique and
- explain the difference between direct and indirect measurement.

Students could explore questions such as the following:

- If we can't see something, how do we know it's there?
- What is the relationship between technological and scientific progress?
- How has the development of new tools affected scientific models of the structure and behavior of matter?

These questions can be applied to different phenomena depending on the context (e.g., biology might include proteins, DNA, ribosomes; chemistry applications might include surfaces, lattice structures).

Also, students should be able to explain the relationships among (1) the tools that enable the study of scientific phenomena, (2) the observations and measurements they provide, and (3) the models that they have informed historically and in the present.

Learning Goal 4
The tools used to study and/or manipulate nanoscale structures interact with individual atoms or nanoscale particles by means of electrical forces.

Specific Prerequisite Knowledge
Students should understand the following:
- Learning Goal 1 in Chapter 7, "Forces and Interactions"
- Learning Goal 1 in Chapter 6, "Structure of Matter"

In order to understand the mechanism of the STM, students need to know certain quantum mechanical ideas (see Learning Goals 1 and 3 in Chapter 8, " Quantum Effects").

Potential Student Difficulties and Misconceptions
Students may believe that
- scanning probe microscopes work similarly to optical microscopes and
- images produced with scanning probe microscopes are the same as "seeing" something through an optical microscope (Harrison and Treagust 2002).

Chapter 11

What Students Should Learn

The development of scanning probe microscopes (SPMs) has allowed scientists and engineers to study and manipulate matter at an unprecedented scale. While optical microscopes extend the sense of sight by magnifying objects too small to be seen, scanning probe microscopes extend the sense of touch. These microscopes actually interact with the sample as they make an image of its surface. The size of the probe determines the potential resolution. Therefore, in order to observe and measure objects at the nanoscale, the tip of an SPM probe must also be of nanoscale size or smaller.

The most prevalent types of SPMs (i.e., AFM and STM) interact with the sample via electrical forces, which are much stronger than the gravitational force between objects on the nano- and atomic scales. An atomic force microscope (AFM) uses a metal probe that tapers down to a point with a radius less than 10 nm; sometimes the point may be a single atom (Hembacher, Giessibl, and Mannhart 2004). This probe scans the surface of the sample and detects the interatomic and intermolecular forces between the probe and the surface to create an image. An AFM can measure surfaces with atomic resolution and has even resolved subatomic features.

Before Learning About Atomic Structure

- Electrical forces dominate interactions on the nanoscale (see Chapter 7, "Forces and Interactions").

After Learning About Atomic Structure

- Students should be able to relate the electrical forces that govern chemical bonding to the electrical forces the AFM uses to observe a sample.

Links to "Tools and Instrumentation" in the National Science Standards

From the earliest grades, students learn that one's own abilities are limited and that tools can facilitate, and are often even necessary for, making and working with some objects. In addition, tools are not only used to create objects but also to study them in order to understand them better. National science standards related to the Tools and Instrumentation big idea are summarized in Table 11.1 on page 149.

What's Missing From the National Science Standards?

Although the national science standards discuss the importance of using tools to investigate phenomena that are otherwise inaccessible, they do not provide explicit links to scale. Scientists often define the scale of a phenomenon by the tool with which they can investigate it (e.g., the optical microscope is required to observe the microscale), so explicitly linking the choice of tool for observing a phenomenon with its scale is an important connection for students to make.

Tools play an important role in scientific and technological progress, yet the standards do not explicitly discuss how particular tools work. Many NSE researchers and educators give priority to having students learn how scanning probe microscopes create images (see Learning Goal 4 of this chapter). If this is prioritized, then these questions arise: Should the way other instruments work also be included in the curriculum? Or should the emphasis be only on the relationship between the tools and scientific and technological advancement? These are questions that must be addressed both for NSE and other disciplines.

Table 11.1
Summary of national science standards related to tools and instrumentation

Description of Content	Standard
Tools	
Tools help extend human capabilities.	*Benchmarks* 8B/3 K–2, p. 188 3A/1 K–2, p. 44 6A/2 3–5, p. 129 3A/2 3–5, p. 45 3A/3 3–5, p. 45 3A/4 3–5, p. 45 *NSES* SI[a] K–4, p. 123 SI 5–8, p. 148 SI 9–12, p. 176
Technology is constantly advancing, which also affects the development of tools.	*Benchmarks* 3A/1 3–5, p. 45
New and better tools can help to improve efficiency, quality, and quantity of manufactured items.	*Benchmarks* 8B/1 9–12, p. 191
Relationship Between Science and Technology	
Science and technology often drive each other.	*Benchmarks* 3A/2 6–8, p. 46 3A/3 6–8, p. 46 3A/1 9–12, p. 47 *NSES* ST– UST[b] 9–12, p. 192

[a] Science as Inquiry
[b] Science and Technology–Understandings About Science and Technology

Acknowledgment

The authors would like to thank César Delgado for helpful discussions and reading of this chapter.

References

American Association for the Advancement of Science (AAAS). 1993. *Benchmarks for science literacy.* New York: Oxford University Press.

Griffiths, A. K., and K. R. Preston. 1992. Grade 12 students' misconceptions relating to fundamental characteristics of atoms and molecules. *Journal for Research in Science Teaching* 29 (6): 611–628.

Harrison, A. G., and D. F. Treagust. 2002. The particulate nature of matter: Challenges in understanding the submicroscopic world. In *Chemical education: Towards research-based practice*, ed. J. K. Gilbert, O. De Jong, R. Justi, D. F. Treagust, and J. H. Van Driel. Dordrecht, The Netherlands: Kluwer Academic Publishers.

Hembacher, S., F. J. Giessibl, and J. Mannhart. 2004. Force microscopy with light-atom probes. *Science* 305: 380–383.

National Research Council (NRC). 1996. *National science education standards.* Washington, DC: NRC.

Chapter 12
Models and Simulations

Big Idea:

Scientists use models and simulations to help them visualize, explain, and make predictions and hypotheses about the structures, properties, and behaviors of phenomena (e.g., objects, materials, processes, systems). The extremely small size and complexity of nanoscale targets make models and simulations useful for the study and design of nanoscale phenomena.

Models and simulations are used throughout the scientific process. Because of their importance in all scientific disciplines, students should develop knowledge of and skills relating to models and simulations throughout the science curriculum. The size and complexity of nanoscale phenomena make models and simulations important for helping students to develop conceptual understanding of NSE.

Students should develop understanding of two broad learning goals for this big idea. Similar learning goals can be applied in many contexts in the science curriculum.

General Prerequisite Knowledge for This Chapter

Prerequisite knowledge common to both of these learning goals is as follows:

- Models are representations of a certain target (e.g., an object, process, or system).

- Models are often used when the target is inaccessible in some way.

- Some characteristics of the target will be represented in a model more accurately than others.

- Models do not necessarily have to look like the target.

- Testing a model's predictions against real data enables a person to assess the usefulness of the model. If necessary, the model should be refined and tested against more data until it more reliably explains and predicts.

Learning Goal 1

Every model has limitations to its accuracy and usefulness. Specific models are designed to make particular aspects of nano-, molecular, and atomic scale phenomena apparent and may not accurately represent other characteristics.

Chapter 12

Specific Prerequisite Knowledge

- Students should understand Learning Goal 1 in Chapter 6, "Structure of Matter."
- Students should have knowledge of electrical forces and the various types of interactions. This knowledge may be necessary to evaluate nano- and atomic scale models (see Learning Goal 1 in Chapter 7, "Forces and Interactions").

Potential Student Difficulties and Alternative Ideas

Students may believe

- that models must look exactly like the target, only larger or smaller (Grosslight et al. 1991; Justi and Gilbert 2002) and/or
- that there can only be one correct model for any given target (Grosslight et al. 1991).

What Students Should Learn

Different models may be useful for representing a given target, as each model represents different aspects of the target more (or less) accurately. The purpose of the model determines which aspects of the target should be emphasized and which are less important. For example, several different models are useful when considering molecules (see Figure 12.1). Lewis structures identify the chemical composition of the molecule as well as certain bond characteristics (i.e., single, double, triple). Ball-and-stick models clearly illustrate the type and arrangement of atoms, but do not represent the relative sizes of the atoms or the distances between them. Space-filling models better represent the relative size and distance between the atoms, but characteristics such as multiple bonds will not be evident. In addition, in more complex molecules, all atoms may not be visible, so a full understanding of the arrangement

Figure 12.1

Multiple representations of carbon monoxide: (a) Lewis structure (b) Lewis dot structure (c) Ball-and-stick model (d) Space-filling or CPK model

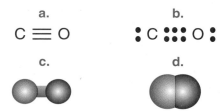

and composition may not be possible. Lewis dot structures illustrate the mode of the interactions between atoms but lack other physical characteristics of the components.

Models and simulations play an important role in developing an understanding of all scientific disciplines. Given any phenomenon under study, students should be able to do the following:

- Explain when and why it is useful to use models and simulations
- Explain the role of models and simulations in scientific and technological progress
- Explain when and why it might be useful to use several different models to represent a target
- Evaluate and justify which model (or type of model) is better for representing different aspects of the target
- Evaluate and justify which type of model is best for representing a given target for a given purpose
- Explain when and why models might change

Before students have a model of atomic structure, they can consider these topics in relation to any scientific phenomena introduced into the classroom. After students have a model of atomic structure, they can begin to consider not only atoms and molecules but also nanoscale targets. They can also evaluate classical versus quantum mechanical models for explaining the behavior of matter.

Learning Goal 2

Various types of models (physical, computer, mathematical) are used to represent, to help us better understand, to make predictions, and to generate questions about the structure and behavior of matter at the macro-, micro-, and nanoscales.

Specific Prerequisite Knowledge

- Learning Goal 1 in this chapter.
- To apply these ideas to nanoscale phenomena, students should understand atomic structure as described in Learning Goal 1 in Chapter 6, " Structure of Matter."

Potential Student Difficulties and Misconceptions

Students may incorrectly believe

- that models are representations of fact. Many students may not understand the important role that models and simulations play in the process of scientific inquiry (Treagust, Chittleborough, and Mamiala 2002; Grosslight et al. 1991);
- that models must look exactly like the target—just be larger or smaller (Treagust, Chittleborough, and Mamiala 2002);
- that models must be able to be touched. Students may not realize that there can be mathematical, computer, and symbolic models (Grosslight et al. 1991); and/or
- that there can be only one model for any given target (Grosslight et al. 1991).

What Students Should Learn

Scientists work to explain the world and they use models and simulations to help them do so. For instance, models and simulations may help develop explanations of the structure or function of a target, generate hypotheses or questions about a target, or help make decisions about improving an existing target or designing a new, alternate one. Models can take many forms. They can be physical representations that can be touched and manipulated or they may be computer-based; they may be static or dynamic. Several different models may represent a given target, each illustrating or emphasizing different aspects of the target. Thus, a model is always a compromise as to what aspects of the target to emphasize. The purpose of the model largely determines its form and its usefulness.

Models are used not only to explain the structure or function of a target but also to make predictions about how a target may behave—even if it does not exist yet. For example, when scientists and engineers are building a new structure, system, or process, models and simulations may help predict their success or failure. They may use models and simulations to explore how a proposed target might behave or how it might react to a different set of conditions. In this way, scientists and engineers can make predictions about properties and behaviors of the final product. Thus modeling and simulations are an essential part of technological development, particularly of design and fabrication. An NSE example is the use of models and simulations to predict how building blocks might interact during a self-assembly process. Figure 12.2 (p. 154) depicts a simple model that predicts how a set of materials may self-assemble.

Chapter 12

Figure 12.2
Illustration of a self-assembly process. Red must be next to white; white must be next to red.

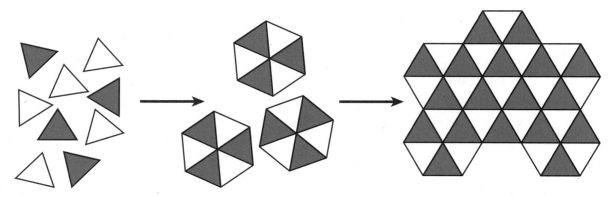

Models are not like facts, illustrating the right answer; instead, they are constantly reevaluated according to new evidence, and they change and evolve as new knowledge is incorporated. Recent examples of scientific models that have changed are good topics for classroom discussion:

- Pluto was recently reclassified from a planet to a dwarf planet (Vedantam 2006).
- Some dinosaurs were likely warm-blooded, which puts their classification as reptiles into question (Fisher et al. 2000).
- Intensive properties (e.g., conductivity, melting point), which traditionally have been defined as properties that do not change with the amount of sample, do indeed change when the size (or amount) of materials transitions through the nanoscale, thus altering accepted models of the behavior of matter.

Students should be able to do the following:

- Construct and choose appropriate models to explain the aspects of the target in which they are interested. Students' justification should include discussion of the purpose of the model, its limitations, which aspects are emphasized and which are not and why, and which aspects are more and less accurately represented.
- Build and use models (and simulations when appropriate) to facilitate the design of various products (e.g., machine, tool, or process). Students should explain how the models are important to the process of design. Students' justifications should include discussion of the purpose of the model, its limitations, which aspects are emphasized, which are not emphasized (and why), and which aspects are more or less accurately represented.

Links to "Models and Simulations" in the National Science Standards

Both the Benchmarks and the NSES consider models to be a critical concept in science literacy. The Benchmarks designate models as a "common theme" that extends beyond a single discipline to all areas of science, mathematics, and engineering and even beyond the physical sciences. Likewise, the NSES discuss models as one of the "unifying concepts and processes" in science (NRC 1996, p. 117). In addition, the NSES link models to the nature of science and scientific inquiry, where building a model or explanation should be the students' goal.

Many specific standards relate to models and modeling. As students move from early elementary to high school, they should build an understanding of what a model is, what it can be used for, how it can be used, and what limitations a given model has. Standards related to models and simulations are presented in Table 12.1.

What's Missing From the National Science Standards?

Although the central role that models and modeling play in all aspects of scientific practice is discussed in both standards documents, the topic is often largely neglected in the science classroom. For example, in chemistry, students are expected to move between macroscopic phenomena, symbolic representation, and a variety of structural models of the microscopic structure. Yet research has documented that students commonly struggle to make sense across multiple representations (Kozma and Russell 1997). Perhaps discipline-specific learning goals related to models should be developed in order to make the connection between a model and the content clearer to students. The use of models is especially important for NSE because nanoscale phenomena are inaccessible due to size and often due to complexity as well.

In the classroom, the educative power of models and modeling is commonly underestimated. Often models are presented to the students by the teachers as a representation of the scientific idea, which may lead students to believe that models are ways of representing scientific laws or facts or, worse yet, that models are the phenomena themselves. However, models and simulations play an important role throughout the scientific process. Scientists use models and simulations to help them visualize, explain, and make predictions and hypotheses about the structures, properties, and behaviors of a broad range of targets. Scientists build and use models throughout the scientific process. It can be argued that models and modeling are the very nature of science, so it is important for students to develop knowledge and skills about them as they develop knowledge related to NSE and other science content.

Table 12.1
Summary of national science standards related to models and simulations

Description of Content	Standard
Using Models	
Models can help us learn about phenomena.	*Benchmarks* 11B/2 K–2, p. 268 11B/3 K–2, p. 268 11B/1 3–5, p. 268
Models help us consider phenomena that are inaccessible in some way.	*Benchmarks* 11B/1 6–8, p. 269
More than one model can be used to represent the same phenomenon. The type of model used depends on its purpose.	*Benchmarks* 11B/3 6–8, p. 269 9C/4 9–12, p. 225

Table 12.1 continued on page 156

Table 12.1 continued

Comparing the model to observations of the target can test how useful the model is.	*Benchmarks* 11B/3 9–12, p. 270
Types of Models	
Models can come in many different forms (e.g., pictorial, physical, mathematical). A model does not necessarily have to look like the target.	*Benchmarks* 11B/1 K–2, p. 268 11B/2 3–5, p. 268 11B/2 6–8, p. 269 9C/4 3–5, p. 223 9C/3 9–12, p. 225
Mathematical models are valuable tools for thinking about scientific phenomena. Like all models, they have strengths and limitations.	*Benchmarks* 2A/1 3–5, p. 27 2C/1 6–8, p. 37 2C/2 6–8, p. 37 11B/1 9–12, p. 270 9B/3 9–12, p. 220 2B/1 9–12, p. 33 2C/2 9–12, p. 38 *NSES* SI* 5–8, p. 145 SI 9–12, p. 175
Graphs, charts, and tables are different ways of representing data and relationships. They can be useful for making sense of data, making predictions, and finding patterns.	*Benchmarks* 9C/3 3–5, p. 223 9B/2 3–5, p. 218 9B/3 6–8, p. 219 9C/4 6–8, p. 224 9B/4 9–12, p. 221
Computers can play a role in building and using models. It is often useful to display models on a computer.	*Benchmarks* 11B/2 6–8, p. 269 11B/2 9–12, p. 270
Simulations	
Modeling and simulations are useful for designing new products and can help scientists and engineers make decisions about factors involved in fabricating new materials or systems (e.g., starting materials, types of processes, environmental factors).	*Benchmarks* 2B/1 9–12, p. 33

* Science as Inquiry

Acknowledgment

The authors would like to thank Harry Short for helpful discussions and reading of this chapter.

References

American Association for the Advancement of Science (AAAS). 1993. *Benchmarks for science literacy.* New York: Oxford University Press.

Fisher, P. E., D. A. Russell, M. K. Stoskopf, R. E. Barrick, M. Hammer, and A. A. Kuzmitz. 2000. Cardiovascular evidence for an intermediate or higher metabolic rate in an ornithischian dinosaur. *Science* 288: 503–505.

Grosslight, L., C. Unger, E. Jay, and C. Smith. 1991. Understanding models and their use in science: Conceptions of middle and high school students and experts. *Journal of Research in Science Teaching* 28 (9): 799–822.

Justi, R. S., and J. K. Gilbert. 2002. Modelling, teachers' views on the nature of modelling, and implications for the education of modellers. *International Journal of Science Education* 24 (4): 369–387.

Kozma, R. B., and J. Russell. 1997. Multimedia and understanding: Expert and novice responses to different representations of chemical phenomena. *Journal of Research in Science Teaching* 34 (9): 949–968.

National Research Council (NRC). 1996. *National science education standards.* Washington, DC: National Academy Press.

Treagust, D. F., G. Chittleborough, and T. L. Mamiala. 2002. Students' understanding of the role of scientific models in learning science. *International Journal of Science Education* 24 (4): 357–368.

Vedantam, S. 2006. "For Pluto, a smaller world after all." *Washington Post*, Aug. 25.

Chapter 13
Science, Technology, and Society

Big Idea:

The advancement of science involves developing explanations for how and why things work and using technology to apply that knowledge to meet objectives, solve problems, or answer questions of societal interest. Because nanotechnology is an emergent science, it provides an opportunity to witness and actively participate in scientific progress and in decision making about how to use new technologies.

NSE is "science in the making" and can be used to illustrate the dynamic nature of science to students (Smalley 2005). Instead of experiencing science in an abstract and historical manner, with NSE, students can witness the advances and struggles of scientists and engineers in real time. They can evaluate how well nanotechnology lives up to the promises presented in the popular media, as well as how accurately the media represent science and technology to society.

NSE provides students with opportunities to play an active role in the processes of science and technology and their relationships with society. Students can learn how to make informed decisions about whether to buy products that incorporate nanotechnology, they can contact politicians about science- and technology-related policies, and they can evaluate how new products might affect their health or the health of the environment.

Experiencing the nature of scientific and technological progress naturally fits into any science class. Likewise, the relationships of science and technology to society can find a place in social studies classrooms. These relationships are given superficial treatment, if any, in most science classes, however, and are generally ignored in grades 7–12 social studies.

Four major learning goals are associated with this big idea (science, technology, and society). The order in which they are presented here is not meant to suggest an order of introducing the learning goals into the curriculum.

General Prerequisite Knowledge for This Chapter

Prerequisite knowledge common across the learning goals associated with this big idea includes the following:

- The work of scientists is to describe, explain, and predict the way the world works.

- Engineers design, build, and analyze products that address practical problems.

- The phenomena (e.g., objects, systems, processes) that scientists study can be biological, physical, or social.

Chapter 13

- Much can be learned about how things work by observing them, and sometimes even more can be learned by purposefully changing something and observing the effects of that change.

- Results of scientific inquiry can sometimes support competing explanations, and different scientific studies sometimes result in different (even contradictory) conclusions. In these cases, further investigation should be undertaken in an attempt to resolve differences, but sometimes decisions have to be made under conditions of uncertainty.

- Although scientists have developed extensive knowledge about the world, much remains undiscovered and unknown. Thus, the process of science will never be finished.

Learning Goal 1

Nanoscale science and engineering (NSE) is an illustration of the dynamic nature of scientific progress and the development of technology.

Specific Prerequisite Knowledge

None beyond the general prerequisite knowledge.

Potential Student Difficulties and Misconceptions

Students may believe either or both of the following ideas:

- Science is not a process, but a static collection of facts (Duschl, Schweingruber, and Shouse 2007; Smith 2000).

- Science is a linear process; all experiments work (Smith 2000).

What Students Should Learn

Science is not a static set of facts, but a dynamic process of building knowledge about how the natural world works. This process is not linear, as both successful and failed investigations can generate new knowledge and questions. Scientific advancement is an ongoing process. For example, the recent discovery of the novel properties of matter observed at the nanoscale has forced scientists to modify their models of the structure and behavior of matter. They are currently developing new knowledge regarding the nanoworld and will continue to adapt their models to better explain nanoscale materials.

> *Results! Why, man, I have gotten a lot of results. I know several thousand things that won't work.*
>
> —Thomas Edison, 1890

Nanotechnology is the application of scientific knowledge about the behavior of matter at the nanoscale to solve practical problems. Design, fabrication, modeling, and prototyping are all part of the engineering process that leads to technological progress. Technological advances have resulted in providing easy access to food, sanitation, health care, communication, and transportation for many people, but they have sometimes given rise to unanticipated and undesirable outcomes as well. The new discoveries that scientists have made regarding the nanoworld are being applied to solve practical problems (e.g., drug delivery) and meet societal objectives (e.g., renewable energy). Efforts are also under way to prevent new risks arising from nanotechnologies (e.g., government regulations) (see Learning Goal 4).

Although scientific disciplines such as biology, chemistry, physics, and Earth science are generally taught separately in the science curriculum, in reality, boundaries blur as interdisciplinary thinking becomes the norm. Historically, when scientists who specialize in one discipline turn their expertise toward the problems of another, rapid advances ensue (e.g., biotechnology). NSE incorporates all scientific disciplines as it represents the study and fabrication of nanoscale phenomena and materials.

It is important that students bring a certain ragamuffin, barefoot, irreverence to their studies; they are not here to worship what is known, but to question it.

—Jacob Chanowski, n.d.

The content within this learning goal can be applied in many contexts. Students might explore questions such as the following:

- What are the implications of changes that have recently been made to the models that scientists use to explain the structure and behavior of matter? (This question can be raised after students have studied atomic structure.)
- How are science and technology related?
- Are products made with new technologies necessarily better than the products they replace?

Learning Goal 2

Scientists, engineers, governments, businesses, and citizens all make decisions that affect the progress of science and technology and how new technologies are incorporated into society.

Specific Prerequisite Knowledge

Students should have basic knowledge and skills regarding decision making, including the following:

- Any decision typically involves weighing advantages and disadvantages. Choices have consequences that are not always positive.
- Due to insufficient resources, not everyone can have what he or she wants. Therefore, the benefits and costs of a decision may not be weighted equally.
- The consequences of choices are not always predictable, no matter how carefully a decision was made.
- A different decision may be appropriate in different circumstances. People may make different decisions because they prioritize differently.

Potential Student Difficulties and Misconceptions

Students may believe the following:

- Only some people play a role in the advancement of science and technology.
- The students themselves cannot play a role in the advancement of science and technology or how it is used.

What Students Should Learn

Technology plays a role in meeting our basic needs for survival (i.e., food, clothing, and shelter), as well as improving our communication, transportation, and medical treatments. As such, introduction of new technologies has the potential to affect many aspects of society. However, technology itself does not impose change on society; it is people—*all* people— who drive societal change. Governments, businesses, and other agencies make decisions about what types of scientific research should

Chapter 13

be prioritized and what types of technological solutions should be applied. Scientists and engineers make decisions about which paths to follow during the process of scientific progress. Individuals—as both consumers and voters—create demand for new technologies that can guide both the path of technological advancement as well as the degree to which technologies affect daily life. These decisions are currently ongoing in regard to NSE. The U.S. government considers NSE a priority and is, therefore, providing extensive funding for NSE research and development (Roco 2001, 2004). In addition, it is predicted that a large number of nano-literate workers will be needed in the future to meet anticipated needs, which also makes NSE an educational priority.

> *It is a capital mistake to theorise before one has data. Insensibly one begins to twist facts to suit theories instead of theories to suit facts.*
>
> —Sherlock Holmes, the fictional creation of Arthur Conan Doyle (1859–1930)

The popular media commonly make claims about nanotechnology—its benefits, its new applications, its promise. However, many of the reports focus on *potential* applications that are not yet reality. In addition, new technologies are not always better than old ones and may not provide added benefits relative to the old. Likewise, additional benefits from the new products may not outweigh the costs (e.g., monetary, individual, societal, environmental). Some individuals or groups benefit from the introduction of new technologies more than others do. It is important for citizens to be able to critically evaluate media reports regarding NSE in order to make informed decisions regarding both. Individuals must gather and consider evidence without relying solely on the decisions of others (e.g., the government, newspapers, television, and online media).

The relationship between science, technology, and society is complex. Here we present some potential questions for students to consider as they develop an understanding of their roles in that relationship:

- How does technology affect my life?
- Are new technologies always better than old ones? How do we know?
- How does the manner in which scientific results and technological advances are represented in the popular media affect the relationships between science, technology, and society?
- How can individuals influence decisions regarding NSE that are made by politicians and the scientists, engineers, and institutions that carry out research and development?
- How can I make good decisions regarding new technologies such as nanotechnology?

Learning Goal 3

Scientific advancement, even a single scientific discovery or new invention, may induce extensive changes in scientific thought and/or contribute to changes in many facets of society.

Specific Prerequisite Knowledge

Students should understand the following:

- Humans are able to make tools and machines to alter their environment. Therefore, they have a significant effect on other living organisms and the environment.
- The changes that humans make to the environment with technologies may create hazards and may affect the rates of natural change.
- The content contained in Learning Goal 1 of this chapter.

Potential Student Difficulties and Misconceptions

Students may believe the following:

- If they want to have "people-helping" careers, students might believe that their choices are limited to roles such as medical professional, social worker, teacher, or policy maker. It may not occur to students that scientists and engineers can also be "people helpers."
- Scientists find answers and then they are done exploring and explaining (Duschl, Schweingruber, and Shouse 2007).
- Scientists never change the way they think something works (Duschl, Schweingruber, and Shouse 2007).

(The last two beliefs above go back to the idea that science is a static set of ideas, rather than a dynamic process.)

What Students Should Learn

Sometimes scientific or technological advances result in major shifts or leaps in scientific knowledge. James Watson and Francis Crick interpreted Rosalind Franklin's data to develop a model of the double-helical structure of DNA. This single model opened the door to knowledge related not only to the mechanism of the storage and replication of genetic information, but also eventually to the regulation of life processes, the treatment of diseases, and many biotechnological advances. The development of the quantum mechanical model changed the way that scientists viewed and studied the natural world. The idea that reality is not necessarily what it seems extended beyond the natural sciences to affect the work of people such as philosophers and artists in the early 20th century. Scientists apply the quantum mechanical model to explain the newly discovered novel properties of matter observed at the nanoscale.

Likewise, the development of new tools (technologies) often makes new worlds accessible, which in turn leads to broad and extensive scientific advances. The microscope and telescope opened unseen worlds and changed the way we considered our place in the universe. When new tools such as scanning probe microscopes were developed to make the nanoworld accessible, a tremendous amount of new information was, and still is, being generated (see Chapter 11, "Tools and Instrumentation," for further discussion). This new information continues to change the way scientists and engineers think about the properties and behaviors of matter.

New inventions and scientific discoveries can contribute to changes beyond the scientific community. For example, Edward Jenner and Jonas Salk each developed vaccines for diseases that affected thousands, perhaps millions of people. Based on their initial work, smallpox has been eradicated from the human population (WHO 1980) and polio is close to eradication. Alexander Fleming discovered penicillin, which began the study and production of antibiotics for the treatment of many types of bacterial infections. Like the development of vaccines, this discovery saved many lives. At the turn of the 20th century, the Wright brothers built and flew the first airplane. A century later, airplane travel has changed the way distant peoples can interact. At the age of 15, Philo Farnsworth outlined a plan for an electronic television. His invention changed the entertainment industry and how we communicate and contributed to the advent and growth of personal computers (monitors). Thus, the work of a single person or a small group of people can affect the lives and values of many individuals, and sometimes all of society.

Chapter 13

The effects that new scientific knowledge or new technology may have on scientific progress, and on society in general, are often uncertain. The introduction of new technologies may be limited to modest improvement of the status quo or contribute to major social or economic changes (Miller et al. 2007). The recently discovered properties of matter at the nanoscale continue to provide scientists and engineers with new ideas and materials that they are applying toward solving problems related to an extensive range of areas, including medical diagnostics and treatment, building materials, energy, and water purification. Many predictions continue to be made regarding the contribution that nanotechnology will make to the quality of people's lives and to the economy. However, imagination often surpasses the ability of scientists and engineers to apply the new technology. Because NSE is a new field, the extent to which nanotechnology will ultimately affect the economic and social environments is unclear.

Questions that students may consider regarding new ideas, discoveries, or technologies and their relationships to scientific progress include the following:

- What determines whether a new scientific discovery is revolutionary, evolutionary, or incremental?
- How often do revolutionary discoveries occur?
- Is nanotechnology evolutionary or revolutionary?

Here are examples of ideas that students might explore regarding how new ideas, discoveries, or technologies relate to society.

- How do science, technology, and society relate to each other?
- Are the effects of nanotechnology only felt in the realm of consumer products?
- How might nanotechnology affect life at home?
- How might nanotechnology affect _____ (e.g., medical treatment, transportation, communication)?
- What are the economic consequences for the introduction of nanotechnologies?
- Are new technologies always better than the ones that they are replacing? What types of things should be considered when comparing two technologies?
- What happens when technologies are rendered obsolete?
- What kind of product may have an effect similar to _____ (e.g., television, personal computers, cell phones)?

Learning Goal 4

Nano-size structures must be evaluated in terms of their risks and benefits to human health and the environment. Because these are new materials, their effects may not be apparent for some time.

Specific Prerequisite Knowledge

Students should understand the following:

- Although the outcome of an event is uncertain, the probability of a particular outcome can be used to make predictions.
- When making informed decisions, people must examine evidence in order to weigh the advantages and disadvantages of the issue in question.
- Evidence-based reasoning should be used to justify decisions. It is important to consider evidence carefully rather than relying solely on the decisions of others (e.g., the government, newspapers, television, online sources) regarding new technologies.

- Technologies are created to solve practical problems and meet objectives.
- In addition to the benefits, new technologies may have drawbacks. These benefits and drawbacks may not be shared equally.
- Regardless of how carefully the decisions regarding the design and implementation of a new technology are made, any given technology may still create new, unexpected problems or benefits.

Potential Student Difficulties and Misconceptions

Students may believe the following:

- Scientific ideas are facts and therefore scientists (or students) have no reason to question those ideas (Duschl, Schweingruber, and Shouse 2007).
- New products and technologies are always better than old ones.
- When technologies and new products are developed to solve problems, there are no side effects or negatives.

What Students Should Learn

Technology is often developed to meet an objective or to solve a problem or question of interest. However, the same technology that solves one problem may cause others. Sometimes the new problems may be worse than the ones the new technology solved.

New knowledge about the behavior of matter at the nanoscale has led scientists to create new technologies, and many more may be forthcoming. To make informed decisions about new technologies, people must look at problems in multiple ways and consider a range of factors. These factors include the advantages and disadvantages of developing and using any new technology. The advantages and disadvantages may be immediate, local, personal, and/or distant in both time and place. In addition, the advantages may benefit (or the disadvantages may cause difficulties) for only a subset of society. Informed decisions regarding new technologies require weighing each of these factors.

When new technologies such as nanoscale materials are developed, it is important to examine the effects they might have on human health, on the health of other living organisms, and on the environment. Even a small change made to a system can result in a larger change in the way the system works. In addition, detrimental effects of a new technology may not be immediately apparent.

Ideas related to risk assessment are associated with a wide range of contexts. Some questions that students could explore include the following:

- Why does it take so long to know if technologies like nanotechnology are dangerous?
- Why should or shouldn't we test new nanoscale materials on animals?
- What effects can nanoscale materials have on living organisms?
- What process and criteria does the Food and Drug Administration (FDA) use to evaluate new technologies (e.g., drugs or devices)?
- What kinds of decisions have government agencies made about nanoscale materials and technologies?
- Is there a difference between natural and engineered nanoparticles as far as their effects on living organisms and the environment?
- Who decides who will receive the greatest benefits and who will pay the highest costs in the development and use of new nanotechnologies?

Chapter 13

- How does the funding for risk assessment of nanotechnologies compare with research and development funding?

Students can develop decision-making skills by considering these and other important questions. In particular, using evidence-based reasoning to justify their conclusions supports scientific inquiry skills.

Links to "Science, Technology, and Society" in the National Science Standards

An important part of science literacy is understanding the nature of science and the nature of technology. Scientific and technological advances affect the evolution of many aspects of society. It is important for students to understand the relationships between science, technology, and society and to see their roles as citizens in those relationships. Table 13.1 summarizes the national science standards related to these critical ideas.

What's Missing From the National Science Standards?

Although the Benchmarks and the NSES do not mention NSE directly, they do thoroughly discuss the nature of science and the relationships among science, technology, and society. Unfortunately, despite the extensive representation in the standards documents, little focus has been placed on introducing these important ideas into the science curriculum. Perhaps that is because science teachers, although they have confidence in their knowledge of this discipline, may lack the training necessary to discuss societal issues in the classroom (Miller et al. 2007).

As members of a society in the midst of a "nanotechnology revolution," students can be part of that revolution. They can witness the processes that scientists use when confronted with new phenomena. They can see how engineers use their understandings to create new applications to address a range of problems. Students can participate in debates about the usefulness and the cost-benefit ratio of these applications to society so that they are prepared to participate in critical decision-making processes.

Table 13.1
National science standards related to the nature of science, the nature of technology, and the relationships between science, technology, and society

Description of Content	Standard
Nature of Science	
Science is a dynamic process.	*Benchmarks* 1B/1 K–2, p. 10 1B/3 K–2, p. 10 1B/3 3–5, p. 11 1B/4 3–5, p. 11 1A/2 6–8, p. 7 1A/3 6–8, p. 7 1A/2 9–12, p. 8 1A/3 9–2, p. 8 1B/2 9–12, p. 13 1B/6 9–12, p. 13 1B/7 9–12, p. 13 *NSES* H&NS[a] K–4, p. 141 H&NS 5–8, p. 171 H&NS 9–12, p. 201
Different methods are used to explore the broad range of ideas, systems, processes, and phenomena that scientists study.	*Benchmarks* 1B/1 3–5, p. 11 1B/1 6–8, p. 12 1B/3 9–12, p. 13 1C/4 9–12, p. 19 *NSES* SI[b] K–4, p. 123 SI 5–8, p. 148 SI 9–12, p. 176 ST[c] 9–12, p. 192
Nature of Technology	
The goals of science and technology are different. Technology applies knowledge to solve problems.	*Benchmarks* 3C/2 3–5, p. 54 3A/1 3–5, p. 45 3A/4 3–5, p. 45 3A/3 6–8, p. 46 3A/1 9–12, p. 47 3A/2 9–12, p. 47 3A/3 9–12, p. 47 *NSES* ST K–4, p. 138 ST 5–8, p. 166 ST 9–12, p. 192–193

Table 13.1 continued on page 168

Chapter 13

Table 13.1 continued

Many factors must be considered when designing and fabricating new technologies. It may take many trials to be successful.	*Benchmarks* 3B/1 K–2, p. 49 3B/1 3–5, p. 49 3B/2 3–5, p. 50 3C/4 3–5, p. 55 3B/1 6–8, p. 51 3B/1 9–12, p. 52 *NSES* ST 5–8, p. 166

Relationships Between Science, Technology, and Society

Because of its focus on problem solving, technology generally has a more direct influence on the lives of individuals and society. Technology has affected most aspects of human life, from basic requirements for survival (e.g., food, clothing, and shelter) to transportation and communication.	*Benchmarks* 3C/1 K–2, p. 54 3A/4 3–5, p. 45 3C/1 3–5, p. 54 3A/3 6–8, p. 46 3C/1 6–8, p. 55 3A/3 9–12, p. 47
A strong relationship exists among science, technology, and society. For example, scientists cannot always choose what they study. In many cases, societal needs and challenges drive the direction of scientific research. In addition, the government and others who fund research set priorities for scientific research.	*Benchmarks* 3C/1 3–5, p. 54 3C/3 3–5, p. 54 1C/3 6–8, p. 17 3A/2 6–8, p. 46 3C/4 6–8, p. 56 3C/5 6–8, p. 56 3C/7 6–8, p. 56 1C/3 9–12, p. 19 1C/8 9–12, p. 20 3C/1 9–12, p. 57 *NSES* SPSP[d] K–4, p. 140 SPSP 5–8, p. 169 SPSP 9–12. p. 199

Plan Vs. Outcome

Introducing something new into a system can have unexpected effects on how the system works. These effects can be extensive and perhaps disruptive.	*Benchmarks* 1C/3 K–2, p. 15 3C/5 3–5, p. 55 3C/4 9–12, p. 57 3C/5 9–12, p. 57 *NSES* SPSP K–4, p. 140 SPSP 5–8, p. 168 SPSP 9–12, p. 199

Table 13.1 continued

Decision Making	
All decisions have trade-offs, so many factors must be carefully considered. Decisions may have benefits for some but negative consequences for others. These consequences may be immediate, or they may affect later generations.	*Benchmarks* 7E/2 K–2, p. 168 7E/3 3–5, p. 169 7D/3 3–5, p. 165 3C/6 6–8, p. 56 7D/1 6–8, p. 166 7D/2 6–8, p. 166 7D/3 6–8, p. 166 3B/2 9–12, p. 52 3C/4 9–12, p. 57 7D/1 9–12, p. 166 7D/2 9–12, p. 166 7D/3 9–12, p. 166 *NSES* SPSP K–4, p. 140 ST 5–8, p. 166 SPSP 5–8, p. 169 ST 9–12, p. 192 SPSP 9–12, p. 199
It is important for citizens to analyze the risks and benefits of the production and introduction of new technologies because they may bring unexpected and extensive consequences.	*Benchmarks* 3C/2 K–2, p. 54 3C/5 3–5, p. 54 3B/2 6–8, p. 51 3C/5 6–8, p. 56 3B/4 9–12, p. 52 3C/3 9–12, p. 57 3C/5 9–12, p. 57 *NSES* ST 5–8, p. 166 SPSP 5–8, p. 169 SPSP 9–12, p. 199
All members of society must be involved in decisions regarding new technologies. In solving one problem, new technologies may create others. For that reason, the benefits and costs of new technologies must be evaluated, which requires decision-making skills.	*Benchmarks* 7D/1 K–2, p. 165 7D/2 K–2, p. 165 7D/3 K–2, p. 165 7D/1 3–5, p. 165 7D/2 3–5, p. 165 3C/3 3–5, p. 54 3C/5 3–5, p. 55 3C/5 6–8, p. 56 *NSES* SPSP K–4, p. 141

[a] History and Nature of Science
[b] Science as Inquiry
[c] Science and Technology
[d] Science in Personal and Social Perspectives

Chapter 13

Acknowledgment

The authors would like to thank Clark Miller for helpful discussions and reading of this chapter.

References

Duschl, R. A., H. A. Schweingruber, and A. Shouse, eds. 2007. *Taking science to school: Learning and teaching science in grades K–8.* Washington, DC: National Academies Press.

Miller, C., D. Guston, D. Barben, J. Wetmore, C. Selin, and E. Fisher. 2007. *Nanotechnology & society: Ideas for education and public engagement.* Tempe, AZ: Center for Nanotechnology in Society.

Roco, M. C. 2001. From vision to the implementation of the U.S. National Nanotechnology Initiative. *Journal of Nanoparticle Research* 3: 5–11.

Roco, M. C. 2004. The U.S. National Nanotechnology Initiative after three years (2001–2003). *Journal of Nanoparticle Research* 6: 1–10.

Smalley, R. E. 2005. Future global energy prosperity: The terawatt challenge. *MRS Bulletin* 30: 412–417.

Smith, D. C. 2000. Content and pedagogical content knowledge for elementary science teacher educators: Knowing our students. *Journal of Science Teacher Education* 11 (1): 27–46.

World Health Organization (WHO). 1980. Smallpox is dead. *World Health* (May): 3–39.

SECTION

3

Next Steps

Chapter **14**
Challenges and Strategies

As we have seen in this book, nanoscale science and engineering (NSE) research has already led to many new products in our lives—for example, electronics, sunscreen and cosmetics, and clothing made of advanced fabrics. Ongoing NSE research focuses on a range of larger societal issues, including sustainable energy, water purification, and medical diagnostics and treatments.

As our society becomes more dependent on NSE technologies, children globally will grow up in a world in which they will need to apply NSE ideas. As consumers, they will need to answer questions such as, What are the effects that using this product will likely have on me or the health of my family? As voters, they will need to consider, What might be the long-range effects of nanoscale waste on the environment? Without a firm understanding of NSE big ideas, young people will not have the foundation for further learning or for making sound decisions that will affect their daily lives and those of their children.

In terms of educating today's students, we have made significant advances in what we know about how people learn (Bransford, Brown, and Cocking 1999; Linn and Eylon 2006); however, these advances are not regularly or systematically applied in school settings. As we argued in this book's Introduction (pp.xi–xv), the current educational system is failing to produce a populace scientifically literate enough to understand the advances of NSE. Students are not being prepared for the workplace of the future.

In this book, we showed how the big ideas of NSE provide a foundation for and guidance to those in a position to fill in these gaps in the current science curriculum. Although we have chosen to address teachers, who most directly influence student learning, clearly curriculum developers, researchers, administrators, and policy makers also must recognize the importance of new directions in science education.

Challenges to the Goal of an NSE-Educated Citizenry

We foresee five challenges to developing an NSE-educated citizenry.

Challenge #1: Ensuring Educational Preparation of All U.S. Citizens

To keep up with growing demands on their scientific literacy, Americans will need a new, 21st-century skill set, of which NSE is an essential component. Evidence for this is ubiquitous. During the decade before this book was written (2009), cell phones and the internet revolutionized the way people communicated and exchanged information. Computer technology is prominent in the workplace and in an increasing number of homes. NSE helped these and other developments to occur.

Students must learn NSE concepts in grades 7–12 so that they become informed decision makers in a global, technology-based

Chapter 14

economy. To become interested in NSE, young people need teachers who will make them aware of the opportunities offered by the nanotechnology revolution

This is an urgent education situation. Why? Because science changes rapidly, yet the technological advances that permeate daily life are not necessarily reflected in classroom learning. Although the call for urgent reform may seem exaggerated, assessment data reveal the degree to which students in the United States are underprepared to live in a world built on science and technology. International assessments provide evidence that U.S. students' performance in science is declining relative to that of students in many other developed countries, and many students are not succeeding on national measures of science success.

On the 2003 National Assessment of Educational Progress, for example, less than one-third of U.S. students in grades 4 and 8 scored at or above proficient levels in math and science. By the 12th grade, only 20% of U.S. students scored at or above proficiency. Of 21 nations for whom data was reported in the 1999 International Math and Science Study (Schmidt, Rotberg, and Siegel 2003; NCES 2004), U.S. 12th-grade students ranked 19 of 21 in math and 16 of 21 in science. To ensure the continued economic prosperity and quality of life that Americans currently enjoy, we must maintain a leadership role in science and technology, a role that hinges on quality science, technology, and mathematics (STEM) education.

Challenge #2: Reforming Science Education

According to the well-known joke, if Rip Van Winkle were to awaken in the 21st century, he'd find everything virtually unrecognizable—except schools. The educational system in this country is simply not keeping pace with changes in science and technology. Educators need to revise the curriculum as well as materials, assessments, and instructional methods to reflect these changes.

In addition, the interdisciplinary nature of NSE (and other emerging science) necessitates erasure of the curricular demarcations customarily supported in U.S. schools. Science education is traditionally presented in a discipline-defined rather than cross-disciplinary manner. That is, biology, chemistry, physics, and Earth science are typically taught in separate units at the middle school level and in separate courses at the high school level. Yet, atoms and molecules, for example, are the foundation of science across these disciplines. An emphasis on the particle nature of matter as a cross-disciplinary big idea would make those interdisciplinary connections clearer.

Interdisciplinary big ideas encourage learners to build integrated knowledge structures, to apply their knowledge to a range of situations, and to develop deeper conceptual understanding than is likely when concepts and ideas are presented in more isolated contexts. In the world outside school, after all, science laboratories that are the source of major breakthroughs are often made up of interdisciplinary, collaborative teams.

Challenge #3: Choosing Which NSE Concepts to Address

Before beginning to incorporate NSE into the STEM curriculum, basic questions must be answered: Which NSE-related topics are most important? Which ones *should* be incorporated into the curriculum? Which ones *can* be incorporated into the curriculum? At what grade level is it appropriate to introduce a given concept? Where in the instructional sequence do concepts logically belong so that they build on what came before and what will follow? How do new ideas related to NSE connect with the ideas that are already a part of the traditional science curriculum? How should new topics be prioritized relative to traditional science concepts?

This book, which came about as the result of a consensus process (see Appendix A for a description of the process), begins to answer the first few questions regarding what content related to NSE is appropriate for grade 7–12 learners, but the other questions are still to be examined.

For NSE concepts to be incorporated into U.S. classrooms, they must be articulated in ways that make sense to stakeholders in education. In addition, new NSE concepts must be recognized as being on a par with other learning goals described in national consensus documents such as the *National Science Education Standards* (NRC 1996) and *Benchmarks for Scientific Literacy* (AAAS 1993) on which school curricula are based. However, to ensure that the already burgeoning curriculum does not result in even more superficial coverage of far too many concepts, challenging decisions must be made about what to include and when. This must be done by reviewing existing standards and benchmarks, considering emergent topics, then evaluating and prioritizing. Choosing to focus on big ideas is one way to guide these important curricular decisions.

Challenge #4: Designing a Coherent Science Curriculum

Identifying the big ideas of nanoscale science is but a starting point for building curriculum coherence. As discussed in the Introduction, *coherence* refers both to aligning instruction with assessment and to sequencing instruction around a small set of ideas that are organized to support learners in developing integrated understanding across time (Schmidt, Wang, and McKnight 2005; Shwartz et al. 2008). Experts in learning recognize that for students to develop sophisticated understanding of complex science, they must build from foundational understandings in ways that relate concepts and principles across disciplines.

Current instructional materials generally do not adequately emphasize connections between new ideas and students' prior knowledge (Kesidou and Roseman 2002). Building on previous knowledge helps learners construct integrated understanding (Bransford, Brown, and Cocking 1999; Kali, Linn, and Roseman 2008) necessary for solving problems and making decisions. To support this type of learning, curriculum materials must be coherent; they must build links among concepts and support the development of integrated understanding over time.

Although big ideas provide the understanding we hope students will reach by the end of their K–12 education, significant work remains to be done to determine how to help learners reach the level of understanding described in this book. For any given big idea, we also need to consider learning sequences, instructional techniques, and assessments that will help students to meet learning goals. However, curriculum materials seldom emphasize explicit connections between ideas, particularly across grade levels, resulting in a piecemeal science curriculum. Moreover, materials often present content in a declarative way, without considering what key learning experiences students need to have had in order to develop deeper levels of understanding of the content. As a result, students experience science as a series of unconnected ideas. Such an approach cannot help students develop understanding of complex ideas such as intermolecular forces or size-dependent properties, for which making connections is of fundamental importance.

Chapter 14

Challenge #5: Teacher Preparation

To successfully introduce NSE into the classroom, teachers must develop associated pedagogical content knowledge (PCK)—that is, knowledge of how to teach a certain content area so that students in grades 7–12 can make sense of it (Shulman 1986). Subject matter knowledge is one critical component of PCK (Magnusson, Krajcik, and Borko 1999). Unfortunately, many experienced teachers studied science well before NSE ideas and the phenomena they explain had emerged or were incorporated into college classrooms. Given that reality, teaching NSE will pose a challenge even to science teachers at the secondary level, who have majored in a discipline and may have advanced degrees in it, but do not have deep understanding of the big ideas of NSE. In fact, as the novel properties of matter at the nanoscale have been discovered and new nanotechnologies developed, scientists have had to reorganize their own knowledge regarding the structure and behavior of matter. Teachers must now do the same thing: make connections among ideas and incorporate new ideas into their current content knowledge.

To meet the goal of treating NSE as a unifying topic to be interwoven within and across disciplines, teachers must develop new curricular knowledge, another aspect of PCK (Shulman 1986). Curricular knowledge involves understanding the goals and objectives of a discipline (Magnusson, Krajcik, and Borko 1999; Shulman 1986) and includes understanding how an individual concept or learning goal fits within the overall curriculum. Because of the interdisciplinary nature of NSE, curricular knowledge related to NSE is especially important.

Teaching content so that students understand it is at the core of successful teaching (Shulman 1986; Magnusson, Krajcik, and Borko 1999). Teachers need to know how to integrate various examples, analogies, phenomena, and activities into the subject they are teaching. They must also be aware of the difficulties that students are likely to have learning the content as well as the types of ideas (including misconceptions) that students may bring into the classroom (Grossman 1990).

Integrating NSE Concepts Into the Existing STEM Curriculum

What should grade 7–12 science education look like in order for these goals to be achieved? Although consensus documents that define science literacy, such as the NSES and Benchmarks, play an important role in establishing the foundation of science education, they do not necessarily reflect emerging science, of which NSE is one example. In part, this is because the nanotechnology revolution was in its infancy when these documents were initially written (the NSES were published in 1996 and the Benchmarks were published in 1993).

Creating a "living document" that reflects new science is an important first step in guiding the development of new educational materials, assessments, teacher preparation practices, and instructional methods that emphasize the problem-solving and collaborative skills necessary for participation in a global economy. In fact, the American Association for the Advancement of Science, following participation in one of the nanoscience workshops described in Appendix A, modified existing learning goals and created new ones related to NSE in the latest version of its strand maps (AAAS 2007).

A related question is *how* NSE should be introduced. In the past, emerging science topics were taught as separate entities, frequently as stand-alone units, and the links between traditional science ideas and new ones were not emphasized. A better strategy would be to systematically integrate new science ideas into the curriculum, creating a more interdisciplinary curriculum in the process. Connections between NSE and traditional mathematics and science must be explicit, addressed not only within a single class but across grade levels as well. To achieve this, materials must be developed that support learning core principles and that align with standards.

Having agreed-upon learning goals for NSE will help ensure that all components of the educational system can be coordinated. That is, once learning goals are defined and developed, then curriculum, instruction, and assessment can be systematically aligned. Learning goals drive state assessments, which, in turn, drive the development of materials, resources, and teacher education. Aligning all parts of the system to learning goals fosters the development of instructional tools and resources, educational experiences for teachers, research studies, and policies focused on these same critical ends (NRC 2001; Wilson and Berenthal 2006). If rationally connected and coherent within and across grades (Shwartz et al. 2008), materials developed based on these learning goals can help students develop a thorough understanding of relevant science concepts and understand the importance of NSE in their lives.

In addition, learning goals must be sequenced such that ideas build on previous knowledge (Bransford, Brown, and Cocking 1999; Kali, Linn, and Roseman 2008). Researchers and policy makers have recently referred to the study of how ideas build on each other to develop more integrated understanding as learning progression research. The sequencing of ideas to build deeper and more sophisticated levels of understandings is thus referred to as learning progressions (Smith et al. 2006; Wilson and Berenthal 2006). We need further research to determine learning progressions, to determine what students *can* learn at various age and grade levels, and to determine which experiences best help them learn challenging concepts.

Future Directions

The big ideas of NSE can begin to provide guidance and vision as to *what* science content should be taught, although establishing *when* particular concepts should be taught will require further research. While the big ideas of NSE are interdisciplinary, cutting across content areas, they are certainly not exhaustive for all of science education. The same process of establishing big ideas, explicating their content, and determining related learning goals could be applied to other big ideas, such as Newton's laws of force and motion, evolution, or certain geological processes.

Concluding Comments

As society becomes more reliant on nanoscale technologies, it is critical that all learners develop an understanding of the big ideas of NSE. By focusing on a few big ideas, teachers and curriculum developers can design instructional materials to help learners understand the core ideas that explain a broad range of phenomena. Future research needs to address how it is that NSE big ideas develop over time and which learning environments best support all students in developing these ideas in a variety of contexts. Future policy must include funding for research and development that addresses our needs for a scientifically literate citizenry for the 21st century.

References

American Association for the Advancement of Science (AAAS). 1993. *Benchmarks for science literacy*. New York: Oxford University Press.

Chapter 14

American Association for the Advancement of Science (AAAS). 2007. *Atlas of science literacy. Vol. 2.* Washington, DC: AAAS.

Bransford, J. D., A. L. Brown, and R. Cocking, eds. 1999. *How people learn: Brain, mind, experience and school.* Washington, DC: National Academy Press.

Grossman, p. 1990. *The making of a teacher: Teacher knowledge and teacher education.* New York: Teachers College Press.

Kali, Y., M. C. Linn, and J. E. Roseman, eds. 2008. *Designing coherent science education.* New York: Teachers College Press.

Kesidou, S., and J. E. Roseman. 2002. How well do middle school science programs measure up? Findings from Project 2061's curriculum review. *Journal of Research in Science Teaching* 39 (6): 522–549.

Linn, M. C., and B. Eylon. 2006. Science education: Integrating views of learning and instruction. In *Handbook of educational psychology,* 2nd ed., ed. P. A. Alexander and P. H. Winne. Hillsdale, NJ: Lawrence Erlbaum Associates.

Magnusson, S., J. S. Krajcik, and H. Borko. 1999. Nature, sources and development of pedagogical content knowledge for science teaching. *Examining pedagogical content knowledge: The construct and its implications for science education,* ed. J. Gess-Newsome and N. Lederman, 95–132. Dordrecht, The Netherlands: Kluwer Academic Publishers.

National Center for Education Statistics (NCES). 2004. *Highlights from the Trends in International Mathematics and Science Study: TIMMS 2003.* (NCES #2005005). Washington, DC: U.S. Government Printing Office.

National Research Council (NRC). 1996. *National science education standards.* Washington, DC: National Academy Press.

National Research Council (NRC). 2001. *Knowing what students know: The science and design of educational assessment,* ed. J. W. Pelligrino, N. Chudowsky, and R. Glaser. Washington, DC: National Academy Press.

Schmidt, W. H., I. C. Rotberg, and A. Siegel. 2003. *Too little too late: American high schools in an international context.* Washington, DC: Brookings Institution.

Schmidt, W. H., H. C. Wang, and C. C. McKnight. 2005. Curriculum coherence: An examination of US mathematics and science content standards from an international perspective. *Journal of Curriculum Studies* 37 (5): 525–559.

Shulman, L. 1986. Those who understand: Knowledge growth in teaching. *Educational Researcher* 15 (2): 4–14.

Shwartz, Y., A. Weizman, D. Fortus, J. Krajcik, and B. Reiser. 2008. The IQWST experience: Using coherence as a design principle for a middle school science curriculum. *Elementary School Journal* 109 (2): 199–219.

Smith, C. L., M. Wiser, C. W. Anderson, and J. Krajcik. 2006. Implications of research on children's learning for standards and assessment: A proposed learning progression for matter and the atomic molecular theory. *Measurement: Interdisciplinary Research and Perspectives* 14 (1 and 2): 1–98.

Wilson, M. R., and M. W. Berenthal. 2006. *Systems for state science assessment.* Washington, DC: National Academy Press.

Resources

The following books and articles were used as general resources in the preparation of this book.

Atkins, P. W. 1990. *Physical chemistry*. 4th ed. New York: W. H. Freeman.

Atkins, P. W. 1991. *Quanta: A handbook of concepts*. 2nd ed. Oxford: Oxford University Press.

Baggott, J. E. 2004. *Beyond measure: Modern physics, philosophy, and the meaning of quantum theory*. Oxford: Oxford University Press.

Birdi, K. S. 2003. *Scanning probe microscopes: Applications in science and technology*. Boca Raton, FL: CRC Press.

Brucale, M., G. Zuccheri, and B. Samori. 2006. Mastering the complexity of DNA nanostructures. *Trends in Biotechnology* 24 (5): 235–243.

Cotton, F. A., C. Lin, and C. A. Murillo. 2001. Supramolecular arrays based on dimetal building units. *Accounts of Chemical Research* 34 (10): 759–771.

Daniel, M.-C., and D. Astruc. 2004. Gold nanoparticles: Assembly, supramolecular chemistry, quantum-size-related properties, and applications toward biology, catalysis, and nanotechnology. *Chemical Reviews* 104: 293–346.

Dirac, P. A. M. 1991. *The principles of quantum mechanics, Vol. 27. The international series of monographs on physics*, ed. J. Birman, S. W. Edwards, C. H. Llewellyn Smith, and M. Rees. Oxford: Oxford University Press.

El-Sayed, M. A. 2001. Some interesting properties of metals confined in time and nanometer space of different shapes. *Accounts of Chemical Research* 34 (4): 257–264.

El-Sayed, M. A. 2004. Small is different: Shape-, size-, and composition-dependent properites of some colloidal semiconductor nanocrystals. *Accounts of Chemical Research* 37 (5): 326–333.

Feynman, R. P. 1995. *Six easy pieces*, ed. R. B. Leighton and M. Sands. New York: Basic Books.

Feynman, R. P. 1960. There's plenty of room at the bottom. *Engineering and Science* 23 (5). *www.its.caltech.edu/~feynman/plenty.html*

Glotzer, S. C., M. J. Solomon, and N. A. Kotov. 2004. Self-assembly: From nanoscale to microscale colloids. *American Institute of Chemical Engineers Journal* 50 (12): 2978–2985.

Gu, Q. F., G. Krauss, W. Steurer, F. Gramm, and A. Cervellino. 2008. Unexpected high stiffness of Ag and Au nanoparticles. *Physical Review Letters* 10 (4): 045502.

Johnson, K. L., K. Kendall, and A. D. Roberts. 1971. Surface energy and the contact of elastic solids. *Proceedings of the Royal Society of London A* 324: 301–313.

Kelly, K. L., E. Coronado, L. L. Zhao, and G. C. Schatz. 2003. The optical properties of metal nanoparticles: The influence of size, shape, and dielectric environment. *Journal of Physical Chemistry B* 107: 668–677.

Resources

Kushner, D. J. 1969. Self-assembly of biological structures. *Bacteriological Reviews* 33 (2): 302–435.

Lagae, L., and W. V. Roy. 2007. Harnessing the electron spin in nano-electronic devices. *MicroNano News* (June): 16–19.

Link, S., and M. A. El-Sayed. 2000. Shape and size dependence of radiative, non–radiative and photothermal properties of gold nanocrystals. *International Reviews in Physical Chemistry* 19 (3): 409–453.

Mott, N. F. 1968. Metal-insulator transition. *Reviews of Modern Physics* 40 (4): 677–683.

Stroscio, J. A., and D. M. Eigler. 1991. Atomic and molecular manipulation with the scanning tunneling microscope. *Science* 254: 1319–1326.

Stryer, L. 1988. *Biochemistry.* 3rd ed. New York: W. H. Freeman.

Wischnitzer, S. 1981. *Introduction to electron microscopy.* Elmsford, NY: Pergamon Press.

Wise, F. W. 2000. Lead salt quantum dots: The limit of strong quantum confinement. *Accounts of Chemical Research* 33 (11): 773–780.

Appendix A
The Process of Determining the Big Ideas

The *National Science Education Standards* (NSES) (NRC 1996), *Benchmarks for Science Literacy* (Benchmarks) (AAAS 1993), and *Science for All Americans* (Rutherford and Algren 1990) argue for a scientifically literate citizenry and schools that support the development of such a populace. In turn, school districts align curriculum, instruction, and assessment with selected national, state, and local standards. Students' knowledge is measured against those standards, and teachers are held accountable for their students meeting the standards. But nanoscale science and engineering (NSE) concepts are not currently explicit in these national consensus documents. To create a nano-literate population, scientists, educators, researchers, and curriculum developers must ask more specifically, "What does it mean to be '*nano*-literate'"?

Big Ideas of NSE: Grades 7–12

In June 2006, the National Science Foundation (NSF) funded a national workshop—the Nanoscience Learning Goals Workshop in Menlo Park, California—that was dedicated to identifying and reaching consensus on the key concepts, or "big ideas," of nanoscience that would be appropriate for grades 7–12. The workshop participants also set out to develop nanoscience learning goals

The three-day workshop was held jointly by the National Center for Learning and Teaching (NCLT) and SRI International. Thirty-three leading scientists and science educators, chosen to represent scientific disciplines that are involved in nanoscale science and engineering research, learning sciences, and science education, participated in the workshop (see the list of participants in Appendix B).

This group of experts included basic and applied scientists (engineers) whose research focuses on problems related to chemistry, physics, and biology. Other participants brought expertise in learning sciences and in both formal and informal science education. They came together with two goals: (1) to develop a consensus on just what the "big ideas" are in NSE and (2) to determine how those ideas might be introduced into the U.S. science curriculum.

The participants identified and articulated the core principles of NSE and justified why they believed each principle to be critical to the discipline. Participants then explicated the meaning of each core principle and developed related grade 7–12 learning goals to support each of the big ideas. For each learning goal they identified the prior knowledge required to understand it and they specified what students would need to know and be able to do to adequately represent their understanding after the teaching was complete. Finally, participants determined how the learning goals aligned with the NSES and the Benchmarks and identified places in these documents that were insufficient regarding

Appendix A

NSE. Below we discuss the smaller steps taken in the process just described.

Brainstorming

Before attending the session, individuals were asked to suggest three ideas or principles they believe to be most important for NSE. Upon arriving at the workshop, the participants took the first few minutes to brainstorm the most important ideas or principles for understanding the field of NSE and those that would be considered critical to the progress of the field of NSE. Ideas were assembled, posted, and shared among participants.

Classifying the Critical Principles and Topics

A subset of participants was asked to group the ideas into related categories. A dozen such categories resulted. All participants then discussed the logic of the groupings and worked to further consolidate them. A tentative consensus of six broad topic areas was reached:

- Size and Scale
- Particulate Nature of Matter
- Properties of Matter
- Self-Assembly and Dominant Forces
- Tools and Modeling
- Technology and Society

Agreement was not unanimous as to these groupings; in fact, several points of contention arose in the discussion. At this point in the process, contentious issues were assigned to subgroups to discuss further, taking into consideration everyone's perspectives. The subgroups then brought back to the whole group more focused points of discussion.

Articulating and Clarifying the Big Ideas

Given the list of six topic areas identified as critical for understanding and advancing the field of NSE, participants divided into six working groups, one for each topic. Each group was purposely made up of scientists, engineers, and educators. The groups were asked to articulate the general topic as a principle or big idea, clarify and elaborate on it, and then provide justification for considering it a "big idea" in NSE. In the articulation process, participants also specified related concepts and possible links and described the prior knowledge needed to understand the big idea.

Although identifying the big ideas of nanoscience was the beginning point of the workshop, the goal was not to frame nanoscience as an entity separate from science more generally. Rather, it was to focus on what students needed to know to understand NSE-related concepts based on the notion that the nanoscale is where the largest gap in educators' and students' understanding of matter lies. This is true both because NSE is an emerging field and because it is not part of most teachers' background knowledge or store of curriculum materials. National science standards address macroscale and microscale concepts, but the nanoscale is virtually absent from these documents; thus it is absent from K–12 curricula.

Small working groups articulated the big ideas. They also expanded and clarified the big ideas by identifying the major concepts and principles underlying each one and by identifying necessary prior knowledge. The workshop leaders asked participants to state the ideas in language that described student learning and to avoid jargon and esoteric language. The goal was that the final document would be accessible to those who were interested in NSE but were not necessarily familiar with the language and ideas of NSE.

Working groups presented the articulation, clarification, and justification of each big idea for evaluation and discussion in the entire group. Groups also reported their decisions about the contentious issues raised during the classification step. At this point, more focused discussion helped the large group come to a general consensus, although not unanimous agreement.

Next, participants returned to working groups to develop Learning Goals that supported the big ideas outlined in the clarification step. Learning goals, in general, define what students are expected to know and be able to do and often have an application component. In this case, multiple learning goals were established for each big idea; the goals would likely span several years of instruction. Because of the interconnected nature of many scientific ideas, a single learning goal may also be associated with multiple big ideas.

Determining Learning Goals

Educators know that learning goals are useful for guiding instructional design, classroom teaching and activities, and assessment. As such, a set of coherent, focused learning goals is important when introducing new ideas into the science curriculum. At the workshop, each working group attempted to think in terms of learning goals by grade-level bands (i.e., grades 7–8, 9–10, or 11–12). This task included expressing precisely what students would need to know to meet the learning goal and how the students should be able to apply that knowledge. In addition, groups considered what prerequisite knowledge is needed in order to understand a particular big idea and to meet particular learning goals. Groups also considered alternative student conceptions (including misconceptions) and potential or documented difficulties (as described in research literature). Ultimately, all of the Learning Goals were presented to the entire group for evaluation and discussion.

Illustrative Phenomena

Scientific research focuses on efforts to explain the world as people know and experience it. Providing students with phenomena that they can personally experience gives them a parallel goal to the learning goal of a lesson and a connection to scientific inquiry. In addition, linking student experiences to instruction has been shown to be a successful motivational strategy (Alexander, Jetton, and Kulikowich 1995). Real-world phenomena can be used as anchoring events for instruction and can provide students with a reason to work toward desired learning goals (Singer et al. 2000).

To this end, workshop participants generated descriptions of illustrative phenomena that could be used in curriculum materials to give students a context for whatever big idea they are studying. For example, growing plants in water alone illustrates that plants do not require an external food source in order to grow. That experiment can be altered to prove that light, carbon dioxide, and water are the necessary requirements for plants to survive. In the same way, identifying familiar phenomena that illustrate aspects of the big ideas can help students learn about nanoscience.

Linking Big Ideas and Learning Goals to Standards

On the final day, working groups refined the learning goals and began to identify links between the NSES and the Benchmarks. The groups suggested ways in which these two documents might be modified to incorporate NSE-

Appendix A

related concepts; the groups also noted ideas that were missing and need to be added.

Refining Workshop Products

After the workshop, its products—statements of the big ideas, the learning goals, links to the standards—were refined by members of the organizing team and then posted on a wiki page for ongoing editing and comment by workshop participants.

Big Ideas of NSE: Grades 13–16

Two months after the June 2006 national workshop, an NCLT Faculty Nanoscale Science and Engineering Education (NSEE) Workshop was held at California Polytechnic State University at San Luis Obispo. Participants discussed what big ideas would be appropriate for grade 13–16 students. Thirty-two faculty members from 17 institutions participated in the workshop. One-quarter of the participants represented community colleges; three-quarters represented four-year colleges and universities.

This group drew up a final list of big ideas that was somewhat different from the 7–12 list developed in the earlier workshop. It was made up of the following nine big ideas:

- Size and Scale
- Surface-to-Volume Ratio
- Quantum Mechanics
- Size-Dependent Properties
- Self-Assembly
- Surface-Dominated Behavior
- Tools and Instrumentation/Characterization
- Models and Simulation
- Societal Impact and Public Education (Wansom et al. 2009).

Ongoing Vetting Processes

Following the June and August workshops, the "Big Ideas of Nanoscience" for grades 7–12 and grades 13–16 were presented at the NCLT center-wide meeting in November 2006. Members of NCLT and participating collaborators debated the big ideas and attempted to reconcile the differences between the two sets of ideas. More specifically, discussion ensued as to whether the grade 7–12 set was complete or whether any ideas should be removed.

The overlap in the principles identified for secondary and postsecondary education is presented in Table A.1.

Lively discussions ensued. The group agreed that Dominant Forces should be its own big idea rather than be combined with Self-Assembly. The Dominant Forces big idea was subsequently renamed Forces and Interactions in order to include the energetic component of interactions. In addition, at another workshop for middle school and high school teachers, the teachers suggested that the term *interactions* could be used to introduce ideas related to nanoscale recognition events before students fully understand electrical forces.

NCLT members also decided that Surface-to-Volume Ratio from the grades 13–16 list should be categorized under one of the other big ideas—either Size and Scale or Size-Dependent Properties/Properties of Matter. The authors of this book ultimately chose to have Size and Scale encompass the mathematical framework that connects to the science content, so surface area-to-volume ratio is included there. Likewise, content related to Surface-Dominated Behavior was subsumed by Size-Dependent Properties/Properties of Matter and Forces and Interactions. The focus on surface-dominated properties moved to Size-Dependent Properties and the important role of induced dipole interactions was included primarily in Forces and Interactions.

Quantum Mechanics was added as a big idea. It is the model that must be used to

Table A.1
Core principles of nanoscale science and engineering identified at two workshops

Nanoscience Learning Goal Workshop (Grades 7–12)	National Center for Teaching and Learning (NCTL) Faculty Workshop (Grades 13–16)
Size and Scale	Size and Scale
Properties of Matter	Size-Dependent Properties
Particulate Nature of Matter	
Tools	Tools and Instrumentation/Characterization
Modeling	Models and Simulations
Technology and Society	Societal Impact/Public Education
Self-Assembly	Self-Assembly
(Dominant Forces)	Surface-Dominated Behavior
	Surface-to-Volume Ratio
	Quantum Mechanics

predict and explain behavior at the nanoscale. (Later, at the 2007 K–12 & Informal Nanoscale Science and Engineering Workshop, the vote was nearly unanimous for quantum mechanical concepts to be included in the grades 7–12 big ideas. For grade 7–14 students, this includes only a basic, qualitative understanding of the quantum mechanical model. Because only some aspects of quantum mechanics are important for explaining nanoscale phenomena, especially at the grades 7–16 level, the big idea was renamed Quantum Effects.)

The Particulate Nature of Matter remained a big idea, but only for grades 7–12. University educators assume that students at the postsecondary level understand the concepts contained within this big idea, although a large body of research suggests that few students develop a deep understanding of accepted models of matter before they reach college (e.g., Nakhleh 1992; Harrison and Treagust 2002; Çalik and Ayas 2005). The authors of this book renamed the big idea Structure of Matter to better encompass

the different levels of organization of matter—atoms, molecules, nanoscale assemblies—that are included in the content. Learning goals for the remaining big ideas support students' developing understanding across grades 7–16. The final consensus for grades 7–12 students was the following nine big ideas:

- Size and Scale
- Structure of Matter
- Forces and Interactions
- Quantum Effects
- Size-Dependent Properties
- Self-Assembly
- Tools and Instrumentation
- Models and Simulation
- Science, Technology, and Society

Based on these discussions, a draft document was composed, edited, and vetted by members of the NSE community, as well as by high school educators. At the same time, the document was posted for review by participants in the previous workshops.

Appendix A

Building the Final Consensus

Finally, in January 2007 the consensus set of big ideas from the three workshops was presented and discussed at the National Science Foundation's K–12 & Informal Education Nanoscale Science & Engineering Education Workshop, held in Washington, DC. This set of big ideas was approved and resulted in this book.

References

Alexander, P. A., T. J. Jetton, and J. M. Kulikowich. 1995. Interrelationship of knowledge, interest, and recall: Assessing a model of domain learning. *Journal of Educational Psychology* 87 (4): 559–575.

American Association for the Advancement of Science (AAAS). 1993. *Benchmarks for science literacy*. New York: Oxford University Press.

Çalik, M., and A. Ayas. 2005. A comparison of level of understanding of eighth-grade students and science student teachers related to selected chemistry concepts. *Journal of Research in Science Teaching* 42 (6): 638–337.

Harrison, A. G., and D. F. Treagust. 2002. The particulate nature of matter: Challenges in understanding the submicroscopic world. In *Chemical education: Towards research-based practice*, ed. J. K. Gilbert, O. De Jong, R. Justi, D. F. Treagust, and J. H. Van Driel. Dordrecht, The Netherlands: Kluwer Academic Publishers.

Nakhleh, M. B. 1992. Why some students don't learn chemistry. *Journal of Chemical Education* 69 (3): 191–196.

National Research Council (NRC). 1996. *National science education standards*. Washington DC: National Academy Press.

Rutherford, J. J., and A. Algren. 1990. *Science for all Americans*. New York: Oxford University Press.

Singer, J., R. W. Marx, J. Krajcik, and J. C. Chambers. 2000. Constructing extended inquiry projects: Curriculum materials for science education reform. *Educational Psychologist* 35 (3): 165–178.

Wansom, S., T. O. Mason, M. C. Hersam, D. Drane, G. Light, R. Cormia, S. Y. Stevens, and G. Bodner. 2009. A rubric for post-secondary degree programs in nanoscience and nanotechnology. *International Journal for Engineering Education* 25 (3): 615–627.

Appendix B
Participants, Nanoscience Learning Goals Workshop, June 14–16, 2006
SRI International, Menlo Park, California*

Carl Batt, Cornell University (nanobiotechnology)

Marcy Berding, SRI International (nanoscience)

George Bodner, Purdue University (chemistry)

S. Raj Chaudhury, Auburn University (physics, science education)

W. Richard Chung, San Jose State University (materials science)

Kyle Cole, Stanford University (Center for Probing the Nanoscale)

Brian Coppola, University of Michigan (chemistry, chemistry education)

Robert Cormia, Foothill-DeAnza Community College (engineering)

Vivian Dang, Boeing Corporation (engineering)

Denise Drane, Northwestern University (education and evaluation)

Ramez Elgammal, University of Michigan (nano-engineering)

Stephen Fonash, Penn State (engineering; director, NSF Nanotechnology
Advanced Technology Education Center)

Jenny Gardner, Oregon Museum of Science and Industry (informal education)

Steve Getty, BSCS (science curriculum development)

Robert Gibbs, National Science Foundation (program officer)

Nick Giordano, Purdue University (physics)

Marni Goldman, Stanford University (chemistry)

Sherry Hsi, Exploratorium (Nanoscale Informal Science Education [NISE]
Network; informal education)

Erik Jakobsson, University of Illinois at Urbana-Champaign (nanobiotechnology)

Jill Johnson, Exploratorium (informal education)

Barry Kluger-Bell, Exploratorium (informal education)

Gregory Light, Northwestern University (education and evaluation)

Carmen Lilley, University of Illinois at Chicago (engineering)

George Lisensky, Beloit College (chemistry)

Thomas Mason, Northwestern University (materials science)

Christine Morrow, McREL (NanoLeap)

Jo Ellen Roseman, American Association for the Advancement
of Science (national standards)

* Conducted jointly by the National Center for Learning and Teaching in Nanoscale Science and Engineering and SRI International and funded by the National Science Foundation.

Appendix B

Maureen Scharberg, San Jose State University (chemistry education)
Dennis Smithenry, Stanford University (chemistry, science education)
Carole Stearns, National Science Foundation (retired program officer)
Robert Tinker, Concord Consortium (computational chemistry)
Jonathan Trent, NASA (nanobiotechnology)
Thomas Tretter, University of Louisville (size and scale)

Organizing Committee and Reporters

SRI International
    Patricia Schank (technology; science education)
    Nora Sabelli (computational chemistry; science education)
    Tina Sanford (chemistry teacher; educational research)
    Anders Rosenquist (science education)

University of Michigan
    César Delgado (science education)
    Joseph Krajcik (science education)
    Christopher Quintana (technology; science education)
    Shawn Stevens (biophysical chemistry; science education)
    LeeAnn Sutherland (literacy)
    Molly Yunker (science education)

Appendix C
Alternative Manufacturing Strategies

Although self-assembly provides a strategy for the efficient and accurate fabrication of nanoscale structures, materials, and systems, the authors of this book do not mean to suggest that it is the *only* way or even always the best way of manufacturing such products.

The self-assembly process does have some limitations. For example, the products fabricated via self-assembly tend to be relatively weak structures. In addition, small changes in the process can manifest in big changes in the product. Likewise, it is often difficult to make small adjustments in the process, so a small change in the specification of the product often means that significant changes must be made to the self-assembly process. Regardless of the limitations at the time of this writing (2009), however, scientists and engineers believe that self-assembly is an important enough concept within the field of NSE to be a big idea unto itself. Despite their position, it should be noted that alternative ways of fabricating nanoscale structures do exist.

Self-assembly is a bottom-up approach to fabrication, involving combining smaller building blocks to make a larger, more complex product. It is one of many ways to potentially fabricate nanoscale products. Currently, there are several top-down and bottom-up strategies that are used to fabricate nanoscale products. Different approaches are more useful for certain types of products. (Most of these fabrication methods likely are too specialized for introduction into the grade 7–12 classroom.)

Table C.1, on pages 190–191, is a summary of some alternate approaches to making nanoscale products. Like self-assembly, these processes have links to other big ideas, including Tools and Instrumentation, Forces and Interactions, and Structure of Matter. With the development of new tools and instruments that make manipulation of nanoscale objects and materials more efficient and accurate, other processes are likely to join self-assembly at the forefront of the manufacturing process.

Appendix C

Table C.1
Some alternatives to self-assembly for fabricating nanoscale products

Lithography

Photolithography
*   Uses light to form a pattern in a thin film (substrate/photoresist) covering a surface
*   Uses: microelectronics
*   Accuracy: ~5 nm

Scanning Probe Lithography
*   Uses probe tip to modify surface during lithography process

Dip-Pen Nanolithography
*   Top-down or bottom-up process
*   Scanning probe lithographic method. The tip of the probe is dipped in "ink" that is transferred to a surface.
*   Used to create nanoarrays
*   Accuracy: ~15 nm

For a general example of the lithography process, see Figure 2.4.

Soft Lithography
*   Uses a "stamp" to transfer a pattern onto a surface

Atom Lithography
*   Involves the deposition of atoms into a designed pattern using laser light
*   Accuracy: ~10 nm

Electron-Beam-Induced Processing[a]

Focused Electron-Beam-Induced Deposition
*   An electron beam initiates the decomposition of a precursor located on a surface.
*   The remaining species is left behind, deposited on the surface.
*   Reaction is localized, only occurring where the electron beam hits the adsorbed species.

precursor adsorbs to surface

electron beam

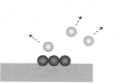

volatile byproduct dissociates from surface

remaining material now deposited on surface

Table C.1 continued

Focused Electron-Beam-Induced Etching
- A chemical reaction occurs between surface atoms and the precursor adsorbed to the surface, brought about by an electron beam
- Reaction is localized, only occurring where the electron beam hits the adsorbed species.

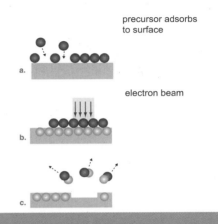

precursor adsorbs to surface

a.

electron beam

b.

c.

Atomic Layer Epitaxy/ Deposition [b]

- Involves depositing a monocrystalline layer onto a substrate surface
- Each layer is a single atom thick and adopts the lattice structure of the underlying surface
- Provides atomic-level control of thickness
- May be used to obtain a homogeneous surface or a designed patterned surface (Patterned Atomic Layer Epitaxy, or PALE)

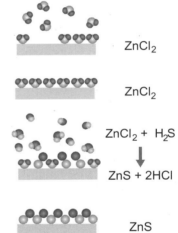

$ZnCl_2$

$ZnCl_2$

$ZnCl_2 + H_2S$

$ZnS + 2HCl$

ZnS

Mechanosynthesis [c]

- Involves the use of mechanical restraints to control the outcome of a chemical reaction

Positionally Controlled Mechanosynthesis
- Involves using the tip of a scanning probe microscope to place individual atoms or molecules into precisely defined positions

Silicon atom removed using a low-temperature, ultra-high vacuum atomic force microscope

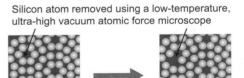

Scanning Probe Tip-Directed Fabrication

- Uses the tip of a scanning probe microscope to position atoms or molecules

See examples in "Tools and Instrumentation" in Chapter 3.

---

[a] Figures adapted from Randolph, Fowlkes, and Rack 2006
[b] Figure adapted from Ritala and Leskelä 1999
[c] Figure adapted from Oyabu et al. 2003

Appendix C

A challenge for NSE is to efficiently fabricate macroscale products that are designed and manufactured with atomic precision. This level of control has thus far been exhibited only in natural physical and biological systems. The ability of human engineers to control matter at the same level of precision and control as in natural and biological systems lies at the heart of the nanotechnology revolution.

Resources

Oyabu, N., Ó. Custance, I. Yi, and S. Morita. 2003. Mechanical vertical manipulation of selected single atoms by soft nanoindentation using near contact atomic force microscopy. *Physical Review Letters* 90 (176): 102.

Randolph, S. J., J. D. Fowlkes, and P. D. Rack. 2006. Focused, nanoscale electron-beam-induced deposition and etching. *Critical Reviews in Solid State and Materials Sciences* 31: 55–89.

Ritala, M., and M. Leskelä. 1999. Atomic layer epitaxy–A valuable tool for nanotechnology? *Nanotechnology* 10: 19–24.

About the Authors

Shawn Y. Stevens is a research investigator in the School of Education at the University of Michigan where her work focuses on assessing and improving student and teacher learning. In association with the National Center for Learning and Teaching Nanoscale Science and Engineering, she is developing a learning progression for the nature of matter as it relates to nanoscience. In addition, she is characterizing how new elementary teachers develop pedagogical content knowledge for science teaching. This work is funded by the Center for Curriculum Materials in Science.

After several years working in industry, Dr. Stevens returned to graduate school at the University of Michigan, where she received a PhD in chemistry. Her graduate research focused on protein•DNA recognition and provided a lead compound that led to the formation of a biotechnology company. As a postdoctoral fellow, she characterized the relationship between structure and function of natural molecular machines before choosing to focus on science education.

LeeAnn M. Sutherland, an assistant research scientist in the School of Education at the University of Michigan, is a specialist in adolescent literacy. For several years she has focused on literacy and learning in science. She is also a co–principal investigator of the Investigating and Questioning our World through Science and Technology project (IQWST). The project, supported by the National Science Foundation, is an effort to create a standards-based, coordinated middle school science curriculum with units at grades 6, 7, and 8 that integrate students' understanding of core concepts in biology, chemistry, Earth science, and physics strands. In the IQWST curriculum students experience phenomena; connect classroom science with familiar, everyday experiences; and extend and apply their understanding as they read, write, and think about science with their peers. In collaboration with colleagues from Northwestern University and the Weizmann Institute of Science in Rehovot, Israel, Dr. Sutherland focuses on integrating literacy practices and science instruction.

Before obtaining a PhD in literacy, language, and culture from the University of Michigan in 2002, Dr. Sutherland taught in the university's School of Literature, Science and the Arts. Prior to that, she was a high school English teacher in rural, urban, and suburban settings in Michigan. Her project websites are *http://hice.org* and *http://hice.org/IQWST*. She may be reached at *lsutherl@umich.edu*.

Joseph S. Krajcik is a professor of science education and the associate dean for research in the School of Education at the University of Michigan. He works with science teachers to create classrooms in which students consider important intellectual questions and find solutions that encompass essential learning goals

About the Authors

and that use learning technologies as productivity tools. He seeks to discover the depth of student learning in such environments, as well as to explore and find solutions to challenges that teachers face in carrying out such complex instruction.

In collaboration with colleagues from Northwestern University, the American Association for the Advancement of Science, and the Weizmann Institute of Science in Rehovot, Israel, and through funding from the National Science Foundation, Dr. Krajcik is principal investigator in a materials development project that is designing, developing, and testing the next generation of middle school science curricula.

Dr. Krajcik is a fellow of the American Association for the Advancement of Science and served as president of the National Association for Research in Science Teaching in 1999. He co-directs the Instructional Development and Educational Assessment (IDEA) Institute and the Center for Highly Interactive Classrooms, Curriculum and Computing in Education (hi-ce) at the University of Michigan. He is also co–principal investigator in the National Center for Learning and Teaching Nanoscale Science and Engineering.

Before obtaining his PhD in science education from the University of Iowa in 1986, Dr. Krajcik taught high school chemistry for seven years in Milwaukee, Wisconsin. His home page is located at *www.umich.edu/~krajcik*. His project websites include *http://hice.org* and *http://hice.org/IQWST*.

Index

Index

Index

Index

relationship to 7–12 curriculum, 50
relationships with other big ideas, **38, 53**
of snowflakes, 46, 138, **139**
static, 46
of supramolecules, 49, **49**
templated, 45, **45**
SEM (scanning electron microscope), 54–55, 56–57, 145
Shape, 7–8, 24
colors of nanoparticles related to, 130
effect on properties, 130–131, **131**
electrical interactions and, 106–107, **106–107**
surface-to-volume ratio and, 7, **7,** 83
Sickle cell anemia, 108
Silver nanoparticles, 130
Simulations, 60, 61. *See also* Models and simulations
Single-stranded DNA binding protein (SSBP), 21–22
Size and scale, 5–10, 77–85
as big idea, 8–9, 77
choosing appropriate tools for, 144
continuum of, 6
in daily activities, 10
definition of, 5
forces and interactions relative to, 8, 18
learning goals related to, 77–83
models and, 59
national science standards related to, 83, **84–85**
what is missing, 83–84
predictions based on, 8
quantum mechanics and, 25, 80
relationship to 7–12 curriculum, 9–10
relationships with other big ideas, **5,** 37, **37, 38, 53**
surface-to-volume ratio and, 6–7, **7,** 8–9, **9,** 10, 39, 82–83, 126
shape and, 7, **7,** 83, 130–131, **131**
worlds defined by, 5–6, **6,** 8, 79–80
Size-dependent properties, 37–43, 125–133
as big idea, 41–42, 125
of gold nanoparticles, **38,** 38–39, 41–42, 127–129, **128–129**
vs. intensive properties, 38, 125
learning goals related to, 81, 82, 126–131
magnetic susceptibility, 41
national science standards related to, 131, **133**
what is missing, 131–132
relationship to 7–12 curriculum, 42–43
relationships with other big ideas, **37**

shape and, 130–131, **131**
size-dominated properties, 40–41
supraparamagnetic limit, 129
surface-dominated properties, 6–7, **7,** 8–9, **9,** 10, 39, **40,** 82–83, 126
Snow, C.P., 67
Snowflakes, 46, 138, **139**
Soft lithography, **190**
Solar energy, 69
s-orbitals, 27–28, **29**
Spin quantum number *(s)*, 28
Spintronics, 33, 121
SPM (scanning probe microscope), 54, 55–58, 145, 147–148
SRI International, 3, 181
SSBP (single-stranded DNA binding protein), 21–22
STEM (science, technology, engineering, and mathematics) education, xii, xiii, 174
integrating NSE concepts into existing curriculum, 176–177
STM (scanning tunneling microscope), 31, **32,** 57, **57,** 145, 146, **146,** 147, 148
Structure of matter, 10–18, 87–96
amino acids and proteins, 15, 18, 89–91, **91**
atoms and their interactions, 10–12, **11**
as big idea, 12–17, 87, 185
biomimetics, 17
bone, tooth enamel, and shell, 15, **17**
carbon allotropes, 12–15, **13, 14,** 91
hemoglobin, 15, **16,** 18, 90
hierarchical, 15, 18, **92,** 92–93
learning goals related to, 87–93
molecules, 89, **90**
national science standards related to, 93, **95–96**
what is missing, 93–94
relationship to 7–12 curriculum, 17–18
relationships with other big ideas, **5, 37, 38, 53**
across scales, 12
Subatomic scale, 8
forces on, 8, 18
quantum mechanics on, 25
Sunscreens, 41, **42,** 69
Supramolecules, 49, **49**
Supraparamagnetic limit, 129
Surface-to-volume ratio (S/V), 10, 39, 184
adhesion properties and, 8–9, 39
learning goal related to, 82–83

NATIONAL SCIENCE TEACHERS ASSOCIATION